ALSO BY ETHAN BROWN

Snitch

Queens Reigns Supreme

SHAKE THE DEVIL OFF

SHAKE THE DEVIL OFF

A TRUE STORY OF THE MURDER
THAT ROCKED NEW ORLEANS

ETHAN BROWN

HENRY HOLT AND COMPANY   NEW YORK

Henry Holt and Company, LLC
Publishers since 1866
175 Fifth Avenue
New York, New York 10010
www.henryholt.com

Lyrics to "Ghosts" by David Sylvian reproduced by permission.

Library of Congress Cataloging-in-Publication Data
Brown, Ethan, 1972–
    Shake the devil off : a true story of the murder that rocked New Orleans /
Ethan Brown.—1st ed.
        p. cm.
    ISBN: 978-0-8050-8893-9
    1. Bowen, Zackery.   2. Murder—Louisiana—New Orleans—Case studies.
3. Murder victims—Louisiana—New Orleans—Case studies.   I. Title.
    HV6534.N45B76 2009
    364.152'3092—dc22   200906698

Henry Holt books are available for special promotions and
premiums. For details contact: Director, Special Markets.

First Edition 2009

Designed by Kelly S. Too

Printed in the United States of America

1   3   5   7   9   10   8   6   4   2

*To the citizens of New Orleans and
the veterans of the wars in Iraq and Afghanistan*

Just when I think I'm winning
When I've broken every door
The ghosts of my life
Blow wilder than before.

—DAVID SYLVIAN, "Ghosts"

CONTENTS

SHAKE THE DEVIL OFF

PROLOGUE

"Hey, Squirrel." Zackery Bowen was hovering over the bed of Greg "Squirrel" Rogers, trying to wake him. "Hey, *Squirrel*," Zack repeated, this time more forcefully. "C'mon, dude. Let's go party." It was 4:00 p.m. on Tuesday, October 17, 2006, and Squirrel was stretched out in his bed in his small, shabby one-bedroom apartment on Burgundy Street in the Lower French Quarter. Squirrel had been out until nearly sunrise that morning and was sleeping off a nasty hangover. Perhaps later that afternoon he would make it over to meet Zack at Cosimo's, a bar nearby at the corner of Governor Nicholls and Burgundy streets. But for now, all he could manage was to sleepily rub his eyes, begin to rise from bed, and say that he'd take a pass on another night of partying.

Once he was up, Squirrel began to focus much more intently on his conversation with Zack. Inexplicably, Zack was dressed in an outfit that he wore when he bartended at the local watering hole Buffa's—a brown plaid Western-style shirt with loose-fitting blue Levi's and bulky black combat boots—even though he wasn't scheduled to work that night. The outfit made Squirrel uncomfortable, particularly because Zack was in the midst of a nearly two-week-long bender in which he'd been treating his closest friends to shots of Jameson's at Aunt Tiki's on Decatur, lap dances at the Hustler Club on Bourbon Street, and twenty-dollar bags of cocaine from Squirrel's stash. Even more curiously, during the partying spree Zack proclaimed to Squirrel that his girlfriend, Adrianne "Addie" Hall, had moved out of the apartment they shared on North Rampart Street on the outskirts of the French Quarter and returned to her hometown of Durham, North Carolina. "Dude," Zack told Squirrel one night, "she tried to rip me off for a bunch of money and then she split." Squirrel had been shocked by the story; Zack and Addie had been inseparable since they got together during the steamy summer months of 2005 before Hurricane Katrina made landfall on August 29. "She split?" Squirrel asked. "*And* ripped you off? That don't make sense." Zack insisted that he was surprised but that was what had gone down. "It *was* strange," Squirrel remembered later. "But these were strange times in New Orleans."

"*Squirrel,*" Zack shouted, snapping Squirrel back from his memories of the past week and into the present. "C'mon, dude. Where is it?" Zack was looking for coke. Squirrel was, after all, Zack's drug dealer, even though they rarely exchanged money. During the fall of 2005, Squirrel had gotten into a bad car accident and Zack and Addie took care of him as he recovered. About six months later, the couple loaned Squirrel nine hundred dollars after he couldn't make his rent. To thank Zack and Addie, Squirrel instituted a special policy for them: they could come by his apartment from time to time and take a small Ziploc baggie or two of coke completely free of charge. "You guys have been so cool to me, from the car wreck to the rent," Squirrel told Zack and Addie. "You're my people. Anything you need, just come by." But by the spring of 2006, the couple was visiting Squirrel's apartment so frequently that they were beginning to "spin out a little bit," according to Squirrel. Addie would kick Zack out of their apartment on Governor Nicholls Street and Zack would then crash at Squirrel's on Burgundy Street. But it wasn't just free drugs that brought Zack to Squirrel's: the men had served in the military in Iraq and Afghanistan, respectively, and felt comfortable talking about what happened in their separate "over there"s with each other. Their military background—Zack had been a sergeant in the army, Squirrel a corpsman in the navy—created a strong bond between them, as had their refusal to leave New Orleans during Katrina even after Mayor C. Ray Nagin ordered a first-ever evacuation of the city on August 28, 2005. "Me and Zack were the survivors," Squirrel remembered later. "Everybody else"—he nearly spat the words out in disgust— *"they're evacuees."*

Yet Zack and Squirrel, strong opposites in outward appearance and temperament, seemed unlikely friends. Zack stood at nearly six foot ten, had long, blondish brown hair and a tanned, dimpled face that easily earned him many male and female admirers. Squirrel—none other than U2's lead singer, Bono, gave him his nickname when he worked as a roadie on the band's "ZOO TV" tour in the early 1990s, because he had an almost preternatural ability to shimmy up towering light rigs—was short and stocky with a close-cropped buzz cut and an unkempt and scraggly reddish brown beard. Zack was admired by their circle as affable, gentle, and lighthearted, a bartender beloved in the French Quarter for his good humor and ability to entertain drinkers with magic tricks pulled from a bag behind the counter. Squirrel was prone to visibly dark moods and could occasionally become publicly violent, even engaging in bar fights in the French Quarter. Zack was so wary of violence and confrontation of any kind that he'd turn and walk away even when angry drunks would throw a punch at him. Still, their involvement in the long wars in Afghanistan and Iraq—and their struggle for survival in Katrina's wake and love for New Orleans—made those differences seem insignificant. So Squirrel didn't mind when Zack grabbed a twenty-dollar bag of coke lying near his bed and left without so much as a thanks.

Zack headed out into the cool, crisp mid-October air of that afternoon, from Squirrel's apartment on Burgundy Street and over to the Omni Royal Orleans hotel on St. Louis Street between Royal and Chartres streets. He strode through the hotel's tacky red-carpet-and-white-marble lobby, rode the elevator to the seventh floor, and made his way past the hotel's sole penthouse suite and to the observation deck along-side La Riviera's rooftop pool bar. When Zack arrived, a popular local Latin dance band—Fredy Omar con su Banda—was setting up its instruments for a three-hour gig to start at 5:00 p.m. Zack then opened up a tab at the bar, sat by the pool smoking, and calmly enjoyed several shots of Jameson's. As Fredy performed the sound check, he couldn't help but notice the tall, blond, and handsome Zack, particularly because it was so early and the La Riviera was nearly empty. "He was smoking and drinking, sitting by the pool, and looking to the sky," Fredy remembers. "Even though he was dressed in just jeans and boots, he looked very elegant, like a rock star." When Fredy started playing, however, Zack began to pace nervously by the pool, arousing the suspicions of a La Riviera bartender, who worried that he was going to walk out on the substantial bill: Zack had been drinking since about four o'clock. Zack, meanwhile, took in La Riviera's expansive view of the French Quarter—the steamboats pushing down the Mississippi, and the iconic, soaring, triple steeples of St. Louis Cathedral in Jackson Square. Zack had been married right in front of the church in 1998 and though the couple had two young children, they separated soon after Zack had returned from Iraq. Zack tried to remember the good times in Jackson Square—the beautiful wedding that attracted so many tourists that they outnumbered invited guests, and the afternoons when he and Lana would hang out on the park benches and feast on shrimp po'boys—but then his thoughts drifted to his failed marriage and, more recently, his turbulent relationship with Addie. To Zack, his twenty-eight years of life had amounted to little more than a successive string of personal and professional failures—from marriage to the military—from which he never seemed to recover.

It was nearly eight o'clock on a Tuesday night and the bar wasn't very crowded. So Fredy ended the band's set. And as they began packing up their instruments, they were approached by the La Riviera bartender, who was angry and anxious. A customer—Zack—had been drinking all afternoon and skipped out on the bill. Even though Fredy didn't know

Zack, he remembered his physical description precisely. "I told my guitar player, 'Let's go look for that dude,'" Fredy recalls. The band took the elevator down to the Omni Royal's garage, packed the remainder of their equipment into their car, and took off into the French Quarter looking for Zack.

Unbeknownst to Fredy, just before eight thirty, Zack had put his final drink down and walked slowly up to the La Riviera's roof railing and back again. Zack then paced from the pool to the edge of the roof, back and forth, two more times. Finally, at eight thirty sharp, all of this according to hotel security tapes, he leapt over the side.

Zack landed with a heavy thud about five stories down, on the roof of the Omni Royal's adjacent parking garage. He died instantly. Just moments later, a frantic hotel guest who saw Zack's body sprawled on the parking garage called down to the front desk and then a panicked hotel manager dialed 911.

"29S, 29S, 29S"—NOPD code for suicide—came the call over the NOPD radios. "A white male has jumped off the upper deck of the Omni Royal hotel."

"This should be interesting," said Detective Tom Morovich, then of the NOPD's Person Crimes division, which handles robberies, stabbings, and shootings. That evening, Tom and his fellow Person Crimes detectives were sitting at the Eighth District police station at 334 Royal Street, just a few blocks away from the Omni Royal, preparing for dinner when the report of the 29S came over the radio. Suicides are common in post-Katrina New Orleans, but the news that someone had leapt off the roof of a four-star hotel seemed bizarre to Tom; a 29S call would have been more likely in a flooded neighborhood like Lakeview that was struggling to rebuild after the levees broke a little more than one year earlier. So he and a small group of detectives headed over to the scene of the suicide.

Tom, a muscular, dark-haired, broad-shouldered native of Empire, Louisiana, who at over six foot five resembled a nightclub bouncer, had weathered Katrina at a makeshift police outpost at the Omni Royal, so he knew the layout of the hotel well. When Tom arrived there, the hotel manager directed him to the parking garage's roof, where they found Zack's gangly body lying faceup, with blood pouring from his mouth and head. A thick trail of Zack's blood mingled with dirty rainwater that had gathered on the hotel's roof from a thunderstorm earlier that week. "I'd seen much worse," Tom remembered later. "This wasn't at all like a suicide where someone hits the cement. Zack's hips were twisted around, but other than that there was little visible damage to his body."

As an investigator from the coroner's office rifled through Zack's pockets, an NOPD homicide detective needled Tom about the case. "No question about it," he said to Tom with a gruff, sarcastic laugh, "this one's gonna be yours."

But then the investigator made a strange discovery: a Ziploc bag in Zack's right front pocket contained army dog tags bearing Zack's full name and a tightly folded sheet of notebook paper that read "FOR POLICE ONLY" on the outside fold. When the coroner's office investigator unfolded the paper, he found that Zack had written a long note. "Here we go," he announced to the cops. "We got ourselves a suicide note." The homicide detective, unsurprisingly, was sure that Tom was going to have to take the case that was suddenly—and most certainly—a suicide. "Whoo-hoo!" he said. "It's *definitely* yours now."

Then the investigator began reading the note aloud:

This is not accidental. I had to take my own life to pay for the one I took. If you send a patrol to 826 N. Rampart you will find the dismembered corpse of my girlfriend Addie in the oven, on the stove, and in the fridge along with full documentation on the both of us and a full signed confession from myself. The keys in my right front pocket are for the gates. Call Leo Watermeier to let you in. Zack Bowen.

When he finished reading the note there was a moment of shocked silence among the NOPD detectives, followed by scattered bursts of nervous laughter. Tom and his fellow detectives thought that the coroner's office investigator had just played a cruel and dark practical joke. But the investigator, looking profoundly disturbed, said that he was reading directly from the note. "Lemme see that," one NOPD homicide detective growled, grabbing the note from the investigator's hands. The detective's eyes scanned the paper and his face went white. This was no joke.

Just as Zack had instructed, the cops rushed to the North Rampart Street home of his landlord, onetime New Orleans mayoral candidate Leo Watermeier. It was just after ten o'clock when officers knocked on Leo's door at 812 North Rampart. Leo, a short, balding man with a slow, easy New Orleans drawl, who usually walked around with arched eyebrows and a wide, loose smile, was shocked to find NOPD detectives looking for a dismembered corpse. "What the hell are you talking about?" he said.

The detectives were cagey about the body in question—they would only say that it was a woman—but Leo let them into his own apartment anyway. "There's no body here," Leo insisted to the cops, "but have a look around." As the detectives toured the ground-floor one-bedroom apartment, Leo opened his refrigerator, stove, and closets for inspection.

"Then they realized, 'This isn't the apartment,'" Leo remembered later. So, Leo walked the cops about one block down the street to the 826 North Rampart one-bedroom unit that he rented to Zack and Addie for $750 per month. The apartment was on the second floor of a Creole cottage above Watermeier's other tenant, the Voodoo Spiritual Temple, run by Priestess Miriam Chamani, an iconic figure in the New Orleans spiritual scene since the early 1990s who had blessed the marriage of Nicolas Cage and Lisa Marie Presley and was much beloved in the neighborhood for quickly resuming her healing rituals after Katrina.

As they neared Zack's apartment, the detectives revealed more about what had brought them there. They told Leo that Zack had just jumped off the roof of the Omni Royal and left instructions directing law enforcement to the apartment he rented from Leo. There, according to the note, they'd find Addie's body. After hearing this, Leo opened the wrought-iron gate, which led to the courtyard beside Zack's apartment, and turned toward home. "I didn't want to go upstairs," Leo explains.

When the NOPD burst into the shabby second-floor apartment, they found a scene both gruesome and inexplicable. Zack had left the window air-conditioning unit on full blast, set to about sixty degrees, giving the tiny apartment the feel of a meat locker. Beer cans stuffed with stubbed-out cigarettes littered the floor, while a tall stack of unopened moving boxes sat near the door. On the apartment's walls, Zack had written a series of spray-painted messages:

"PLEASE CALL MY WIFE."

"I LOVE HER."

"I'M A TOTAL FAILURE."

"LOOK IN THE OVEN."

Then, on the ceiling above Zack and Addie's bed, there was another message that seemed directed at some other force, one more difficult to address than the detectives of the NOPD:

"PLEASE HELP ME STOP THE PAIN."

"There was something particularly disturbing about that last message," Tom remembered later. "I imagined that Zack had spray-painted it just after he had killed Addie and stared at it every night before he went to bed." After taking in Zack's final message, Tom moved toward the kitchen, where he saw a huge silver arrow spray-painted over the range, pointing downward toward the oven. When Tom pulled the door open, he discovered Addie's small legs—which were charred a deep black from being cooked—stuffed into a tinfoil turkey pan. Tom then turned toward the range's front burner, where he found a deep cooking pot, and peering inside he discovered a thicket of human hair and Addie's head. A large cooking pot on the back burner held her hands and feet. Finally, Tom opened the refrigerator and found Addie's legless and armless torso packed separately into a bloodstained, black garbage bag.

"None of the cops who were on the scene had ever seen anything this disturbing," Tom told me. "In fact, we all had to take breaks outside the apartment that night. What we were seeing was inconceivable. It was like we were living inside a movie. It was just that eerie." At a press conference the next day, NOPD chief of detectives Anthony Cannatella still seemed to be reeling from the murder scene at 826 North Rampart. "I would imagine that he was in some serious mental anguish and pain," Cannatella said of Zack to the reporters that day. "I couldn't fathom to think what caused him to do it."

Why was Zackery Bowen, a former army sergeant, a veteran of two wars (Kosovo and Iraq), and a beloved bartender and deliveryman in the French Quarter, in such unimaginably deep emotional pain? And what drove him to commit this incomprehensibly brutal crime? Few of the journalists in the local New Orleans or national media seemed to be interested in answering these questions that day, or the days soon after. Instead, they portrayed Zack as, at best, a freakish, drug-addicted French Quarter resident who simply flipped out after Katrina, at worst, as an archetypal New Orleans–style madman (that he lived in an apartment above a voodoo temple played perfectly into the caricature) in the tradition of the neighborhood's long history of brutal killers—whose "ghastly deeds" are showcased during popular "Haunted History" walking tours. The *New York Post*, in keeping with its house style, ran a story about Zack with the headline "GAL PAL GUMBO," a headline in the British tabloid the *Daily Mirror* wrongly declared "MAN COOKS AND EATS GIRL-FRIEND," while even the usually tame Associated Press placed the murder-suicide in the context of a city in which "Carriage drivers regale . . . tourists nightly with phantasmagoric tales of black magic, debauchery and murder." Local media coverage of the murder-suicide wasn't much more restrained: the *Times-Picayune* ran a front-page story about Zack with the large and garish headline "BOYFRIEND CUT UP CORPSE, COOKED IT."

Meanwhile, many New Orleanians, weary from a constant stream of stories about mental health problems in the post-Katrina city—several of which had described them as in a deep "Katrina Funk" or, worse, as being "Katrina Crazy"—seemed intent on portraying Zack as an outsider. Andrei Codrescu, NPR commentator and author of *New Orleans, Mon Amour: Twenty Years of Writings from the City*, told me that the murder-suicide "seems midwestern [and] not New Orleans to me, more Milwaukee than French Quarter." The *Times-Picayune*, meanwhile, quoted an LSU Medical School psychiatrist who emphasized that neither Zack nor Addie were New Orleans natives with roots there or a home in any flooded part of the city. Similarly, the late New Orleans blogger Ashley Morris simply proclaimed that "Zackery Bowen was a Californian, from Los Angeles. He was *not* a New Orleanian."

New Orleanians have a strict definition of who can be considered a native. As Joshua Clark wrote in his Katrina memoir *Heart Like Water*, "there is no way to be from New Orleans unless you first came into the light here." So it's undeniable that Zack Bowen was not a New Orleanian—he was born in Bakersfield, California. But Zack lived in New Orleans from the mid-1990s until his death in 2006 and was a proud resident of the city: he told friends and even landlord Leo Watermeier that he was so die-hard in his love that he couldn't imagine ever leaving New Orleans. And while many New Orleanians do have familial roots in the city going back generations, some of the city's most devoted citizens have come from other parts of the country or even the world, from nineteenth-century newspaper columnist Lafcadio Hearn (who was born in Greece and lived in New Orleans only ten years) to *Times-Picayune* columnist Chris Rose (who was born and raised in Maryland), whose columns about his post-Katrina mental health struggles captured the city's on-the-brink mood and were eventually a finalist for the Pulitzer Prize.

Zack and Addie were not great artists or writers, but they loved New Orleans deeply, and it was discomfiting that they were treated like freakish outsiders worthy only of scorn and disdain. The couple were mocked for everything from their artistic aspirations—Zack played the drums; Addie wrote poetry and was a seamstress—to, more bizarrely, their seemingly mundane thoughts on the beauty of their adopted city. After

Katrina, Addie enthused to a reporter that "we've been able to see the stars for the first time." After she was murdered, Addie's remark about the stars brought a nasty rebuke from New Orleans novelist Poppy Z. Brite, who wrote on her blog that while "I feel bad for the girl . . . I can't quite forgive that remark about how beautiful the stars were over New Orleans in the nights right after the storm. Stars are horrifying things in general and should never, ever be seen over New Orleans. Our night sky is supposed to be purple." While it was understandable that New Orleanians sought to distance themselves from the gruesome tale of Zack and Addie, surely these two young people had lives that did not need to be attacked at any opportunity, and sad ends that did not deserve to be ridiculed.

———

I came across the story of Zack and Addie entirely by accident: my wife and I happened to be in New Orleans celebrating our fifth wedding anniversary just days after Zack's body was found on the roof of the Omni Royal's parking garage in October 2006. We'd honeymooned in 2001 in New Orleans, so we had headed down to the beleaguered city for a four-day vacation even though we knew it might make for an uncomfortable anniversary. It was a catastrophe, after all, that had brought my wife and me to New Orleans in the first place. We were married near Woodstock, New York, just a few weeks after 9-11, and fearing that we could be stuck outside the country if another terrorist act occurred, we decided to spend our honeymoon in the States. We chose New Orleans simply because it was one of the few cities in the States that neither of us had visited. We spent our weeklong honeymoon in the grand suite of the Soniat House, a gorgeous, small historic hotel with a sprawling courtyard on Chartres Street in the Lower French Quarter frequented by celebrities like Brad Pitt and writers like Greil Marcus. (Marcus, whose *Mystery Train* was a major inspiration for me to become a writer, happened to be staying at the Soniat House while we were there.) Though even New Orleans was subdued so soon after 9-11, we had a fantastic and unforgettable time, waking up around noon every day and downing the Soniat House's intense chicory coffee and flaky biscuits warmed on a hot stone, and then, much later, at sunset, decamping to our balcony to watch groups of tourists riding in horse-drawn carriages and Goths clad in long, black cloaks taking ghost tours down below. We also fell in love with the sensibility of the citizens of New Orleans: their stunning generosity and friendliness, which to New Yorkers like us could seem at first like a put-on; their dark sense of humor (one night my wife and I shared a laugh with a cabdriver whose permit number was 666); and a nightlife and music scene that spanned everything from after-hours Goth clubs like the Whirling Dervish, to the plush lounge El Matador on the corner of Esplanade and Decatur, to the rowdy French Quarter rock club the Shim Sham Club (all three establishments unfortunately now closed), to the great street musicians like Glen David Andrews, a slim, bald-headed singer and trombonist who would belt out standards like "Cabaret" and "St. James Infirmary" in his Satchmoesque growl right in the middle of Jackson Square.

Our fifth-anniversary, post-Katrina trip to New Orleans turned out to be much less fun than our honeymoon. The flight to New Orleans was so turbulent that the pilot had to change our route to the city mid-flight. I was bleary-eyed, groggy, and shaken from the rough ride when we arrived in New Orleans. As I walked through the streets of the French Quarter that fall afternoon I noticed that while the neighborhood appeared mostly physically unscathed by the failure of the levees, signs of Katrina remained everywhere more than a year after the storm. On one desolate French Quarter street near North Rampart, someone stacked Katrina debris into a truck and placed a sign on it reading "NAGIN'S LIMO." Even Jackson Square was eerily quiet on Halloween night—a shock, because during our honeymoon in 2001, Halloween revelers had packed Jackson Square shoulder-to-shoulder. Indeed, five years later the city was nearly a true ghost town: the Louisiana Recovery Authority estimated that New Orleans's population stood at 190,000, down from nearly 500,000 before the levees broke.

Back then, there was a palpable sense of exhaustion and depression in

New Orleans; a University of New Orleans poll conducted in the fall of 2006 found that nearly one-third of the area's residents were considering moving out of the city. The national and even international media furor over Zack and Addie was an unwanted distraction for New Orleanians, taking away much-needed attention from far more vital issues, such as its still inadequate system of levees, Louisiana's inept "Road Home" program (designed to provide compensation to Louisiana home owners affected by Hurricane Katrina or Hurricane Rita), and its skyrocketing murder rate.

Still, the locals' famously pitch-black humor managed to cut through the thick atmosphere of despair: on Bourbon Street there were T-shirts for sale insulting Allstate and FEMA, while a free, widely distributed, *Onion*-like satirical newspaper called the *New Orleans Levee* brilliantly skewered local politicians and the big insurance companies alike ("Mayor Rolls Out Floating Streetcars"; "Allstate Called On to Change Its Name to Somestates").

As our trip to New Orleans came to an end, I rediscovered my love for the city; it was suffering in countless ways but also undergoing a civic renaissance. This was born out of necessity: with federal, local, and state governments failing them, New Orleanians were forced to rebuild on their own. Katrina also put under a spotlight the renegade spirit of a city that had endured great fires and floods, and Spanish and French rule; during the first Carnival season after Katrina, Ashley Morris famously paraded down the streets dressed as a mime under a sign reading "BUY US BACK CHIRAC!" I also began to wonder if the cartoonish media coverage of Zack and Addie—as well as the disdain with which the couple were treated—meant that a much more significant story of Zack's survival on the streets of Kosovo, Baghdad, and New Orleans was being missed.

So I extended our trip by a few days and began conducting interviews with Zack's and Addie's friends in the French Quarter. When my wife and I returned to New York a week later in early November, I began the slow process of tracking down Zack's army buddies. By the spring of 2007, I had begun to realize that the story of Zack Bowen was not that of a voodoo-inspired, drugged-out French Quarter killer but of an Iraq veteran who could not cope with the memories of fighting in some of the most intense combat of the war, from the assault on Baghdad in March 2003 to the first sparks of the insurgency that summer. Zack was also heartbroken that he received a general (under honorable conditions) discharge from the army during the fall of 2004. His discharge jeopardized his postmilitary benefits administered by the Department of Veterans Affairs. When Zack finally returned to New Orleans in early 2005, he exhibited many of the symptoms of PTSD (post-traumatic stress disorder): mood swings, nightmares, flashbacks, and feelings of stress and anger when reminded of his wartime trauma. Whenever the subject of the Iraq war came up, Zack closed himself off emotionally, even to the closest members of his family. "When Zack came home he just wasn't the same," Zack's older brother, Jed, remembers. "He was never enthusiastic or energetic. He didn't like to talk much and everything was *blah*." Zack's untreated PTSD triggered a free fall, from the dissolution of his marriage to trouble at a string of low-paying jobs to an abusive relationship with Addie that ended so tragically.

After researching Zack's story through the spring of 2007, I found it hard to imagine a life that contained more of the tragedies of our era than that of a combat veteran who suffered the consequences of the federal government's disastrous policy decisions in both Baghdad and New Orleans. Zack is one of the few Americans who witnessed firsthand, with such a level of sustained exposure and intimacy, two of the biggest debacles in recent U.S. history. And the policies manifested in both New Orleans and Baghdad—in which contractors, not soldiers, first responders, or citizens, reap the benefits of the postwar and post-Katrina recovery—are inextricably linked, right down to an American construction company (Parsons Corporation) that was given lucrative contracts by the U.S. government in both cities. As Naomi Klein wrote in her dissection of "disaster capitalism," *The Shock Doctrine*: "Within days of the storm it was as if Baghdad's Green Zone had lifted off from its perch and landed on the Bayou." There are also strong parallels between the struggles of Iraq vets and those of New Orleanians. As New Orleanians confront PTSD and a skyrocketing murder rate, Iraq and Afghanistan veterans struggle with psychological wounds and a staggering increase in suicides among their ranks. In a cruel irony that binds vets and New Orleanians, the deepest suffering—and the greatest loss of life—often occurs after the wars and the storms have passed.

As the summer of 2007 began, I decided to move to New Orleans to pursue Zack's story full-time. Since honeymooning in New Orleans, my wife and I had dreamed of moving there; in 2003, we'd even looked at small houses in the Bywater and Faubourg Marigny neighborhoods. But when we arrived in New Orleans in July 2007, we found a city that was both far more inspiring and much more dangerous than we had expected. On a steamy late July afternoon, we pulled into the French Quarter in a rental car packed with boxes and luggage and began moving into our apartment, a two-bedroom duplex in an 1830s Creole town house on Burgundy Street. My wife had flown down to New Orleans alone that spring to rent the apartment, so I'd never seen the place, and it was remarkable to walk through the town house's narrow hallway to a leafy courtyard with an imposing, cast-iron fountain, swaying palm trees, and beautiful, bright purple bougainvillea growing along its walls. Standing in the courtyard that afternoon, I felt as though I had been transported to Central America.

When I headed out into our Lower Quarter neighborhood to run an errand that night, my sense of displacement grew as I passed dimly lit blocks with drug dealers and drunks lurking in the shadows. About two blocks from our apartment, I brushed by a transvestite who hobbled out of a beat-up old Chevy in high-heeled stilettos, rapping, "I'm ill / I'm ill / I'm ill when I'm on these pills." (I'd later find out that New Orleans is home to a gay rap scene dubbed "Sissy Bounce.") As I made my way down one dark Lower Quarter Street, I realized that I hadn't seen a single cop apart from the clusters of officers posted on the busiest corners of Bourbon Street. I'd soon discover that our Lower Quarter neighborhood was in the midst of a wave of violent armed robberies. Despite the violence and ugliness, I immediately felt that New Orleans was a tonic to what had become the safe and staid culture of the New York City that we'd left behind.

As my wife and I unpacked our belongings, I found that my identity was blurring with Zack's; he had even been misidentified as "Zack Brown" in a *New York Times* story about Hurricane Katrina. My wife and I took over our lease from a New Orleans attorney and his wife. As we acquired our keys on move-in day, the attorney told me that he went to high school with Leo Watermeier. The attorney's wife, meanwhile, mentioned that Zack had regularly delivered groceries to their apartment. As I explored the Lower Quarter during our first week in New Orleans, I discovered that our apartment was dead center in what had been Zack's existence. Matassa's Market, where he worked delivering groceries, was down the street on Dauphine; Zack and Addie's North Rampart apartment was around the corner; and the one-bedroom unit Zack shared with Addie during Katrina was about three blocks away on Governor Nicholls. About one month after moving into our new apartment, I had a close friend of Zack's and a coworker of his at Matassa's, Capricho DeVellas, take over the ground-floor one-bedroom unit in our three-story building (my wife and I occupied the top two floors). Capricho told me that he had become weary of living in his apartment on Burgundy Street in the Marigny, where he and Zack had spent so much time together; it had been in Capricho's Burgundy Street apartment that Zack bartended for one last time before killing himself.

As the fall began and the oppressive heat of the summer subsided, I started tracking down Zack's friends, family, and former military buddies in California, Georgia, Alabama, Indiana, Pennsylvania, Ohio, Giessen, Germany, and in my new adopted hometown of New Orleans. The brutal murder-suicide of Zack and Addie had shattered dozens of lives across several continents, and as I spoke with everyone from Zack's wife to his mother to his drug dealer, I felt as though I was at least putting the recollections of one life back together again.

SANTA MARIA

He knew himself too well not to realize the meaning of what he was feeling; yet his self-knowledge, born of a habit of incessant reflection, did not enable him to escape the morass in which his feelings were bogged.

—RICHARD WRIGHT, *The Outsider*, 1953

Early in the afternoon of Wednesday, November 1, 1995, the candidates for Santa Maria High School's homecoming king and queen—Marcos Cortez, Jay Robbins, Jimmy Draper, Zackery Bowen, Christina Villavicencio, Michelle Wilcox, and April Sharp—posed for a school newspaper photo standing in a pumpkin patch adorned with jack-o'-lanterns and thick corn husks. A long-haired, seventeen-year-old Zack stares glumly at the camera, his chin resting on top of his hand. For months Zack had been obsessed with being anointed homecoming king. As he posed for the photo on that early November day in Santa Maria, a medium-size California town of nearly a hundred thousand residents located about seventy-five miles north of Santa Barbara, Zack was nervous and fidgety. Sensing his anxiety, Zack's mom, Lori, had tried repeatedly to lower his expectations about homecoming. The other boys competing for homecoming king, Lori calmly explained to Zack, had excellent grades and solid college plans. Lori wasn't underestimating her son—Zack was popular in school and had decent grades—but he had no postgraduation plans. With his long mane of blondish brown hair, his awkward demeanor (partly a result of physically towering over his classmates), his affinity for dark, grinding metal bands like Metallica and Tool, and after-school activities that centered mostly around bashing out beats on a hulking drum kit in his house, Zack was far from the homecoming king type.

Lori's predictions about the homecoming results were, unsurprisingly, correct. On Friday, November 3, 1995, after being introduced by the MC as a senior who "plans on making a career out of music," Zack, who was dressed strangely in black pants, a white dress shirt, and a long, flowing black cape, and was shifting nervously on his feet, stood side by side with the other candidates for king and queen under the bright lights of Santa Maria High School's football field. A billboard for a Santa Maria hair salon called Hair Studio 1 was directly behind him, a fitting backdrop for the long-haired, shaggy Zack. While the other candidates delivered serious speeches on school spirit—one candidate for homecoming king implored his fellow students to attend the school's football practices to marvel at "the pride and dedication that people have when they're out there"—Zack grabbed the microphone on his turn and suggested that Santa Maria High School institute a "mandatory two-hour nap period." The students and parents packing the bleachers laughed halfheartedly at Zack's joke. Lori enthusiastically shouted *"Go, Zack!"* from the stands, but it was clear from the embarrassed look on Zack's face that he knew the odd little gag wasn't appropriate and, worse, would likely dash his chances for being elected homecoming king. A few moments later, the homecoming queen candidate beside Zack made a short, rushed speech ("Thanks to all the people who helped me publicize all this week, especially the sophomores and freshmen—thank you;

vote for me, Michelle Wilcox!"), and the parents of the candidates joined them all on the football field to wait for the big announcement. Then, the MC cheerily announced that Jay Robbins and April Sharp—who were dressed in more traditional, formal attire: a black tuxedo and a shiny black-and-white silk taffeta dress—were homecoming king and queen. With Lori standing by his side, Zack smiled wanly and clapped politely as his competitors were crowned.

"Zack was just crushed by losing homecoming," Lori remembered later. It was a blow to his already shaky self-esteem and confirmed his outsider status at Santa Maria High School. Botched joke about mandatory nap time aside, Zack could always be counted on to make his fellow students laugh, but ultimately, it seemed, they didn't really understand or have much in common with him. Soon after homecoming night, Zack became distracted during his classes, sending his grades plummeting. Lori had been pleasantly surprised by how well Zack had done in school his freshman and sophomore years (earning A's in difficult subjects like geometry), and she was devastated that Zack suddenly reversed his hard-won progress during his senior year. Worst of all, Zack began talking about dropping out of Santa Maria High School and moving in with his dad, Jack, in Washington state. Lori and Jack had gone through a bitter divorce in the early 1990s, and their two sons (Zack and his older brother by three years, Jed) lived with Lori and visited Jack only sporadically after the split. So Lori was surprised that Zack suddenly wanted to move in with his dad. She was especially upset because Jack was not a strong parental figure; he was a dad who behaved like "one of the buddies" around Zack and Jed. But Zack could not be dissuaded and in early 1996, the second half of his senior year, he dropped out of high school, packed up his room, and headed to Jack's home in Washington.

Though Zack's sudden departure from Santa Maria was dramatic, it was in keeping with the gypsy spirit of his family. Lori and Jack had married when she was only twenty-one. They had seemed like kindred spirits during their brief courtship; he worked as a bellhop in Redondo Beach, California, and dreamed of traveling throughout the West Coast and

Pacific Northwest; she had spent her adolescence in Southern California attending Led Zeppelin and Jethro Tull concerts and protesting the war in Vietnam. Jack had seemed interested in Lori's ideas about everything from psychedelic rock to the war. "I think the reason I liked Jack was that he was one of the first guys I dated who didn't want sex," Lori remembered later. "I matured really young and everybody I went with wanted sex. Jack, on the other hand, wanted to talk to me and get to know me." The couple was married in 1972 and their first child, Jed, came three years later. Zack arrived after another three years, on May 15, 1978, at 6:50 p.m. at the Greater Bakersfield Memorial Hospital in Bakersfield, California.

When Zack was just a few months old, Lori and Jack decided to finally pursue their dream of living on the road. The family bought a VW bus and hauled Zack and Jed through small California towns like Torrence where Lori and Jack had friends. One summer in the late 1970s, when a friend who lived in a small, idyllic rural Idaho town asked Lori and Jack to help him on a home he was renovating, the Bowens dropped everything. "Jack and I got in our VW and zoomed up to Idaho for the summer," Lori remembers. "It was gorgeous." While in Idaho, Jack, who had long harbored artistic ambitions, began contemplating trading the family's itinerant lifestyle for a life in academia. "Jack wanted to be a speech and drama teacher," Lori explains. "I was so impressed." Jack then attended a small college in Chico, California, and received a BA in drama, but clashed with his professors in a teaching program soon afterward. Depressed and disappointed, Jack moved the family back to Bakersfield, where he took a job at an oil company. "Jack hated it," Lori explains, "he wanted to be back in the limelight." Jack's frustrations with his job began to affect his treatment of the family; Lori was often left to care for Jed and Zack alone. "When my mom came by our house she would be so upset because there was no milk in the refrigerator for the boys," Lori remembers. Soon, Jack stopped working entirely. "I almost left him," Lori explains, "but the boys were little; I stuck it out." At Lori's urging Jack found a job, but it was not what Lori expected: he worked as a bartender in Bakersfield strip clubs. "I was like, 'This isn't how it's supposed to be,'" Lori remembers.

Pressured again by Lori to find more meaningful employment, Jack reluctantly returned to the oil business in 1980, working at a drilling company in Ojai, a tiny, beautiful California town of about eight thousand residents surrounded by rolling mountains and filled with gorgeous Spanish architecture. "We were making about seventy thousand dollars per year and we had a little farm with chickens," Lori remembers. "It was a wonderful time." With Jack thriving in his job, the Bowens decided to stay put in Ojai for the next five years.

The stability they enjoyed during their time in Ojai meant that the family could replace their pull-up-the-tent-stakes, improvisational jaunts around the country with long vacations. During one trip to Whidbey Island in Puget Sound, about thirty miles north of Seattle, the Bowens fell in love with the island's soaring cliffs, sprawling, dark blue tide pools, and homespun music and arts festival culture. So in 1985 the Bowens moved to Whidbey, happily anticipating that the island could create the same sense of togetherness they'd experienced in Ojai. But soon after settling into their new home, tensions between Jack and Lori emerged. "Jack wouldn't get home until three a.m.," Lori remembers. "He was staying out all night with his buddies." Lori and Jack attempted to keep their marriage together, but by 1990 Lori had had enough. She left Jack, taking Zack and Jed with her to Santa Maria, California. "I wished I would have stayed in Washington," Lori remembers, "but I was so hurt and devastated."

The transition from Whidbey Island to Santa Maria was difficult for everyone: Lori was adjusting to life as a divorcée and Zack and Jed were entering their teenage years. "Zack was awkward and very bashful," Lori remembers. "And Zack's teachers were split on Zack. It was either 'I love this child' or 'I hate this child.'" Jed, meanwhile, was developing a personality very different from his younger brother's: he was quiet and thoughtful with a bone-dry sense of humor, while Zack was alternately shy and goofy. Zack's jokiness with his classmates was his way of covering up for his shyness and a feeling that he was different from everybody else. Zack and Jed even differed on musical tastes: Zack loved heavy metal and grunge, while Jed was the rare white kid in the early 1990s to be immersed in hip-hop. "Zack liked all that angry-white-boy music," Jed says dismissively. "I listened to Run-DMC and Eric B. and Rakim."

Much of Zack's awkwardness stemmed from his long, lanky frame; with a size 17 shoe, he even had difficulty walking correctly. As he reached his senior year at Santa Maria High School, Zack was plagued by self-doubt and, more worrisome to Lori, was finding his own behavior so regrettable that he was constantly apologizing to his friends and family. Zack would frequently proclaim in a strange, stiff manner that he'd made "quite a few errors in my past," even though his most glaring faults were at worst mediocre grades.

As trivial an incident as it might have been in the context of a much longer life, the sting of losing out on homecoming night in November 1995—and to have done so with such a potent mixture of sincere but awkward courage, social miscues, and the fear of public rebuke that must lurk in the corners of any teenager's heart—was particularly hard for Zack to bear. Zack was finally, provably, the failure he'd always imagined himself to be. That meant it was time to leave Santa Maria and start anew somewhere else.

———

Jack Bowen was also ready for a fresh start. As soon as Zack arrived at his home at the beginning of 1996, the pair set out on an extended cross-country road trip. Jack mapped out a route that would include party-spot destinations such as Savannah, Georgia, and Fort Lauderdale, Florida, with a final, longer stop in New Orleans before the return home to Washington state. Because Jack had experience bartending in Southern California nightclubs, he thought that New Orleans might be the ideal place for he and his son to spend a few months. For Zack it was thrill enough to go to such a strange and exciting place as New Orleans with a father he hadn't spent much time with since his early teens. But while Savannah and Fort Lauderdale were a rushed blast of drinking and partying, their first few weeks in New Orleans were, for Zack, a letdown: the pair lived in a run-down apartment on Carondelet Street in the Uptown section of New Orleans. Zack enrolled himself in a public high school, where he was once again an outsider. "I'm the only white kid there!" Zack groused to Lori during a phone call one night. Unsurprisingly, Zack dropped out of high school after just a few months, but unlike just before and immediately following his departure from Santa Maria High School, this time he felt much more confident about himself and his future. Zack was on the cusp of turning eighteen years old, and the persistent awkwardness of his teenage years was finally fading. The baby fat on his cheeks was disappearing, giving his face a strong, chiseled profile. Now when Zack flashed his dimples he looked less "aw shucks" and more sexy. He was growing comfortable in his massive frame. At nearly six foot ten, Zack was impossible to ignore, and strikingly handsome. Girls were responding to him when he flirted, and in the French Quarter bars he frequented—even though he was below the drinking age—he was getting attention from gay men, too.

In the summer of 1996 Zack started working a series of jobs on Bourbon Street where he could put his good looks to use. He served "go cups"—plastic cups used to take drinks "to go" on the streets of the French Quarter—from a bar window. Manning the go cup windows, Zack hawked beers and shots of liquor to revelers wandering on Bourbon Street. "Hey, ya'll!" he'd yell in a slightly southern twang. "Want a beer? A shot of Jack?" The sight of an astonishingly tall, blond-haired eighteen-year-old hanging out a go cup window was tempting for many of the women who frequented Bourbon Street. One night that summer, Lana Shupack, a twenty-eight-year-old stripper who danced in topless bars in Dallas and Houston, spied him leaning out a go cup window and quickly heeded his call. "Come on in," Zack had said to Lana and a female friend of hers that night. "Ya'll want a shot of Jägermeister?" Lana and her friend were vacationing in New Orleans that week and were up for a few shots, so they had Zack pour them the Jägermeister. After downing their shots, Lana's friend whispered, "I think he's gonna be my toy

for the next couple of days." But because Zack was attracted to Lana—
slim, pretty, busty, with long brown hair and a purring, smoky voice—
Lana's friend stepped aside and let them get to know each other. Three
days later, Lana and Zack went on their first date.

"He was just gorgeous," Lana remembered later, "an Adonis."

————

Lana Shupack was born in Florida on September 21, 1969, and at just
five days old, she was adopted by a Jewish family in Bayside, Queens.
Because Lana's father, Carl, owned a car wash in the Jamaica section of
Queens, the family could afford a solidly middle-class lifestyle. But that
sense of security came to an end when Lana was nine years old: Carl lost
the business under mysterious circumstances and moved the family to
Houston, where he worked as a stevedore. Lana was unhappy in her new
hometown, and by her early teens she'd rebelled against her Jewish
upbringing and what she felt to be her father's oppressive style of parent-
ing. At fourteen, she moved out of her parents' home and got her own
apartment across town.

By her late teens, Lana began stripping in Houston clubs like Caligula
21 in order to make ends meet. The money turned out to be a lot better
than she had ever imagined—she says she often brought home more than
two thousand dollars per night—so she never had to worry about finding
a day job. During the rare moments when she was restless with life in
Houston, Lana and her stripper girlfriends would hit the road and, as
Lana remembers it, "any city with a topless bar." By her early twenties
Lana was so familiar with the network of strip clubs in the South and
Northeast that she was able to time her road trips to periods when the
clubs would be especially busy (for example, she'd head to Myrtle Beach
during golf season in the springtime). When Lana was twenty-four, she
hastily married—and then quickly divorced—a man whom she had met
in one of the strip clubs in which she worked. She describes this relationship as "very volatile, very violent, very crazy." Soon after her marriage dissolved, Lana moved to Mexico City, where she lived on and off

for about three years. She says that she fled Mexico City after she was falsely implicated in a gun-running case.

After Mexico City, Lana landed in Dallas and started stripping again. But Lana despised the city's bourgeois pretensions. "In Dallas, people drive BMWs and eat bologna sandwiches as they're driving because they can't afford the BMW they're riding in," Lana explains. "I hated it." A stripper friend suggested that they take a road trip to New Orleans. Desperate for a change, Lana joined her on the long trek toward Louisiana. "I met Zack during our very first night in New Orleans," Lana remembers.

When Lana returned to Dallas after her brief courtship with Zack, he "called and called and called and begged me to come back [to the French Quarter]," Lana remembers. A few weeks later, Lana returned to New Orleans, renting a temporary apartment above the Big Daddy's strip club on Bourbon Street; the plan was to hang out with Zack and maybe dance a few nights a week at the local strip clubs. That fall, Lana and Zack dated constantly—"we were inseparable," Lana says—but by the end of 1996 Lana began to distance herself from Zack after he confessed that he was only eighteen years old. "I had absolutely no idea that he was eighteen," Lana remembered later, still sounding shocked at the memory of discovering Zack's age. "I figured that because he was bartending he had to be at least twenty-one." Then, in early 1997, came another surprise: she was pregnant with Zack's child. Lana decided to keep the baby but fretted for months over how to break the news of her pregnancy to Zack. Finally, in early March, she told Zack about the baby. Unsurprisingly, he was conflicted about how to handle becoming a teenage father.

Still living with his father on Carondelet Street, Zack sought advice from his mother. On March 10, 1997, Zack sat down at the desk in his bedroom, took out a pencil and notebook paper, and wrote a long letter to Lori:

Mom,

Well, the letter I never wanted to write so soon is upon me. This is the letter informing you of my unexpected venture into fatherhood. I've made quite a few errors in my past and this is one of the biggest I've had to deal with. But, this is what I get for being young and stupid.

The mother was as surprised as myself, but not as regretful. For she wanted to have this child. After hours of pleading defenses such as: I'm too young; I don't want to father this child; and, why not wait for someone who shares the same feelings as you, she was still unmoved . . . and much to my dismay.

She is a 28-year-old ex-stripper (as of now) who I regret ever meeting. I know this isn't the ideal mother, and neither of us wanted parenthood which was why she was on the pill the entire time. But I guess science sometimes fails. That's no excuse and I know it, but it's the best I've got.

I believe she will make a good mother who will love this child, but I just wish she could have waited for an older, more responsible person than myself to share this with. But, now I'm stuck. I'm going to stay in New Orleans until the child is born and see it through part of its infancy but in no way will I be its daddy.

I could have chose [*sic*] the easy way out and ran [*sic*] from this, like I have all my other problems, but I couldn't do that to her. I have a responsibility to uphold and dammit, I'm going to do it. I figure that if I want to play the gamble, then I need to be willing to uphold the consequences.

Well, I know this troubles you and hurts you, but there's nothing I can do about it. So give me a call to discuss it. I'd like your support in this so think it over before you talk to me. I know I've screwed up and I don't need to hear it from you. Please understand.

Love always,
Zack

When Lori received Zack's letter she was more upset by the sad, self-critical tone of the writing than the news of the pregnancy itself. "He seemed trapped," Lori remembered later. Lori felt equally helpless when Zack followed up the letter with a frantic phone call. She told Zack that his choices were either to "stay with the child and raise it or let it go and wonder what happened to the child." With evident frustration in his voice, Zack responded that he hadn't a clue which choice to make. "I can't answer this question for you," Lori forcefully told Zack that day. "Honey, you gotta make up your own mind."

Zack reluctantly decided to commit himself to fatherhood, but as Lana's pregnancy progressed, she purposefully kept him at arm's length. "I was very cold toward him," Lana admits. "I thought he was too young. I know I'm glad I wasn't saddled with a baby at eighteen. So I'm sure he was terrified, freaked out, and scared to death." Lana didn't even call Zack when she went into labor on July 13, 1997, and had to be rushed by a friend to Touro Infirmary in New Orleans. Nor did Lana let Zack know right away when his son—whom she named Jaxon—was born at 7:34 p.m. that evening. "He didn't know about Jaxon until after he was born," Lana explains. "A few weeks later, I had a friend call Zack when I was in the shower. And when I got out of the shower, there he was."

When Zack saw Jaxon for the first time, his feelings about fatherhood were instantly transformed from a tentative, halfhearted embrace to a full, almost overbearing acceptance. "The minute he had that child," Lori remembers, "he was hooked. He would carry Jaxon on his shoulders and even take the kid into the bar when he was bartending." Zack's love for Jaxon also strengthened his bond with Lana. "After I had the baby," Lana remembers, "he wouldn't leave me alone. So we officially got together when Jaxon was six weeks old." Jaxon's arrival forced Zack to become more serious about his future; in addition to bartending at watering holes in the French Quarter, he took a job bartending at the Pontchartrain Hotel on St. Charles Avenue. The job offered health benefits, and for the very first time Zack felt like a truly responsible adult. At the outset, Lana was slightly put off by Zack's sudden zealousness about his relationship with her and Jaxon; she wasn't sure if he really wanted a long-term relationship or was simply on an ecstatic high since becoming a first-time father. "If you are going to be in this baby's life," Lana warned Zack, "you can't stay for a month and then disappear for six months. You need to really think about this."

By the fall of 1997, however, Zack did seem committed—to Lana, to Jaxon, and to working multiple jobs to keep the family financially afloat. "I want to be with the baby," Zack told Lana, "and I want to be with *you*." To prove his devotion to his new family, Zack moved Lana and Jaxon in with him in an apartment in the Carrollton neighborhood Uptown.

Zack was a proud new father but was also just a teenager immersed in the boozy world of French Quarter bars, which often meant late-night hours and drink- and drug-laden after-parties with coworkers. Late in the evening of January 28, 1998, Zack was hanging out on a French Quarter street with a fellow bartender who was smoking a joint and carrying a Coke can fashioned into a bong. An NOPD officer happened to be passing by just as Zack's pal took his first few tokes. Zack's friend was arrested for marijuana possession, and assuming that the Coke can belonged to Zack because his friend was smoking the joint, the cop booked Zack for possession of drug paraphernalia. Though the charges against Zack were dropped soon afterward—the makeshift Coke can bong did indeed belong to his friend—Zack felt profoundly embarrassed by the arrest: he'd been trying so hard to create a respectable, settled-down life for himself, Lana, and Jaxon in Carrollton. So he called his brother, Jed, for advice, even though the two had never been very close. During the phone call with Zack, Jed was unsparing in his criticism of his younger brother. "You've got nothing there," Jed told him plainly. "No education, a dumb bar job, and a kid." Jed had enlisted in the army in the fall of 1994, and during the phone call he suggested that the wayward Zack do the same. To Jed's surprise, Zack said he would consider it.

In the weeks after the arrest, Zack poured even more energy into his relationship with Lana. It wasn't long before he proposed to her. "You want health insurance?" Zack asked Lana one night. "If we get married you can have health insurance." It was a decidedly unromantic way to propose, but it was steeped in the sort of pragmatism that Lana liked to see in Zack. She agreed to marry him and the pair set an October 10, 1998, wedding date.

As their wedding day approached, Zack took on double shifts at his hotel and bar jobs, all the while attending to Lana's and Jaxon's needs. During his rare few hours off—which often came during the middle of the day—Zack would take Lana to Jackson Square for a picnic of shrimp po'boys accompanied by a bottle of red wine purchased at a liquor store on nearby Decatur Street. Zack was thrilled about his upcoming wedding to Lana, but he was even more excited by his son, a bright and creative twelve-month-old who loved to draw. "Jaxon," Lana remembered later, "was going to be better than Zack and I ever were."

Zack was also thriving at work: just before the wedding he won a "most creative drink" contest at a French Quarter bar; the prize was a free trip to Belize, which Zack and Lana decided to take as their honeymoon that fall. "The drink wasn't anything special," Lana explains. "It was just some Sauza Tequila, orange juice, and Cointreau. He won the contest on his personality. Zack was such a showman. People loved him."

Zack and Lana's Jackson Square wedding was the capstone to a year in which Zack had striven so hard to be a good father and partner. Lori and Jed flew in from California and Zack felt especially touched by their presence. As Zack and Lana took their vows, he broke down in tears. The emotional ceremony—held in the middle of a tourist destination—brought throngs of onlookers.

"It was a gorgeous wedding," Lana remembers. "I think we had more tourists than guests. There were dozens of people standing all around us filming us with camcorders." The entire day seemed to symbolize the promise of what Zack's life, which already had been marked by setbacks—from dropping out of Santa Maria High School to the drug arrest earlier that year—*could* be. Still, there were hints of more challenges ahead. Just before the wedding, Lana had discovered that she was pregnant with their second child. When Zack sheepishly delivered the news to Lori by phone in the days before the wedding—"Uh, mom, she's pregnant again"—Lori upbraided him for rushing too quickly toward a bigger family just as his life was beginning to stabilize. "Shit!" Lori cried. "No, Zack, no! That is not what your life is supposed to be. Now you're really trapped."

Lori was right: though Zack was devoted to Lana and Jaxon, the new baby on the way intensified the pressure on Zack to excel in his multiple jobs. After Zack and Lana returned from their short honeymoon in Belize, Zack threw himself even harder into his work, bartending at both the Pontchartrain Hotel and the Sheraton Four Points hotel on Poydras Street in the New Orleans Central Business District. The arrival of Zack and Lana's daughter, Lily, on June 12, 1999, felt different for Zack than Jaxon's birth almost exactly two years earlier. When Jaxon had been born, Zack was not yet committed to Lana or to fatherhood. With Lily, Zack was a loyal family man from day one. Yet Lily's birth encouraged another self-appraisal for Zack. As Zack pondered his future, he thought about the conversation he'd had with Jed. *"You've got nothing there. No education, a dumb bar job, and a kid."* So, during the fall of 1999, Zack enrolled in a GED program, and on March 29, 2000, he earned his high school degree.

Almost two months later—on May 12, 2000—Zack headed over to an army recruiting station at 4400 Dauphine Street, at the farthest end of the Bywater neighborhood of New Orleans. There, Zack filled out exhaustive paperwork, which required him to disclose his entire educational and employment history, provide copies of his marriage license and the birth certificates for himself and his children, and, embarrassingly, to document his sole brush with the law. Fortunately, in a "determination of eligibility" memo, a military attorney wrote that Zack's arrest for drug paraphernalia in the French Quarter was a "ridiculous charge" that had been quickly dismissed. The military attorney also described Zack as "excited and motivated to be joining the army" and recommended that he "should be afforded the opportunity to enlist." Indeed, on May 12, Zack enlisted in the army for an eight-year term that would begin two weeks later, on May 24. That day, Zack became Private E-1 Bowen.

Lana remembers, "He wanted to make a better life for the kids. He wanted to make a better life for *us*. He did all this so that I wouldn't have to strip and he wouldn't have to bartend."

"Besides," Lana adds, "there was no war."

TWO

COURTESY OF THE BOWEN FAMILY

KOSOVO

Reports of Serb war crimes in Kosovo—including the detention and summary execution of military-aged men, destruction of civilian housing, and forcible expulsion—continue to mount. Kosovar Albanian refugees report mass executions in at least 85 towns and villages throughout the province since late March, as well as mass graves. . . . Numerous refugee reports indicate Serb forces are taking steps to reduce forensic evidence of their crimes. This includes execution methods that would allow the Serbs to claim their victims were collateral casualties of military operations and disposal of bodies that will hamper war crimes investigations. Kosovar Albanian refugees continue to report both mass and individual summary executions throughout the province. Refugee reports of Serbian mass executions claim over 6,000 ethnic Albanian deaths; the number would be far higher if we added the countless tales of individual murder. The organized and individual rape of ethnic Albanian women by Serb security forces is continuing to be reported by Kosovar refugees. . . . We also have clear indications of the magnitude and intensity of the Serbian effort to displace the ethnic Albanian majority in Kosovo. At

least one million Kosovar Albanians have left the province since the
Serbs launched their first security crackdown in March 1998, with
most having fled since March 1999. Based on the scope and intensity
of Serb activities throughout the province, some 480,000 additional
Kosovars appear to be internally displaced persons (IDPs). In sum,
over 1.5 million ethnic Albanians—at least 90 percent of the estimated
1998 Kosovo population of the province—have been forcibly expelled
from their homes.

—U.S. State Department report on the
ethnic cleansing of Kosovo, June 4, 1999

In early June 2000, Zack shipped out for basic training at a military
police school in Fort Leonardwood, Missouri. The transition from bartending in New Orleans to the strictly regimented life of boot camp was
surprisingly smooth. After all, since becoming a dad he had ably managed working several jobs and contributing to the care of his two children. Zack also felt as though he was fulfilling a family tradition by
enlisting in the military—Jed and Milton, Jed and Zack's grandfather,
had served in the army, too.

"My father served in World War II and later the Korean War," Lori
remembers, "and he even spent basic training at Fort Leonardwood. So
I copied all of my dad's letters and sent them to Zack when he was in
basic training." Zack was moved by his mother's gesture, as he had been
by his grandfather's death in 1993, when he composed a poem for Lori—
called "Fragile Life"—to mourn his passing:

A life so tender and fair comes into this world full of curiosity.
As it grows, it learns.
It blossoms into a beautiful person full of ambition
It will meet someone it loves and make more fragile lives.
This process will repeat again with this new life.
But long since forgotten is the first life.

Life is painful and unfair,
Unfair to the original life who has grown old and gray unnoticed.
The first life just a picture on the mantel of life.
But one day this picture will fall and shatter into thousands of pieces . . .
. . . And the life is gone.
Blown away like sand blowing out over the ocean,
forgotten by all but its loved ones.
ZAKK 12-10-93
In memory of Milton Arthur Younken
Grandfather to me . . . friend to all. He will be missed.

On June 5, 2000, Zack thanked his mom for sending his grandfather's correspondences from Fort Leonardwood by sending her a letter that sounded uncharacteristically optimistic about his new life in the army. Perhaps because he was following in his beloved grandfather's footsteps at Fort Leonardwood, the self-deprecating style of his earlier letters was gone, replaced by a new sense of self-confidence.

Mom,

Hello from boot camp (Day 4). Sorry I haven't written yet, but it's been a quick four days with little time to spare. Anyhow, I'm having a blast! All we've done so far is shoot rifles, run and sit in classes and march (with some terrible push-ups thrown in there). I'm doing good, I miss the hell out of Lana and the kids. But I guess that gives me something extra to drive me. Well don't have much time to write so I have to go. Love from all my drill SGT's (which [*sic*] are actually really cool). I miss you.

Love,
Zack

Zack grew even more enthusiastic about life in the military when, after successfully completing boot camp in October 2000, the army sent him to a military base in Giessen, Germany, a town of about seventy-two

thousand approximately thirty miles from Frankfurt. When Zack had
enlisted the previous spring he'd asked that his initial assignment be in
Europe, and he was excited that the army had granted his request. "Zack
and I loved to travel," Lana remembers. "Like me, he was a free spirit. He
loved the idea of being able to pack up your things and just go. So he
was thrilled to go to Germany."

In Giessen, Zack joined the 527th MP Co., part of the 709th Military
Police Battalion. The 709th has a long and storied history in Europe: it
was activated on April 9, 1942, at Camp Niantic, Connecticut, where it
trained for service in World War II. In 1943, the battalion guarded German POWs, and in August 1944 it landed on Omaha Beach, Normandy.
Later that month, the 709th entered Paris, where it operated the Paris
Detention Barracks and provided installation security and traffic escort
for supply movements. After the war, the 709th was stationed in Hanau,
Germany, as part of the Eighteenth Military Police Brigade, where it
provided law enforcement services in and around Hanau. Throughout
the Cold War, the battalion provided law enforcement services to communities around Germany, and in the early 1990s it deployed to northern Iraq, where it assisted in humanitarian relief to Kurdish refugees. In
the mid-1990s, the 709th Military Police Battalion deployed to Bosnia-
Herzegovina during fierce ethnic fighting, where it provided security in
and around U.S. base camps and Bosnian election support. By the end
of the decade, the 709th Military Police Battalion deployed three companies to Bosnia and three companies—including the 527th MP Co.—
and the Battalion Headquarters to Kosovo.

The 527th MP Co. is comprised of five platoons with approximately
forty soldiers in each platoon; in total, there were about 250–275 military police officers in the 527th. As a soldier in the Fourth Platoon, Zack
had various duties in Giessen, including patrolling the perimeter of the
base, checking on the commissary (which was in downtown Giessen,
several miles from the base itself), and filing reports on any accidents—a
dull grind. But Zack was hugely popular among his fellow soldiers in the

527th because he turned the army barracks into a nightclub of sorts for their off-hours enjoyment. He set up a drum set and several guitars in his room, and the musically inclined members of the company would come by and jam with him. One of those MPs was Sergeant Jeremy Ridgley, a hulking native of Columbus, Indiana, who shipped out to Giessen right around the time that Zack arrived.

"When I met Zack he was a private just out of basic training," Jeremy remembers. "He was a drummer and I was a guitarist and we just got along instantly and started jamming in the barracks. It was almost addicting being around Zack because he was such a bright personality." Zack regaled his fellow soldiers—many of whom came from conservative backgrounds in small towns in the South and the Midwest—with wild stories from the French Quarter bar scene. Zack bragged that he had slept with nearly a hundred girls prior to marrying Lana and he passed around photos of Lana dancing in topless bars. When the soldiers from the 527th partied in Giessen nightspots like Babajaga's—a college bar popular with the military—Zack would get behind the bar and start mixing drinks himself. Giessen is a college town—Giessen University and the University of Applied Sciences Giessen-Friedburg are both located there—and Zack, young, blond, and often high-spirited, in love with typical college-kid fare, like the Dave Matthews Band and the stoner retro 1970s movie *Dazed and Confused*, fit in perfectly.

During the fall of 2000, Zack befriended a small, close-knit group of English-speaking Giessen natives, showing off his cocktail-making skills and even his Mardi Gras beads. Zack and his new German friends toured the twelfth-century castles in Giessen and even took in a German-language production of *Hair*; Zack explained to his Giessen friends that he wanted to go to the show because his mom had once been a hippie. Katharina Friedrich, a Giessen native among the locals whom Zack befriended that fall, remembers him as a compassionate, giving friend with a great sense of humor. Zack would invite his friends out for dinner, meet them at a bar beforehand holding an armful of MREs (military meals ready to eat), and then jokingly announce, "Dinner's served." When his Giessen friends were sick, he'd make them peppermint tea with honey at their apartments. And he constantly compiled lists of music, movies, and books that they needed to hear, see, and read before they died. (Jimi Hendrix's albums made the lists, as did most of the work of onetime New Orleanian Gothic novelist Anne Rice.)

"Zack was unbelievably considerate, almost to a fault," Katharina remembers. "By Christmas he became part of our family." Zack was open with his new friends about his reasons for joining the military. "He felt he hadn't accomplished anything before he joined the military," explains Katharina, "and he wanted health insurance for his wife and kids." She also recalls Zack rhapsodizing about Lana—"'She's the one I want to grow old with,'" he'd say—as well as his undying love for New Orleans. "'New Orleans,'" Zack proclaimed, "'is *my* town.'"

Zack had become so close with his Giessen friends that soon after Christmas he suggested they take a New Year's Eve trip to Paris. Early in the morning on December 31, Zack piled Katharina and several of their friends into a rental car and began the almost four-hundred-mile drive from Giessen to Paris. The group arrived in Paris well after midnight as a freezing rain was pounding the city's streets. "Everyone was in a terrible mood," Katharina remembers, "everyone except for Zack."

Even though the weather was abysmal, Zack was thrilled to be in Paris for the first time and he demanded to have his photo taken in front of the Eiffel Tower. In the photos taken early that morning, Zack, dressed in black jeans, black combat boots, and a heavy black sweater, looks giddily happy, whether posing near the Eiffel Tower and the Arc de Triomphe or leaning coolly against light posts and street signs with a wide grin on his dimpled face. His short, severe, military-style buzz cut—with hair on the sides of his head shorter than the thick clump of hair on top—resembles a Mohawk. With their Paris sightseeing complete, Zack and the crew piled back into their car in the early afternoon on January 1, 2001, for the six-hour drive to Giessen. The brief, spur-of-the-moment trip—even though it was damp, dark, and rainy—would be a paradise remembered compared to Zack's next destination.

————

On January 10, 2001, Zack and his fellow soldiers from the 527th MP Co. deployed to Kosovo to take part in a peacekeeping mission conducted by NATO's Kosovo Force (KFOR). KFOR had been in action since June 1999 and its objectives were to deter hostility between military and paramilitary forces from the Federal Republic of Yugoslavia (FRY) and the Kosovo Liberation Army (KLA), maintain a secure environment in Kosovo, and confront the humanitarian crisis there. The bodies of thousands of ethnic Albanians had been found in mass graves across Kosovo by international monitors, and hundreds of thousands of refugees had fled the city.

The 527th was based at Camp Bondsteel, a 955-acre military base near the small town of Uroševac, the snowcapped peaks of eight-thousand-foot Mt. Ljuboten towering behind it. Living conditions at Camp Bondsteel were spartan: soldiers were housed in what the military dubbed "SEA Huts," tiny wooden huts built in Southeast Asia (hence the acronym "SEA"). Each morning, the Fourth Platoon would receive its mission brief and then roll out on patrol in Humvees. Zack served as a gunner in a Fourth Platoon Humvee, which patrolled the city of Kosovska Mitrovica, one of the oldest settlements in Kosovo, which dates back to the fifteenth century and was dominated by tensions between Serbs and ethnic Albanians, to support French peacekeepers in the area.

By March 1999, Serbian forces had expelled most of the Albanians from the city. When Zack arrived in Kosovska Mitrovica, the situation on the ground was not much more stable. Because the French had failed to quell large-scale riots between Serbs and Albanians, Zack dubbed their mission "Operation Save the Frogs," according to 527th sergeant Eric Royer. "Back then, the French were getting their asses handed to them by the locals," Eric remembers. "As soon as the Americans showed up, it stopped."

Indeed, in the beginning the Fourth Platoon's missions seemed so easy and frictionless that Zack would lead the entire platoon in a sing-along of 1980s New Wave duo Soft Cell's "Tainted Love" as they patrolled the streets of Kosovska Mitrovica. "Zack would sit up on top of the Humvee and act like he was playing drums and then getting us all sing-ing 'Tainted Love,' just to keep everybody awake and smiling," Eric remembers. "I loved Zack. You couldn't ask for a better gunner. He was real responsible; he'd be the first person to take apart his weapon at the end of the day. At the same time, when we were back at Camp Bondsteel he didn't mind cranking up the tunes or breaking out the hooch. By the end of our first few weeks together, we were joined at the hip."

But the Fourth Platoon was soon assigned a grimmer series of tasks, uncovering mass graves of ethnic Albanians and confronting some of the most violent Serbs.

"We had a lot more face-to-face contact with the Serbs than we ever expected," remembers Specialist Todd Rauch of the 527th's Second Pla-toon, "and in Zack's case, because this was his first deployment, he didn't know quite how to handle them." Jeremy Ridgely, the Second Platoon sergeant whom Zack had befriended back on the base in Giessen, says that the hard months in Kosovo offered one of the toughest tests of the 527th's ability to confront the bleak realities of war. "We all took part in bagging mass graves," Jeremy remembers. "It was pretty rough stuff to deal with."

One day during the early spring of 2001, Zack handed a few pieces of candy to a young Albanian girl. The next day, Zack and his fellow sol-diers were told that she had been killed by the Serbs simply for interact-ing with an American. The incident sent Zack reeling, thinking especially of his own young daughter, Lily. He became less boisterous after the incident; the "Tainted Love" sing-alongs were rarer, and at the gun of the Humvee Zack seemed lost in his thoughts.

In an undated letter to his grandmother that spring, Zack described a classic soldier's lament—boredom mixed with intense fear—that filled his time in Kosovo:

Hello, how are you? I'm fine, just fighting the odd case of extreme boredom and extreme stress that everyday life in Kosovo puts on one's nerves. I'm always tired and worn out from the hectic schedule that I work. A normal workday usually lasts between 12 & 14 hours, then we have to do P.T., and by the time you shower and try to eat, it's time to go to bed. We get a day off about once every two weeks, but all we do on those days is sleep and play catch-up with going to the p.x., getting haircuts, and trying to call home. The lines for the phones are ridiculously long so it takes awhile to get through. Life on Camp Bondsteel is pretty odd, you have to have a weapon and ammo on you at all times so it's kind of hard to get used to. When we go out on patrol, we go out as a six-person squad with one interpreter. Each team drives a Humvee out with a gunner, a driver, and a teamleader. I'm a gunner. I sit in a hole in the top of the truck with a machine gun and watch for the bad guys. We conduct walking patrols of the little towns, do random searches of vehicles and people for weapons, and other police stuff. It gets really cold at times and is really boring. But, we don't have much longer here; only 2 months! The countryside is pretty here, but all the towns are run-down and blown-up or burnt down! Well, I have to get ready for work in a minute so I'll have to go now. I love you. Zack

Pressures far away, at home, were also eating away at Zack's morale. Lana was still living in New Orleans, working long shifts at the local bars, caring for Jaxon and Lily on her own. Though Lana desperately missed Zack, she found herself too listless and depressed to start on the army paperwork that would allow her and the kids to live on the base in Giessen if Zack returned from Kosovo as scheduled later that spring. Zack spent his days on twelve- to fourteen-hour shifts patrolling Kosovo,

and his nights consoling Lana by phone. In a long, rambling letter written to Lori on March 24, 2001, Zack vented his frustrations about Lana
and the mission in Kosovo:

Mom,

Hello, how are you? First off, let me say how truely [sic] sorry I am for
not writing sooner. My life has been turned completely upside down
lately and I'm running to keep up. I average a 10-14 hour workday here,
and still try to find time to do PT, eat, sleep . . . you know, the extras in
life. I'm in an extremely stressful situation here and my situation with
Lana isn't helping. I know that I've put her in a strange position, but she
doesn't seem to want to accept the fact that the only reason I did this
whole thing was to better our family. . . . [It's] really stressful, then I get
a wife who never writes or sends packages, rarely wants to talk on the
phone because she's been at work all day and is "tired," and on top of
that doesn't want to get the paperwork done so I can get her to Germany! . . . OK, Kosovo. This place really sucks! It's dirty, run-down, all
the buildings are blown up. . . . My job is as a gunner. . . . I ride on top
of a Humvee with my head and torso sticking out, sitting behind a
machine gun, looking for bad guys and worrying about running over
land mines. . . . I'm learning a lot about my job and what it means to be
a cop. Some of the stuff we do is fun, but most of it is boring and scary.
We respond to about two riots a week where people throw rocks and
Molotov cocktails and stuff. We mace them, hit them with batons, or
shoot them with rubber pellets. . . . We've been called away from our
sector twice so far, once to Mitrovica in the French sector to respond to
bad rioting, and once to the mountains of Macedonia to reinforce the
infantry companys [sic] trying to hold back the Serbian troops and
protect the refugees. It's all pretty exciting, but it's dangerous and
I'm always worried. I just wish things would work out, but I only have
2½ more months until I can go get the family and bring them over to
Germany. I can't wait. Jaxon barely remembers who I am anymore. I
don't know, I guess this will all work itself out in the end. We'll just see

what happens. Anyhow, I've got to get ready to go to work. I love you, take care.

Zack.

PS—I've enclosed some pictures and a newspaper clipping of beautiful Kosovo. I hope it paints a better picture than I have.

THREE

COURTESY OF KATHERINA FREIDRICH

GIESSEN

Nothing is so damaging to a great nation as overbearance, overexten-
sion and overkill, especially in the pursuit of alleged interests that are
not clearly defined and enunciated or are not really being threatened
or trampled upon. For by attempting to control everything you eventually lose the power to control anything because you will squander
the capital, the assets that endow you with power in the first place.

—WALTER A. MCDOUGALL, "How Should Americans
Prepare for the Most Likely Challenges Facing Them in the
Next Generation?" *American Diplomacy*, December 1999

When Zack returned to Giessen on May 24, 2001, he was worn out,
depressed, and worried that Lana, Jaxon, and Lily would never make it
to Germany. A promotion from private to specialist that month lifted
his spirits, but Zack still felt weighed down by his worries at home. So,
to distract himself from his faraway and increasingly unsatisfying domestic life, Zack took the youngest soldiers from the 527th out on patrol to

school them on the basics of military police work. "When you first start patrolling as a lower-ranking person you get assigned to go out with someone who knows the ropes," explains Second Platoon specialist Todd Rauch, who was then just eighteen years old. "I went out with Zack and he taught me how to patrol as well as the layout of the areas in which we were patrolling. Zack was a great cop, he knew exactly what to do. Being really young at the time, the best part about Zack was that he would never talk down to you; he'd always find some kind of common ground with you. So if I was going out on patrol in Giessen and I had the choice, I'd always patrol with Zack."

Todd and Zack made an odd pair. At twenty-two years old, Zack was only a couple of years older than Todd when he took him out on patrol. But with his lanky, six-foot-three frame, red, rounded cheeks, and soft brown eyes, Todd looked no older than fifteen. And whereas Zack had enlisted in the military primarily for practical reasons, Todd had been groomed for military service for much of his life. A native of Mattoon, Illinois—a small town of about nineteen thousand residents in the south-central section of the state—Todd enthusiastically enrolled in Mattoon High School's Junior Reserve Officers Training Corps (JROTC), a federal program sponsored by the armed forces in which high school students participate in activities such as color guard and drill. By Todd's senior year, he was competing nationally in drill teams and being courted by the Third United States Infantry (aka "the Old Guard"), which guards the Tomb of the Unknowns at Arlington National Cemetery and escorts deceased army service members to their final rest in Arlington. But Todd didn't want to perform ceremonial duties in the military; he sought to enlist in a company that might see combat. So after a stop in Fort Leonardwood in 2000, he joined the 527th in Giessen.

When Zack and Todd finished their patrols for the day, Zack would head back to the barracks where he shared a room with Sergeant Eric Royer. "Our room was the spot," Eric remembers. "One week it would be margarita parties, another it was Bloody Marys. We had the entire barracks locked down. Everyone wanted to hang out with us." For Zack, the booze-fueled revelry at the barracks and busy days on patrol had begun to be complicated by profound physical and emotional pain. At size 17, his feet were so large he'd been forced to wear ill-fitting combat boots since the beginning of his enlistment, and this had led to a painful case of hammertoe. During the spring of 2001, the pain in Zack's feet became unbearable and he stopped wearing combat boots entirely, preferring instead to hobble around Giessen in beat-up old tennis shoes. That Zack had what the military dubs a "soft shoe profile" made him stick out uncomfortably from the other military police officers at Giessen. So Zack had the army make a special pair of combat boots just for him later that spring.

But as the summer of 2001 began, Zack's hammertoe had become debilitating and army doctors recommended surgery to correct the condition. That July, Zack underwent a painful but successful surgery, which involved removing bone and cartilage at the joint to eliminate pressure on the toe, relieve pain, and, ultimately, straighten the toe. When Zack was given a few weeks of medical leave by the army, he rushed back to New Orleans to see Lana.

In New Orleans, Zack and Lana argued so intensely about Lana's failure to follow up on the military paperwork arranging for her and the kids to come to Giessen that Zack worried their marriage would collapse. By the end of the month, Lana issued a stern warning to Zack: "You're not leaving here without me and the kids." Zack then rushed to complete the forms himself and by August, Lana, Jaxon, and Lily were all living in family housing with Zack at Giessen.

Making a transition from civilian to military life is difficult for anyone, but it was particularly fraught with problems for Lana. Before she even arrived at Giessen, most of the soldiers in the 527th were aware that she worked as a stripper. It didn't help that Lana often mailed Zack photos of her and her girlfriends working in New Orleans in order to cheer him up in Kosovo. "We'd take pictures of ourselves at the strip bars," Lana remembers, "and when the flash went off we'd say, 'This is for you, Zack!' So all the guys over there with Zack knew I worked in a topless bar." Lana, naturally, worried about what the MPs at Giessen might think of her and, indeed, she immediately struck Sergeant Jeremy Ridgely as someone who was "rough around the edges. I could tell that she'd definitely been a wild child growing up." Lana was particularly concerned about fitting in with the other military wives at Giessen, whom she suspected were likely to be less tolerant of her background than their husbands would be. "I knew I wouldn't fit in real well with the military wives," Lana remembers. "And I didn't."

So as Zack went out on patrols in Giessen, Lana and the kids would take day trips to nearby Heidelberg and even weeklong jaunts to Spain, France, and Italy. "Most of the women came from sheltered backgrounds and were scared to leave the base," Lana remembers, "but I wasn't afraid. I'd just take off with the kids and we'd drive all over Germany." The frustrations of life in family housing were also tempered by Zack's popularity among the soldiers. Zack and Lana would host cookouts and they'd hit the college bars of Giessen with Zack's closest friends, like Jeremy and Eric. Lana was able to befriend a military wife in the barracks who was willing to babysit Jaxon and Lily on occasion. So, as September 2001 began, Lana began to feel at ease in Giessen.

Then came 9-11. Lana and Zack were at home in Giessen family housing watching TV when the first plane hit the World Trade Center. As the towers fell, Lana felt for the very first time that Zack's decision to enlist would have profound consequences for them. Zack, conversely, seemed strangely sanguine about the effect that the terrorist attacks would have on his life.

While Lana was transfixed that day by the events unfolding in New York City, Washington, D.C., and across the nation, Zack walked in and out of their living room, seeming distracted, glancing at the TV only sporadically. Perhaps, Lana thought then, Zack didn't want to face the consequences that the terrorist attack would bring to their family. But in the days following 9-11, changes to their day-to-day life at Giessen made the prospect of a dramatically altered future impossible for them to ignore.

Immediately security was ratcheted up around Giessen. Trunks and undercarriages of vehicles entering the base were inspected. Occasionally, the army brass would deny all entries and exits to and from the base. A few parents stopped sending their kids to schools off the base entirely, preferring to homeschool them instead. Lana, meanwhile, felt a strong sense of kinship toward Europeans because they had reacted with an outpouring of sympathy toward the American victims of the terrorist attack, from the famous *Le Monde* headline (*"Nous sommes tous Américains,"* or "We Are All Americans") to candlelight vigils in Berlin. "I had no doubt we were going to war," Lana remembers. "But at least we had the world behind us."

———

War did come soon after 9-11—in Afghanistan—but in 2002 the 527th MP Co. was still stationed in Giessen, performing its rote duties, such as patrolling the perimeter of the base. "Things seemed good with Zack and Lana over there," Lori remembers. "The kids were in school in Giessen. And Zack and Lana were traveling all the time—they'd send pictures from the Eiffel Tower. They had finally gotten out of the rut of New Orleans."

By the late fall of 2002, Zack had also expanded his circle of friends in the company to include a new, young soldier in the 527th: a nineteen-year-old private named Rachel K. Bosveld, or "Boz," as some of her fellow military police officers nicknamed her. While Zack was much beloved in the 527th partly because he could bartend, play the drums and guitar, and get his entire platoon singing along to hits like "Tainted Love," Rachel also became instantly popular in the company due partly to her talents: she drew intricate tattoo designs in a notebook that she seemed always to have in her possession, and played string instruments such as the violin and viola and would jam with Jeremy and Zack. A diminutive teenager who stood barely over five feet tall, Rachel, like Zack, stood out physically from the company. And she was one of only a few women in the 527th, which made the male soldiers protective of her.

Though Rachel did not take to some of the nitty-gritty details of soldiering easily because of her small size and free-spirited demeanor, she could always be counted on to enliven the humdrum routines of patrolling Giessen. One afternoon while out on patrol in a hulking ASV (armored security vehicle), Rachel dared her fellow soldiers to leap off the vehicle with her into a roadside puddle so dense with muck that it looked as though it could consume anyone unlucky enough to step into it. When no one took the dare, Rachel leapt off the vehicle by herself and ended up in waist-deep mud to the roaring laughter of her fellow MPs. "About ten seconds later," Jeremy remembers, "we got our asses whipped by our sergeant. Rachel could have really hurt herself out there."

Rachel had always loved risk and adventure. She was born on November 7, 1983, and adopted by Mary and Marvin Bosveld of Berlin, Wisconsin, just four weeks later. "We all just fell in love with her," Mary remembers. "We all knew then that she was gonna be a keeper." Rachel's early childhood was idyllic—her two older brothers adored her and the Bosvelds lived on a small farm in Berlin. "We had ten acres of land," Mary explains, "the kids had lots of toys and dirt bikes, and because we didn't have a TV—we didn't want the kids to be influenced by the media—there was a lot of tree climbing and drawing." When Rachel was six years old the family moved to Oshkosh, Wisconsin, a medium-size town of about sixty-two thousand residents on Lake Winnebago, approximately eighty miles from Milwaukee. Rachel remained content to immerse herself in art, music, and writing.

But just before Rachel started high school Marvin and Mary divorced, with Mary staying in Oshkosh and Marvin moving to Waupun, Wisconsin, a small town of about eleven thousand people, thirty miles southwest of Oshkosh. Rachel managed to make the best of the split: she lived with her mom in ninth and tenth grade and with her dad as she finished her last two years of high school. But as Rachel approached her senior year, she began to worriedly discuss her future with Mary.

Craig, Rachel's older brother by about twelve years, had enlisted in the army. They had been especially close growing up, and Rachel wondered if she should follow in his footsteps. "If Craig can do that," Rachel told Mary, "that's what I should do. And I can get my education paid for." Mary was steadfastly against the idea of Rachel joining the military—Marvin was a Vietnam vet, and having one child in the army was more than enough for Mary. Besides, Mary worried that Rachel was abandoning her talents for a military career—she played violin, had acted in Waupun High School Drama Club productions, and had talked with her mom about studying graphic art in college. Rachel was also contemplating joining the military at a dangerous moment—just after 9-11—which deeply frightened Mary.

"I want to make a difference," Rachel told Mary then. "Then join the Peace Corps," Mary shot back.

Rachel would not give any ground in the argument with her mother—instead, she pressed further, arguing that the participation of women in the U.S. military had a special meaning in the country's war against fundamentalist Islam. "I want the women over there to know that they could one day have the same opportunities as me," Rachel explained. "They don't have to wear veils on their face. They could have the same opportunities and freedom I have." Sensing that Rachel would not back down, Mary gave up the argument. "It was like talking to a brick wall," Mary remembers, "and I realized that, at eighteen, she simply did not realize the magnitude of what she was doing. She was so positive and gung ho about the military."

Soon after graduating high school, Rachel enlisted in the army, heading to basic training in Fort Leonardwood, Missouri, just as Zack and Specialist Todd Rauch and so many others had done before her. Rachel's letters to Mary from basic training were characterized by an exuberant, gee-whiz optimism about her new life in the military.

"Mom, I got to go through the gas chamber twice!" Rachel wrote of a training exercise in one exclamation point–filled letter. "And I asked if I could do it again!" By June 2002, as she neared completion of basic training, Rachel had developed a cartoonishly simplistic attitude about military service that Mary found disturbing. "Only miserable creatures,"

Rachel wrote to Mary in one letter, "care about their personal safety." In the early fall of 2002, when Rachel arrived in Giessen with the 527th MP Co., her patriotic spirit was unflagging. "If I go to war," Rachel told her mother, "I'll have made a big, big difference."

———

As Rachel settled into life in the Giessen barracks, rumors swirled around the base that war with Iraq was imminent. "The Iraq war," Specialist Todd Rauch remembers, "started as a rumor."

The rumor, of course, was based in fact: that year, President Bush repeatedly demanded that Iraq fully comply with UN resolutions requiring that Iraq allow weapons inspectors access to alleged weapons production facilities. In August 2002, high-level Bush administration officials had drafted a top-secret document laying out the objectives of a potential war in Iraq called "Iraq: Goals, Objectives and Strategies." The goals of the war, according to the document, would be to eliminate the threat of weapons of mass destruction (WMDs), prevent Saddam Hussein from supporting terrorists, and, more optimistically, "build a society based on moderation, pluralism and democracy."

The soldiers of the 527th, of course, were not privy to the Bush administration's top-secret plans for a war with Iraq. Yet by the early fall of 2002, they had reason to suspect that war was probable when informed of at least one unusual—though limited—new mission in the Middle East being planned by their superiors in the army. "We were supposed to go to Israel on a PSD [personal security detachment]," Todd explains. "We were going to head over to Israel and serve as bodyguards for ambassadors and the like."

That fall, several soldiers from the 527th were prepped for the forthcoming PSD in Israel. "Guys were being pulled from our platoon," Todd remembers, "and told to go and buy suits, polo shirts, dress shirts, khaki pants, and dress shoes in preparation for the PSD. It got down to the day when we were supposed to leave. But then, suddenly, the mission got dropped."

The scrapping of the PSD did not, of course, mean that the Iraq war plans were being scuttled. By the early fall of 2002 tensions between the United States and Iraq were ratcheting up significantly. On September 12, 2002, President Bush addressed the United Nations General Assembly and blasted the Hussein regime for defying the demands of UN weapons inspectors, and also accused the Iraqi government of secretly harboring WMDs. President Bush then presented a long list of demands to the Hussein regime, among them to "immediately and unconditionally forswear, disclose and remove or destroy all weapons of mass destruction, long-range missiles and all related material."

About one month later, on October 16, 2002, the United States Congress passed the "Authorization for Use of Military Force Against Iraq Resolution," describing the Hussein regime as "a continuing threat to the national security of the United States" with the "demonstrated capability and willingness to use weapons of mass destruction." Because of its suspected WMDs—and its failure to cooperate fully and unconditionally with UN weapons inspectors—the Hussein regime was deemed by the UN to be in "material breach" of a series of previous UN resolutions. Meanwhile, a new U.S. Army general—David McKiernan—had moved to the Camp Doha base north of Kuwait City to work on plans for the land campaign in Iraq, which were code-named by the army brass "Cobra II," after an army operation led by General Patton during World War II. The Iraq war was moving quickly from rumor to reality, and this was not lost on the soldiers of the 527th or their kin. "By the late fall of 2002, we were ready for Iraq," Lana remembers. "We knew Zack was going. We had no doubt."

As 2002 came to a close, unmistakable physical signifiers of the coming war with Iraq began to appear in Giessen: vehicles on the base were painted desert colors. By mid-January 2003, the 527th MP Co. slowly began the process of shipping out to Kuwait. "We received orders to go to Kuwait for up to one year," Todd remembers. "So we started packing our rooms up and painting the barracks. It was surreal. I remember taking a shower one afternoon and thinking, 'Is this really happening?'"

Finally, soldiers from the 527th were packed into a bus and driven to a nearby airbase for a flight to Kuwait. "I said good-bye to a German girlfriend I had at the time, which was painful," Todd remembers, "but once I left the base I had no emotions. It was just business. I had nothing else to worry about except our mission in Kuwait." For three of the kind of simultaneously restless and boring days known only to those who have served in the military, the 527th slept in an airplane hangar in Germany until they were told curtly: "Pick up your stuff." As Todd remembers, "Within fifteen minutes we were on a plane." To the soldiers' surprise, they were not loaded on a C-130 military transport aircraft but instead onto a civilian double-decker 747.

"Hundreds of soldiers carrying all sorts of weaponry from 9 mms to SAW [squad automatic weapon] machine guns to grenade launchers were all packed into this huge commercial 747," Todd explains. "I remember thinking, 'I will never see anything like it again in my life.'" The crush of soldiers and their weaponry quickly filled the main seating area, so a steward began enlisting soldiers to sit upstairs in what was normally the business-class section. As the 747 prepared for takeoff on the airbase's long runway, Todd was yanked from his seat by the steward and taken upstairs. "I'm a low-ranking guy, an E-4 specialist, and here they have me sitting next to a full-blown colonel," Todd remembers. "While everyone else is trying to watch a movie screen way ahead of them, I'm sitting there with a screen of my own with nine movie channels." When the 747 was in the air over Europe, the colonel seated next to Todd turned to him and asked, "Have you been up in the cockpit yet?" Todd wasn't sure how to respond. "I didn't know we *could* go in the cockpit, sir," he stammered meekly. The colonel put his hand on Todd's shoulder and smiled, putting the young specialist at ease. "Go up there, knock on the door, and talk to 'em." Todd rose from his seat, walked down the aisle, and then knocked on the cockpit door; the pilots let him in and they regaled him with stories about flying missions in Vietnam. "It was," Todd remembers, "a first-class flight to the war."

Upon arriving at Kuwait City International Airport, however, Todd and his fellow soldiers from the 527th realized that they would no longer be enjoying the luxuries and freedoms they'd grown accustomed to at the base in Giessen. As the 747 came to a stop on the runway, Todd watched weary-looking soldiers scurry up to the plane and take luggage from the cargo holds. The 527th was then escorted off the plane and onto buses that had their windows blacked out, a precaution—they were told—against any potential terrorist attack as they made their way to the base, Camp Doha, about twenty miles from the airport. "It was creepy," Todd remembers. "No one could see out—and no one could see in."

Grim conditions continued at Camp Doha. Sandstorms with up to fifty-mile-per-hour winds blew constantly, sometimes for days on end. The sand tore at the soldiers' skin. Worst of all, patrols were even duller than they had been back in Giessen. "We'd sit and do security at the front gate," Todd remembers, "and then when a water truck came in we'd drive around with it on the base to make sure the driver wasn't planting a bomb somewhere." Topping it all off, Scud missile attack drills ran repeatedly: "Exercise! Exercise! Exercise!" blared a voice over the loudspeaker. "Put on your protective masks. Seek cover." The drills forced soldiers to don gas masks and rubber suits to protect from a potential chemical weapons attack. The chemical suits were unbearably hot even though the temperature hovered at around 80 degrees in Kuwait, and the drills made the time there all the more painful. "Kuwait was a horrible waiting game," Jeremy remembers, "and we lived every day with the fear that Scuds were being fired at us, so we'd be forced to run out and put on our chemical suits. Imagine sitting in an oven and having people shout at you all day as bombs are falling. That's what Kuwait was like. After a few days, we hated Kuwait so much that we were ready to get to Iraq and do our thing."

But Zack was not eager for the war with Iraq to begin. Unbeknownst to even close friends like Jeremy and Todd, he had befriended a tiny group of Iraq war skeptics in the 527th led by Larry Berreman, a gruff, plain-talking staff sergeant who had served in the army since 1984 and been stationed at points all over the map from Panama to Korea and beyond. "We all firmly believed that there were no weapons of mass destruction," Larry explains, "and that even if Saddam did have chemical weapons he did not have an effective delivery system."

The suspicions of the skeptics in the 527th—whom Larry dubbed "the band of rebels"—were confirmed when Camp Doha came under attack. "When we were in Kuwait we had five missiles fired toward our camp," Larry explains, "and *none* of them—not one—had chemical weapons."

Zack, Larry remembers, was just as critical of the ideological foundations of the Iraq war as were his fellow band of rebels, whom Larry describes as "politically minded people who did not buy into government propaganda." "Zack and I were in complete, one hundred percent agreement," Larry explains. "The reasoning for the war was wrong. If you want to argue that we should remove a dictator and free the Iraqi people, fine. But we felt that the public was being fed a line of crap about weapons of mass destruction and that was wrong."

Back in Giessen, Lana was consumed with worry over Zack's safety in Kuwait and busy caring for Jaxon, then six, and Lily, three and a half, at the family barracks. "I didn't hear from Zack at all when he was in Kuwait," Lana remembers. "Until one day when I was with the kids shopping at the PX. Jaxon had put a pair of tennis shoes in our shopping cart without me noticing. When I pushed the cart out the door, I was stopped by a security guard: 'Ma'am, did you pay for these shoes?' I hadn't realized that the shoes were in the cart and said, 'I'll pay for them right now.' The guard didn't care—he wanted to charge me for shoplifting." Lana was furious that she could face criminal charges at such an enormously stressful time for her and her family—the 527th was one of the first companies to ship out to Kuwait, and with the Iraq war imminent she, Jaxon, and Lily were all emotional wrecks. Lana had the guard at the PX call Zack's commander in Kuwait, who insisted that the guard let Lana go and not file any criminal charges. That night, Lana received her first call from Zack in Kuwait.

"Do I have to send Jaxon shoplifting," Lana scolded Zack, "in order to hear from you?" Zack promised to begin calling and writing more regularly—but he said little else to Lana. He was quiet and distant; perhaps, Lana thought then, the war was already changing Zack even though the war itself had not begun.

Lori, meanwhile, attempted to distract herself from her concerns about the war and her son's safety by putting together care packages for him that included baby wipes, talcum powder (for his boots), sunscreen, and even copies of *Playboy* magazine, which the soldiers of the 527th appreciated. Early that spring, Lori—who was then living in Nipomo, California, a small town near Santa Maria—was profiled in the *Santa Maria Times* in a piece headlined "NIPOMO MOTHER WATCHES, WORRIES; HER SON IS ON THE ROAD TO BAGHDAD BATTLE." "Every couple of minutes my mind cuts back to him," Lori told staff writer Emily Slater. In the article, Lori was described as a former Vietnam War protester who worried constantly about the possibility that Zack would be killed in combat. "This is the first day I haven't cried," Lori admitted. "My son is in this and he may die. This is real." When asked by Slater about her position on the showdown with Saddam, she seemed torn. "War is the most horrible thing to go through," Lori told the reporter, "but Saddam is a horrible man . . . a war at the sake of my son? I don't know."

FOUR

COURTESY OF THE BOWEN FAMILY

BAGHDAD

You are about to remove the regime of Saddam Hussein and eliminate the threat of his weapons of mass destruction. He is a brutal
dictator whose regime has a history of reckless aggression, ties to ter-
rorism, attempts to dominate a vital part of the world and a history of
developing and using weapons of mass destruction. . . . Your courage
will be tested but you will draw strength from those on your left and
right. You will not falter. I know that all of you will represent yourselves, your units and your respective countries with honor and valor
in the days ahead. . . . I have total confidence in you. There is no finer
team gathered anywhere in the world; no team more capable of
addressing the task at hand. We are comrades in arms and I have
unbounded pride in leading you. Trust your instincts, training and
leadership in the days ahead. You are warriors in a historic campaign
that will benefit our families, loved ones and our countries, as well as
the people of Iraq. Strike fast and hard!

—GENERAL DAVID MCKIERNAN, in a March 19, 2003,

message to all personnel supporting Operation Iraqi Freedom

On March 17, 2003, President Bush gave a televised address from the White House's Red Room in which he implored Saddam Hussein and his sons Uday and Qsay to "leave Iraq within forty-eight hours" or face a "military conflict commenced at a time of our choosing." Specialist Todd Rauch remembers, "We were all sitting around a little radio listening to President Bush's speech, and we just couldn't take our ears off of it. Some of the guys couldn't even stop *staring* at the radio. I remember thinking, 'This is what we're gonna do. We're goin' into Iraq. There is no other way.'"

The Iraq war began in earnest two days later on March 19, when, after receiving intelligence that Saddam and his sons were at the Dora Farms compound on the outskirts of Baghdad, forty Tomahawk cruise missiles fired from naval destroyers and submarines were launched at the compound. The missiles were meant to "pulverize every structure in the vicinity," according to *New York Times* military correspondent Michael R. Gordon. When the missiles hit their target U.S. Air Force chief of staff General Michael Moseley shouted, "Bitchin', dudes, bitchin'."

"It looked like the Air Force might have won the war," Gordon wrote in his book about the Iraq invasion, *Cobra II*. Yet neither Saddam nor his sons were in Dora Farms during the attack.

Meanwhile the 527th, the MPs riding in ASVs (armored security vehicles) and Humvees outfitted with .50-caliber machine guns, started moving slowly toward the Iraq-Kuwait border as part of a massive 250-vehicle convoy. As the 527th amassed at the border, it joined the army's Third Infantry Division. "We were the eyes and ears of the convoy," Todd remembers. At dawn the next day, the 527th and the Third Infantry Division crossed the border into Iraq, with the 527th being the first army company to employ the ASV in Iraq.

"War as we know it started today," Private Rachel Bosveld wrote in her diary then. "I hope it's a short one." The soldiers of the 527th did not have much time to contemplate how long the war was going to last. Moments after crossing the Iraqi border, the company came into contact with the enemy, though it was impossible to tell if they were regular members of the Iraqi army, Saddam's Republican Guard (the elite troops of the Iraqi army), or the fedayeen, a paramilitary organization loyal to Saddam's Ba'athist government.

"We went over a hill and saw a vehicle," Todd remembers. "And when we got closer we saw that the truck had a .50-caliber machine gun mounted on it. When we got even closer we saw men in civilian dress along with women and children in the vehicle. We didn't know what to call them." So the soldiers of the 527th fulfilled their standard policing duties—they stopped the vehicle and detained its occupants—and pushed northward in the desert.

As the 527th moved toward Baghdad, they came upon another odd sight: an Iraqi man driving a massive dump truck piled high with thick bales of hay and, even more strangely, the carcasses of dead goats. The military police officers stopped the vehicle, pulled the driver out, and then began methodically moving all of its cargo onto the desert sand. The 527th worked for nearly twelve hours emptying the hulking dump truck of all its contents. As their task was completed they found nine rocket propelled grenade (RPG) launchers and several Russian-made high-caliber machine guns—all buried deep beneath the hay and dead goats. The MPs seized the truck and briefly detained the driver before releasing him and, once again, pushed on through the desert toward Baghdad.

The incident with the dump truck was followed by even more strange encounters: Zack and the Fourth Platoon nearly crashed into a herd of camels that had rushed onto the road. The platoon also had to deal with small-arms fire coming from seemingly all directions. "As we drove, we heard gunfire hitting our vehicle," Staff Sergeant Larry Berreman remembers. "It was a steady 'ping-ping-ping' sound but we couldn't see anybody shooting."

Later on, a truck loaded with tomatoes was found to be carrying RPG launchers, and after stopping an Iraqi man driving a tractor, Jeremy found that he was suspiciously clean and well taken care of for a farmer. "He was dressed like a farmer but he had very well-kempt manicured hands," Jeremy remembers. "And because he was wearing sandals I could see that his toes were pedicured." As he inspected the "farmer," Jeremy quipped to Todd: "Ever seen a farmer with prettier feet?" The farmer, Jeremy and Todd quickly discovered, was a member of the Republican Guard. Gunfire was not exchanged during these encounters, but they nonetheless greatly unnerved the 527th. Operation Iraqi Freedom had only just begun and it was already clear that in this conflict the line between soldier and civilian was often going to be blurred.

Morale among the 527th was also sapped by the lack of necessities provided to them by the military. In the planning of the Iraq war, then secretary of defense Donald Rumsfeld insisted that a small, light force could overthrow the Hussein regime. But on the ground Rumsfeld's vision—dubbed the "Rumsfeld Doctrine" by some journalists—amounted to war on the cheap. Soldiers rode in aging vehicles, so they often had to affix "hillbilly armor" (slang for pieces of scrap metal and bulletproof glass) to their vehicles in an attempt to adequately protect themselves. There was also insufficient body armor for the soldiers to wear, and the 527th lacked basics such as sufficient drinking water. In the first few weeks of the war, water was so scarce that the soldiers subsisted on one bottle of water per day. "My morale is still good but could be better," Rachel wrote in her diary on March 23. "I spend all day thinking about going home and all the things I wish I would have done had I known I'd be going to war. I will get to do them all once I get home. I will make sure of that."

Later that day, the 527th approached Tallil Airbase, about 190 miles southeast of Baghdad. The airbase had several aircraft shelters and two huge runways that were still damaged from heavy bombing during the first Gulf War in the early 1990s. The 527th anticipated resistance in Tallil because a garrison for the Eleventh Iraqi Infantry Division was known to be close by, as was a weapons storage area in Nasiriyah, a city of about three hundred thousand residents on the Euphrates River that had already been the site of fierce fighting between the Iraqi army and First Reconnaissance Battalion Marines. But as the company neared the

Tallil-Nasiriyah area in the early morning hours of March 24, they experienced a series of small, unexpected problems.

First, tents that were tied to the back of Zack and Larry's Humvee fell off the vehicle when it made a sharp turn. Zack and Larry had to make a U-turn in the Humvee and drive back several miles to pick up the tents. Then, more ominously, the 527th spotted a convoy of empty Humvees far in the distance that looked as though they had been ambushed by Iraqi forces; the company later found out that the convoy belonged to the army's 507th Maintenance Company and had indeed been ambushed when they made a wrong turn into enemy territory. Eleven soldiers from the 507th Maintenance Company were killed in the ambush and five others—including a nineteen-year-old private named Jessica Lynch—were captured. "The signs on the road that night had been switched by the enemy," Larry remembers, "so we went out late that night and re-signed the route."

The ambush of the 507th Maintenance Company seemed to further indicate that the Iraqi army would mount fierce resistance in Tallil. "Tallil was our first major fight of the war," Todd remembers. "There was a lot of resistance from the Iraqi army, and artillery rounds from Americans were dropping all over the place." Air strikes from coalition forces had already so decimated Tallil and the surrounding areas that the charred, burnt bodies of Iraqi soldiers lay scattered all over the roads. "When we rolled up to an airfield there was a Toyota truck with five Iraqis burned up inside of it," Larry explains. "Zack took a look at them and said, 'Wow, *crispy*.' He was joking but that was the only way to handle it—it was pretty damn gross."

Soon after the 527th arrived in Tallil, entire battalions of the Iraqi army surrendered and the 527th set up POW camps and dug graves for the dead. Among the detainees was another Republican Guard member dressed like a farmer. "When we stripped him down he had green army pants underneath his civilian clothing," Todd remembers. "He also had a two-way radio and a bag full of cash." The swiftness with which the enemy was vanquished in Tallil fostered a sense of exuberance in the company; as Rachel wrote in her diary on March 25, "We're here making history for the 527th MP Co."

From Tallil, the 527th moved north toward Tikrit, the birthplace of Saddam Hussein. The trip to Tikrit was filled with more pitfalls than the fast route to Tallil. One afternoon in late March, as Todd and Jeremy were riding in their ASV, the vehicle lurched suddenly to the left and then to the right, prompting a warning from Jeremy, who was riding up top manning the .50-caliber machine gun. "You guys got this?" Jeremy asked Todd and their team leader, who was at the wheel of the ASV. Before Todd could answer, the ASV swerved wildly off the road, went airborne, hit the ground, and then rolled over four times and crashed into an embankment. In the accident—which was sparked by a broken axle on the ASV—Todd broke his nose, Jeremy suffered a concussion, and their team leader broke two fingers. "We all should have died," Todd remembers.

Though the Second Platoon was injured and the ASV was destroyed, Zack and his fellow military police officers in the Fourth Platoon kept moving toward Tikrit.

"We were out of the mission," Todd remembers. "We had to sit in the desert and wait for parts for our vehicle." For about one week, the Second Platoon waited for help and endured sandstorms, scorpions, and living conditions that were primitive even by the low standards in Iraq. They dug toilets in the sand, and the persistent sandstorms made even their bathroom breaks miserable. "We were in hell," Jeremy remembers. "When I took a shit there'd be scorpions fighting underneath me. And the sandstorms never stopped. Sand would end up in my shirt, trousers, and other places you wouldn't want to imagine."

When an army convoy finally rescued the Second Platoon after one week in the desert, the Second Platoon began driving toward Tikrit and encountered strong resistance along the way. Yet again, the enemy was not wearing a uniform. "The Iraqis were shooting RPGs at American soldiers from tractors," Todd remembers. "So when we reached a town just outside Tikrit we were given orders to find any moving vehicle and make it not work. We pulled spark plugs from *every* vehicle. It was so hard because you saw families farming who were barely making it. Their only transportation to go from their house to the market was their tractor. And there we were pulling spark plugs. But we had no other choice."

After the firefights outside Tikrit, the Second Platoon moved toward Baghdad to rendezvous with the rest of the 527th. It was the second week of April, and as the Second Platoon drove into the Iraqi capital, they immediately noticed an enormous U.S. military presence. "You could see the military everywhere," Todd remembers. "It looked like Baghdad had fallen."

Baghdad had indeed fallen to coalition forces the week before—on April 9. The 527th had missed the toppling of the Hussein regime, but few in the company felt they had been left out, as they arrived in Baghdad having experienced fighting in Tallil and Tikrit. "We didn't take a single fatality during the march to Baghdad," remembers Sergeant Charles Shepard of the 527th. The company was now focused on its immediate mission in and around Baghdad: setting up police stations and training the Iraqi police force in Baghdad and nearby cities like Abu Ghraib, about twenty miles west of the Iraqi capital. "We knew then," Todd remembers, "that things were about to get rough."

FIVE

COURTESY OF TODD RAUCH

ABU GHRAIB

I have not been out of the capital, but it is clear that Baghdad is the biggest problem. . . . Re-forming the Baghdad police has begun, but it needs to be accelerated. . . . The police need to start patrolling with sympathetic soldiers rather than with one police car sandwiched between two Humvees. . . . There are hundreds of small problems needing attention . . . and security is both the most important and the most sensitive. There will be an instinct in Washington to allow [Coalition Provisional Authority head Paul] Bremer time to find his feet and reach his own conclusions. But that will take another week or more—and the clock is ticking.

—JOHN SAWERS, Tony Blair's envoy in Baghdad,
in a May 11, 2003, memo on Baghdad security

In the beginning, day-to-day life in Baghdad was not as difficult as the soldiers of the 527th had expected. The entire company lived in a palace formerly occupied by one of Saddam Hussein's vice presidents on the outskirts of Baghdad. The palace had working toilets and showers, electricity, and even a few luxuries such as a screening room with a wide-screen TV where soldiers could watch DVDs. The military police officers moved a pair of tattered, floral-printed couches to an outdoor area behind the palace where they would hang out and smoke cigarettes. When the soldiers were bored, Zack would bring his guitar to the back of the palace—which was dubbed "the Back Porch"—and entertain everybody. Staff Sergeant Larry Berreman remembers, "That was the best part of every day."

In Baghdad, the 527th rediscovered its sense of unity because its closest-knit soldiers—Zack, Rachel, Larry, Jeremy, and Todd among them—were back together after weeks of being scattered throughout the Iraqi desert. Better still, the mission of establishing legitimate law enforcement in Baghdad was well suited for the military police officers; the days of firefights with RPG-toting farmers in the middle of the desert were behind them. "Did Zack and I believe in the war?" Larry asks rhetorically. "No. But we were totally behind the mission. And to us, the mission was opening up schools, protecting Iraqi kids at school, helping the Iraqis build up their law enforcement." For the youngest soldiers of the 527th—like Rachel—the first weeks in Baghdad at Saddam's vice presidential palace were a heady, hopeful time unburdened by any doubts that they could assist in putting Iraq's broken infrastructure back together again. "They [the Iraqis] love that we are helping them get back on their feet," Rachel wrote in her diary on May 11. "This will soon be a rich society with our help."

Yet the optimism of the 527th MP Co. began to fade as the oppressive summer heat enveloped Baghdad in June. As the 527th aided the Iraqis in rebuilding their police force, they soon discovered that the city's law enforcement was far more dysfunctional than they had believed it to be. Many of the cops in Baghdad were inept, corrupt, and all too willing to provide insurgents with intelligence about the Americans for a little cash.

"When you stood right in front of the Iraqis, they loved you," Larry remembers, "but when you turned around it was another story." The streets of Baghdad were also extremely hostile and volatile, primarily because in the months before the war began Saddam Hussein had emptied nearly all of Iraq's prisons. On October 20, 2002, Saddam issued a sweeping amnesty declaration that included "prisoners, detainees, and fugitives . . . including those under sentence of death" inside or outside of Iraq. "When Saddam Hussein ordered the prisons empty," Jeremy explains, "all the prisoners who left the Abu Ghraib prison just blended right in with the population in Baghdad." The freed prisoners had access to looted weaponry, readily available in the black markets that filled Abu Ghraib. "Back then, Abu Ghraib was the Wild West of Iraq," Sergeant Charles Shepard explains. "We'd head out on patrols and get into constant firefights."

As the soldiers of the 527th fanned out around Baghdad in an attempt to restore order to the shattered city, Zack was stationed back at the palace running operations for the company. During the summer of 2003, Zack had been moved to operations because his feet were racked with pain; that summer, he'd discovered that the hammertoe surgery he'd undergone in 2002 was not entirely successful. Zack occasionally had difficulty even walking, so going out on patrol in Baghdad was out of the question. "Zack was in the 'headquarters element' and not a platoon because he couldn't keep up," Larry explains.

Every morning, Zack prepared the company for its missions out in the field. "He was very well trained and he knew exactly what to do," Todd remembers. "Everyone respected him." Zack's days were spent filing paperwork and driving the company's lieutenants into Baghdad to check on the 527th's progress in training the Iraqi police: Zack would busy himself with any task that could keep him off his feet as he struggled through fourteen- to eighteen-hour days. Zack's hard work was quickly recognized by his superiors in the army: that summer he had been awarded a "driver and mechanic badge." Zack was also adept at maintaining peace in the palace, which was crowded with hundreds of hot, sweaty, and stressed-out soldiers. "It was an incredible strain because each soldier had about three feet of personal space," Todd remembers. "And in that three feet you had to put your cot. So you just had room to stand up or lie down. Adding to the frustration and irritation was the fact that everyone worked on different schedules. It was like living in an enormous version of *The Real World*."

Zack wasn't satisfied with his role in operations: he didn't like being separated from most of the 527th and, more important, his distance from combat greatly embarrassed him. "Zack did not want to be back at the palace in ops," Larry explains. "He wanted to be out in a platoon. Zack referred to himself as a BOB" (back-office bitch).

The round-the-clock grind of administrative tasks in operations at the palace left little time for Zack to write or call Lana or Lori. The few phone calls he made to Lana were short and the quality of the connections was extremely poor. Lana remembers, "It was inevitable that every time I would hand the phone off to Lily, the line would go out and Lily would shout at the phone, *'Daddy, Daddy, Daddy, don't go.'*" But on July 18, 2003, Zack did manage to write a rushed letter to Lori from the palace that conveyed the intensity of day-to-day life in Baghdad:

> Mom,
>
> Hey what up? Not much here. I know, I know. I should have written sooner, but I'm just not good at keeping up with correspondence. So, I'm sorry. Now that that's over, let me tell you how things are here. We live in Saddam's Vice President's entertainment facility. It's actually very nice. At first, we didn't have anything, but now we've got running water, toilets, showers, power, hot food for breakfast and dinner, a PX that's open once a week, phones that never work, a movie theater with a big screen and DVD, and all of the other amenities. But still no AC yet. All that's fine and dandy, but I'm never here to enjoy it. I go out every day and drive our LT [lieutenant] out to our platoons and police stations. That usually takes 12 hours a day. Then the PLT SGT [platoon sergeant] usually has some other busy work for me. So overall I usually run an 18-hour day.

Yes, I've been getting letters/packages from you and everybody else. Thank you. No, there isn't anything I need. All the guys say you're the coolest mom in the company 'cause you send Playboys. The guys send their thanks. I've been taking lots of pictures and I'll send them back to Lana to get developed and she'll send you some.

It's very hot here (surprise, it's the fucking desert). Today's high was supposed to be 120 and with full BDU's [battle dress uniform], body armor, 30 lbs. of extra ammo, helmet, rifle, pistol and everything else.

Well, I've gotta go to sleep so I can get up and do it all again.

Love ya,
Zack.

Fortunately for Zack, the long hours that he put in operations back at the palace soon paid off: on July 28, he was promoted from specialist to sergeant. But Zack's success was quickly overshadowed by devastating news arriving from Giessen. Lana was sick and had been diagnosed with a severe case of hepatitis C, a blood-borne infectious disease affecting the liver that would soon need to be treated with interferon therapy, which involves injecting the patient with interferon, a protein naturally made by the body to fight off a virus like the flu. The extra interferon, while highly effective in treating hepatitis C, also causes fever, chills, joint aches, hair loss, and low white blood cell count, and there's the possibility of seizures or acute heart or kidney failure. The therapy would make Lana's task of caring for Jaxon and Lily on her own difficult if not impossible. "I looked like I was dying," Lana remembers, "and everyone on the base thought I was dying. I was already so sick that I couldn't take care of myself or the kids."

That summer, Zack was allowed to fly back to Giessen to visit Lana— but only for a few days. "He held me while I shook and was delirious with a fever of 105," Lana explains. When Zack arrived in Baghdad, Lana hoped that he would be able to return to Giessen at the time when she would likely be at her sickest from the interferon therapy. But just as Zack settled back at the palace outside Baghdad, the symptoms of Lana's

hepatitis C worsened, much more quickly than her doctor had anticipated. Her doctor informed her that it would be dangerous to delay the
interferon therapy any longer, and because he had just returned from
leave, Zack was not permitted by his superiors to go back to Giessen.

Lana panicked. "I can't put this off any longer," Lana told Zack during a phone call. "So now there's a chance that I could die while you're
in Iraq." Zack understood the huge medical risks that Lana faced, but
even if he had been granted leave he would have been torn by the profound sense of duty he felt toward his fellow soldiers of the 527th. "He
wanted to be with his guys, to fight beside them in Iraq," Lana remembers. "They were all in it together."

But unbeknownst to Lana, and regardless of his feelings of duty to
serve, the decision by Zack's superiors to deny his request to care for her
appropriately in Giessen had soured Zack on the military. One afternoon that summer, as Zack and Larry smoked cigarettes out on the
palace's back porch, Zack admitted that as far as he was concerned his
military career was over. "He was fed up with the army," Larry remembers. "He was done." According to Larry, Zack went on to explain that
the army wasn't "something I wanted to do. It was just a necessary evil at
the time." But with a war Zack never believed in keeping him from his
gravely ill wife, Larry says that Zack was suddenly "questioning where his
life was going." As they finished up the pack of smokes, Zack told Larry
that once he was out of the army he'd invite him to New Orleans and
show him a great time in the French Quarter. "He assured me that when
he got out I could come out and visit him," Larry remembers, "and
there'd be a big fatty and we'd both kick back some scotch."

———

As Zack's opposition to the Iraq conflict hardened, Rachel Bosveld
began questioning for the very first time the basis for the war. Back in
basic training at Fort Leonardwood, Rachel had written to her mother
that "only miserable creatures care about their personal safety," but once
she faced small-arms fire, RPGs, roadside bombs, IEDs, and mortar

attacks while out on patrol with the Second Platoon in Abu Ghraib, she had been forced to think repeatedly and at length about her own mortality. By the middle of the summer of 2003, Rachel had become convinced that she was not going to survive her tour in Iraq. A terrifying nightmare that summer seemed to portend her worst fears.

In the nightmare, Rachel is sent home from Iraq on leave. While there she decides to book an appointment at a spa to unwind. As Rachel prepares for the appointment in her bathroom, she hears her mother, Mary, cooking, downstairs. But as Rachel descends the staircase, she notices that she has aged forty years. When Rachel opens the front door to go outside, "the next thing I know I'm walking toward the palace [in Baghdad] we are staying in and it is full of people I have met over my lifetime of years. I frantically search through the people as if I'm searching for someone. But who?" Rachel wrote in her diary. Inside the palace, Rachel finds a high school friend and the pair begin singing together and then suddenly, Rachel is outside the palace again. "It's weird because now everyone is in military clothes. Then there's me in civilian clothes and I'm still singing." Near the palace, Rachel sees her grandfather who had died before she shipped out to Iraq. She begins to yell to him, and when he doesn't respond she runs toward him. Her grandfather disappears into the palace and walks up a staircase with Rachel following close behind. "At the top of the stairs I see my family. My dad and brother are dressed in black suits and the rest of my family is dressed in dark colors, too. They saw me but they hadn't heard me. My brother was very nervous. I called to my grandpa again and my brother and they can't hear me. I called to them again and they turned around and stepped back . . . my heart stopped and I caught my breath. They looked at me and stepped towards me, they knew me and yet . . . everyone just watched but they couldn't hear me." The nightmare deeply unnerved Rachel, and she began to lose focus on her patrolling duties. "I'm such a quitter," Rachel wrote in her diary. "What's happened to me?"

For the 527th, distractions and weariness, always unwelcome to any soldier, were arriving at a perilous time. As the summer wore on, Abu

Ghraib was becoming increasingly difficult to police: its sprawling open-air souk on a road leading to the Abu Ghraib prison—emptied of Saddam's prisoners and now filled with America's—was teeming with vendors selling produce and looted weaponry. In and around the souk, there was also a swarm of gamblers, armed robbers, and Iraqis looking to eliminate their own enemies by falsely implicating them in RPG attacks on American soldiers. "There were constant robberies, and when people would shoot dice and the game went wrong, there would be a huge gun battle afterward," Todd remembers. The road that ran down the middle of the market had been the site of so many roadside bombs and IED attacks on American forces that it was dubbed "the Gauntlet" by the soldiers of the 527th. Inside the market, anti-American vendors would, according to Jeremy, "step outside their store, spray some rounds into the air, and then jump back inside just to draw us into shooting at civilians in the crowd." The 527th was struggling to work with the incompetent—and, they would later find out, abusive—soldiers of the 800th Military Brigade and 372nd MP Co. who were running the Abu Ghraib prison. "One time we had detained several Iraqis and called over to the prison to have them picked up," Todd remembers, "but when the soldiers arrived they just put all the prisoners in a truck without searching them. We were like, 'Are you gonna search these guys?' and they said, 'Naw, we trust you.' I knew then that these guys were retarded, complacent, and just not doing their jobs right."

One excruciatingly hot July afternoon, Jeremy, Todd, and Eugene DeMinico, a military police officer from the 527th's Second Platoon, were patrolling the Abu Ghraib market when a massive riot broke out. The soldiers attempted to control the crowd but, with most of the vendors in possession of high-powered weaponry, this proved impossible. "*Everyone* in Abu Ghraib had an AK-47 or an RPG launcher back then," Jeremy remembers. So the Second Platoon decided that the riot was uncontrollable and began pulling out of the market. As the military police officers made a hasty retreat in a Humvee, the angry rioters turned on them, sending dozens of rounds of small-arms fire and RPGs their way. "A crowd of about fifty people all bore down on us, yelling, shooting, and throwing rocks," Jeremy remembers, "and our guys had to fight 'em all off." The Second Platoon made it back to the palace without incurring any injuries, and later that day, several Second Platoon soldiers received an Army Commendation Medal for Valor.

The difficulties in patrolling the Abu Ghraib market—which by August was packed with a strange, combustible combination of vegetable vendors, gamblers, petty thieves, and weapons dealers—were compounded by the incompetence of the Iraqi police. "We'd teach them all the law enforcement basics, like how to infiltrate a house," Todd explains. "We'd say, 'Close off all exit points and then flush the people out.' And we'd explain how to handcuff somebody and how to stop a vehicle. But they just didn't get it. The police had such a long history of corruption and incompetence that it didn't seem like they'd *ever* get it." One afternoon, Todd was on patrol in the Abu Ghraib market with a group of Iraqi police when he noticed that a guard who was usually posted in the market was missing and, more ominous, that much of the market had been emptied of its vendors. "Where's the guard?" Todd shouted at one of the Iraqi police officers, who shrugged his shoulders in response. "Where is everyone in the market? Shit, something is going down!" Todd swerved the Humvee off the road in the middle of the market. Just moments later an RPG was fired at them. "This RPG came screaming toward us," Todd remembers. "It went about four feet over our heads." Though Todd and the Iraqi police officers he was patrolling with were spared any injury in the RPG attack, one of the Iraqi cops in their Humvee shot wildly with an AK-47 in the direction of the insurgents, injuring Todd in the process. "He'd had his gun too close to my head when he was shooting," Todd explains, "and when the gun kicked back it slammed into my head. I wanted to take the AK-47 and throw it back in the Humvee. I could have died." Because the weapon was fired so close to his ears, Todd was deaf for several days afterward. In the wake of the incident, Todd wondered if one of the Iraqi police officers had tipped off insurgents to their presence in the market that day—and he worried that both the Iraqi police and its army would never be ready to assume the security of their own country. A meek apology from the Iraqi police officer who injured him did nothing to assuage his concerns. "Don't be sorry," Todd scolded him. *Be careful.*

———

By early August, insurgent attacks on the 527th were almost routine. "One afternoon, I was smoking a cigarette outside an Iraqi police station and an RPG hit the tree above me," Todd remembers. "I was so used to it at that point that the only thing I was pissed off about was the fact that I couldn't smoke my cigarette."

Rachel, however, could not adjust to living under the constant threat of attack. "We're constantly under fire," Rachel wrote in her diary then. "Last night we were shot at by two men stealing trucks. Oh well, we're alive. That's what matters most, going home in one piece." Zack, meanwhile, was enduring the long slog of eighteen-hour days back at the palace, coping with intense pain in his feet and, most worrisome of all, dire reports on Lana's health. "I was so sick that Lily would hold my hair as I threw up," Lana remembers. "And my doctor was sending messages to Zack's superiors saying that he has to come back from Iraq because I might not make it." Yet Zack's superiors refused to allow Zack to return to Giessen even after Lana enlisted a Red Cross official to send a letter to Zack's company about her medical condition. The letter from the Red Cross only hardened the resolve of Zack's superiors. "That Red Cross letter really ruffled some feathers," Larry remembers. So Zack was left to wonder if his wife might die as he sweated it out in the palace.

For Todd and Jeremy, and the other soldiers of the 527th, a change to night patrols that August heightened the dangers of patrolling the Abu Ghraib district. That summer, Baghdad's power-generating ability was about 3,200 megawatts, well below its prewar level of 4,000 megawatts, which often left the city shrouded entirely in darkness during nighttime. "We were working totally without lights," Todd remembers, "so you literally couldn't see your hand in front of your face when you were out in

Abu Ghraib. When the lights went off there was nothing you could do but hope that nothing happens." Just after sundown on August 21, 2003, Todd led a Second Platoon patrol into Abu Ghraib. As their ASV passed under an overpass that had often been used by insurgents to toss incendiary devices at the troops below, the driver swerved dramatically into the left lane, anticipating and hopefully avoiding a potential attack. But seconds later, a Coke can attached to a long string was dropped ominously from the overpass; it dangled for a few seconds in front of the ASV before it was pulled up again. "Did you see that?" Todd said to his fellow military police officers. They said that they had. Because insurgents were often hiding powerful incendiary devices inside seemingly innocuous items like Coke cans, Todd feared that the Second Platoon was about to be hit. So Todd ordered the ASV's driver to stop in order for the entire patrol to get out of the vehicle and search the area for insurgents. Sure enough, Todd and several soldiers from the Second Platoon came under small-arms fire as soon as they exited the ASV. Insurgents were firing at the Second Platoon to provide coverage for the hasty retreat of the man who had dangled the Coke can.

Frustrated but glad to be alive, Todd and his fellow soldiers finished the short drive to the Abu Ghraib police station. "We were all pretty wired by what happened," Todd recalls. "So we grabbed dinner and then went outside to smoke some cigarettes. But as we stood out there smoking, an RPG hit the ground about thirty feet away from us." The RPG attack was followed by a mortar and then more small-arms fire. "Let's search the area!" Todd shouted, and paired off with an Iraqi policeman. As Todd and the Iraqi cop walked slowly through the desolate streets of the Abu Ghraib district, he noticed a massive electricity generator that was flickering on and off. "It was very suspicious," Todd remembers. "It would go off for five seconds and then on for seven seconds. It was also throwing some light on us which made us cast a shadow. I decided to not be a shadow so I told the Iraqi police officer following me to take cover over by a big fuel tank nearby." Seconds later, the fuel tank exploded in a huge ball of fire: an insurgent had attached a cell-phone-triggered explosive device to it. When the insurgent dialed the cell's number the device exploded.

Shrapnel from the mortar tore through the Iraqi policeman's torso, killing him instantly. Huge hunks of shrapnel passed *through* the Iraqi cop and slammed into Todd's right shoulder, right hand, and back. As Todd lay on the ground beside the dead man, he took small-arms fire from insurgents hiding in the darkness. One bullet pierced his right thigh. In the chaos, Todd managed to pull a flashlight from his pants pocket to inspect his wounds. In the harsh glare of the flashlight he saw that his right hand was damaged and he also saw that one soldier from the 527th standing nearby was on fire: pieces of shrapnel had struck live rounds that the soldier wore on his chest. "The rounds were literally cooking on his chest," Todd remembers. So Todd's team leader—who had been unhurt in the blast—ran back to the Abu Ghraib police station to get help. As Todd waited for medical attention to arrive, he fashioned a tourniquet around his arm to help stop the bleeding. A few minutes later a group of military police officers arrived on the scene, and realizing that Todd would die if his wounds went untreated, they threw him in their Humvee and sped toward a medical facility in Baghdad. As Todd lay in the Humvee he attempted to examine his injuries, which were much more severe than he had thought: the explosion had severed three-fourths of his right hand while the pieces of shrapnel in his back had torn his rotator cuff. When Todd arrived at the medical facility, Jeremy was there waiting for him.

Jeremy remembers that Todd was looking "shaken, pale, and mangled" but in good spirits. To make sure that Jeremy understood he was conscious and determined to survive, Todd reeled off a quote from his favorite movie *Forrest Gump*. "That's a million-dollar wound," Todd said to Jeremy while gesturing toward his own shredded right hand.

That night, Todd was sedated for surgery and when he woke up the next morning he was lying on a gurney by a large open window in the medical facility. "There was so much heat and sunshine that I felt like I was baking," Todd remembers, "so they moved me to a different part of the facility." After Todd was moved to a cooler, darker place he was told that he would be flown to Landstuhl Regional Medical Center in Germany later that day. During the trip to Landstuhl, as he lay in a C-130 transport plane attached to a morphine drip, Todd thought back to his flight to Kuwait a few months earlier in the business-class section of a 747. He wondered how the rest of the 527th would handle his departure from the company. "I was one of the first soldiers seriously wounded from the 527th," Todd remembers. "I knew my stuff, so I knew that the feeling would be, 'If he can get injured, any one of us could be next.'"

SIX

COURTESY OF TODD RAUCH

RAMADAN

In Baghdad . . . two men on a motorcycle unloaded an explosive
device at an exposed water main. As they sped off, a blast tore a foot-
wide hole in the pipe. Water gushed into a street below, depriving
300,000 homes in the sweltering capital of running water. Boys frol-
icked in an instant lake that stretched 500 yards along an underpass,
while adult onlookers fretted about interrupted water supplies. . . .
Reports of ambushes on U.S. soldiers continued apace throughout
central Iraq. . . . Two U.S. soldiers were wounded by gunfire as they
left a restaurant in Baghdad. . . . U.S. officials also reported that
someone threw a hand grenade at the Turkish Embassy in Baghdad
two days ago. . . . The embassy stands a few houses away from the
Jordanian Embassy, which was destroyed by a car bomb attack on
Aug. 7. . . . U.S. officials stress that, nonetheless, the violence is con-
tainable. . . . "What are people going to do? Electricity and now the
water!" said Wamidh Hassan, 24, as he watched the youthful
horseplay and admonished no one in particular: "They can play now,

but soon there will be no water left." Hassan said he blamed "Saddam and America."

—DANIEL WILLIAMS AND ANTHONY SHADID, "Saboteurs Hit
Iraqi Facilities; Oil and Water Lines and Prison Targeted
in New Ambushes," *Washington Post*, August 17, 2003

Todd was right about the effect of the Abu Ghraib market attack on the 527th's morale. On August 22, an anxious and depressed Rachel wrote to her mother, Mary, back in Wisconsin, asking her to pray for Todd and the rest of the company. "I'm sending you a piece of black ribbon that I want you to wear for a while," Rachel wrote. "The IP [Iraqi policeman] who was killed was one of the best. Please wear this in memory of the IP and in memory of the injured. Love you always. Keep us in your prayers."

The market attack was all the more frightening because by late August it was becoming clear that the larger war effort was itself going badly. Just two days before Todd was injured, a spectacular car bomb attack on the Canal Hotel in Baghdad killed twenty-two people, including Sérgio Vieira de Mello, the UN high commissioner for human rights. Investigators believed that the bomb was constructed from munitions looted from Iraq's prewar arsenal. The suspect in the bombing was Abu Musab al-Zarqawi, the head of the so-called al-Qaeda in Iraq terrorist organization. Yet the most ominous aspect of the incident was not al-Qaeda's alleged involvement but that security had deteriorated in Baghdad to the point of near anarchy. Worse, Paul Bremer, who was then head of the U.S.-led Coalition Provisional Authority, had disbanded the Iraqi military in May 2003, a move that put 250,000 young Iraqi men out of a job. These unemployed and irate Iraqi soldiers then looted unguarded Iraqi bases and secured a supply of bombs and other critical materials used to make thousands of improvised explosive devices (IEDs), which were then potently turned against U.S. forces and even UN diplomats.

"After Todd got hit," Jeremy remembers, "shit hit the fan. The attacks doubled." Rachel, meanwhile, was terrified enough of the growing intensity of anti-American sentiment in Baghdad to have soured on the war completely by early September. "More and more people want us to go home," she wrote to her father, Marvin. "Believe me, we want to go home." The 527th worried especially about the potential of a huge attack on the upcoming second anniversary of 9-11.

For Todd, who had been moved from Landstuhl in Germany to the Walter Reed Army Medical Center in Washington, D.C., to undergo a series of nearly one dozen surgeries and a long rehabilitation, September 11 was going to be the most thrilling day in his young life. President Bush was scheduled to visit Walter Reed on 9-11 as part of a series of events commemorating the anniversary of the terrorist attack, including an early morning service at St. John's Church in Washington, a wreath-laying ceremony at Arlington National Cemetery, and a moment of silence at the White House at 8:46 a.m., the moment the first plane hit the World Trade Center. The president would meet with Todd and about thirty other soldiers at Walter Reed; along with ten other soldiers, Todd was going to be awarded the Purple Heart by the president.

But early in the afternoon of September 11, Todd found himself nearly overcome with anxiety about the president's visit. He was feeling self-conscious about his appearance: he was rail-thin—at over six feet tall he weighed only about 145 pounds—and he still didn't have use of his right hand. "My mom fed me a sandwich that day," Todd remembers. "I think that was my lowest point. I was thinking, 'Here I am, a twenty-year-old man and my mom is feeding me a sandwich.' I just lost it." He was also feeling guilty about Zack, Rachel, Jeremy, and the soldiers of the 527th who were fighting in Iraq without him. "Maybe I let this happen," Todd remembers thinking. "Maybe I should be back in Iraq. I let the 527th down. Now someone else is gonna have to do my shitty job over there."

But as soon as President Bush arrived at Walter Reed, Todd, a fervent Iraq war supporter and Bush fan, was swept up in the moment. When the president and Laura Bush made it to Todd's room—which was packed with five other soldiers who had been brought by visiting generals into the room to meet the president—he asked each soldier, one by one, "What's your name? How did you get hurt?" Todd felt the president was sincere and thankful. "You knew that he cared," Todd remembers. "It wasn't that you were honored to meet him; he was honored to meet you." Just before the president left Todd's room, he asked all the soldiers if they had any questions for him. "It got really silent," Todd remembers. "You could tell the generals in the room didn't want us to ask any questions. But I raised my hand anyway. All eyes were on me and the generals were looking at me like, *'Don't say anything stupid.'*" Todd explained to President Bush that the soldiers of the 527th had insufficient drinking water during the six-week march to Baghdad—sometimes as little as one bottle per soldier per day—and that the irregular supplies from water trucks were so heavily chlorinated that they often made the entire company sick. What, Todd asked the president, could be done to ensure that the soldiers in Iraq had access to cleaner water? "I thank God every day," President Bush proclaimed to Todd, "that we're fighting them on their land and not on our own land." Todd remembers being confused by the answer, but he didn't press the matter further because the president was about to leave. "I wasn't gonna play twenty questions with the big guy."

———

When September 11, 2003, passed without incident in Baghdad, the 527th felt that they had finally been blessed with some good fortune. But early in the afternoon of September 12, while Rachel was riding in a Humvee near a police station in Abu Ghraib, an insurgent fired an RPG at her vehicle and scored a direct hit. The fuel line of the Humvee exploded upon the RPG's impact, engulfing the entire vehicle in flames. Rachel's team leader—who was at the wheel of the Humvee—pushed open the driver's-side door and was able to exit. But Rachel—who was seated in the backseat of the Humvee behind the driver—could not open the door next to her. She shoved her small frame against the door and it still wouldn't budge. Rachel then threw herself against the door again and, mercifully, it flew open. A unit on patrol nearby swept in and escorted Rachel, the Humvee's gunner, and her team leader to a medical facility for treatment. The gunner and team leader had taken minor shrapnel wounds, while Rachel escaped injury. Yet with this incident coming so soon after Todd's wound and evacuation, the 527th began to sense that its no-fatality record was about to come to an end. "This is a story I only want to write one time," Rachel wrote in a letter to her older brother, Craig, in September after the Humvee attack. "The grenade must have struck our fuel line because almost instantly our entire vehicle was in flames. There was fire and smoke everywhere . . . everything was melted or destroyed . . . [except for] a personal bag with a notebook in it . . . strange, huh? Maybe it's a sign of knowing how many great things I have in life."

Yet in the days following the incident, Rachel had persistent headaches from the remaining effects of the RPG blast, and she threw up constantly from stress. While out on patrol in Abu Ghraib, Rachel was so listless that she found it difficult to get out of her Humvee; occasionally she would fall asleep in the vehicle's backseat. Jeremy was alarmed by Rachel's sudden laxness in conducting patrolling duties. "She would roll her eyes when given orders," Jeremy remembers, "and I'd say, 'Pay attention. You cannot afford to roll your eyes at *any* information right now.'" One 527th MP Co. sergeant, according to Jeremy, was more direct with her: *"You are going to die in Iraq,"* he snarled at Rachel.

Tensions in Baghdad were ratcheted up even further at the outset of October. The Muslim holy month of Ramadan was about to begin and the soldiers of the 527th feared that insurgents would mark the beginning of the holiday with a fusillade of attacks on the company. Jeremy, meanwhile, was becoming increasingly concerned that an Iraqi policeman working in their ranks was providing insurgents with key intelligence about the 527th's movements. In early October, a parking area in front of the Abu Ghraib police station was rocked by a successive series of mortar attacks, stoking Jeremy's fears even further about the possibility of there being a corrupt Iraqi cop in the company. "We got mortared about three nights in a row," Jeremy remembers, "and each night they [the insurgents] would move the mortar closer and closer to parking spaces. *Someone* had to have been telling them where the mortars were impacting each time." Jeremy told the company to avoid using the parking spaces in front of the Abu Ghraib police station. "If you have to use the parking area," Jeremy instructed, "get your ass inside and get some security on the roof."

But early in the afternoon of October 26, a group of military police officers—including Rachel, Private Christopher Busby, and Sergeant Shawn Monroe—pulled into the parking area in front of the police station and then sat idly in their Humvees, talking and resting. Somehow, they had either not received or heeded Jeremy's warning about the mortar attacks, and because Jeremy was enjoying a day off, he was not there to tell them to move quickly inside the police station. Rachel, Christopher, and Shawn sat in their Humvees—which were turned toward one another—with the doors flung wide open in an attempt to cool off from the stifling early fall Iraqi heat. As they relaxed and chatted, Shawn had his leg propped up in one Humvee's open door, Christopher had one foot dangling out the door of another vehicle, and Rachel sat on the driver's side of her Humvee, with her door closed. A mortar landed directly between the two vehicles, rocking the ground with a boom and sending shrapnel flying in all directions.

The impact of the mortar was instantaneous and devastating. Part of Christopher's leg was sheared off. Shawn's leg was so mangled that it later had to be amputated. A pin-size piece of shrapnel struck Rachel's heart. As she lay pale and lifeless in the Humvee's front seat, a combat lifesaver from the 143rd MP Co., which had been on patrol nearby, ran toward Rachel with his first-aid bag. The combat lifesaver and several members of the 143rd tried to revive Rachel as Christopher and Shawn were taken to a combat-support hospital. When the 143rd's attempts at reviving Rachel were unsuccessful, Sergeant Jimmy Thorne of the 527th stepped in and tried. "Hang in there, Boz!" he screamed. Because mortar and IED attacks were often followed by small-arms fire from insurgents, Jimmy also had to protect Rachel from a potential second attack amid all the chaos. "As Thorne did mouth-to-mouth on Rachel, a vehicle flew by that he thought was carrying the spotter," Jeremy remembers, "so he got up and pumped some rounds into the vehicle. Then he went back to mouth-to-mouth."

Despite the combined efforts of the 143rd and 527th MP Cos., Rachel would not come back to life. She died several weeks shy of what would have been her twentieth birthday on November 7. Rachel, the first female military police officer to die in combat in Iraq, was the first fatality from the 527th MP Co.

Rachel's death—and the serious injuries suffered by Shawn and Christopher that day—nearly shattered the company's already brittle morale, with Jeremy and Zack among the most affected by her passing. "I was supposed to be at the police station that day," Jeremy remembers, "but I was talking to my wife on video teleconference. I would have made sure that nobody parked there, and as a result, nobody would have been hurt. The fate of the whole thing really, really bothers me." To honor Rachel's memory, the 527th built a makeshift rifle range near the spot where she was killed.

———

For Zack, the loss of Rachel was particularly hard to bear; he'd felt a special kinship with her because the pair had kept up morale in the 527th with their creative endeavors (Zack with his music, Rachel with her tattoo artistry). "Losing the girl from his company," Zack's father-in-law, Carl Shupack, remembers, "that was very painful for Zack. That was a turning point." At the same time, Zack was consumed with fears over Lana's health; she was in the midst of the interferon therapy and it was not yet clear if she would survive the treatments.

Unbeknownst to Lana and most of the 527th, Zack was mourning yet another loss that October. Late that summer, Zack had "adopted" a young Iraqi boy named Rashid (not his real name) whose family owned a small shop across the street from one of the Iraqi police stations in Baghdad. Nearly every afternoon when Zack was at the police station with a lieutenant from the 527th, inspecting the progress the company was making in training the Iraqi police, Rashid would bring Zack cans of Coke and bags of ice from his family's store. To thank Rashid for his help, Zack taught him English, which Rashid picked up effortlessly. "He was a smart little bugger," Staff Sergeant Larry Berreman remembers, "and Zack took to him like you wouldn't believe." Larry says that Zack forged such a strong relationship with Rashid because he felt that it was a good deed that would help him overcome his own opposition to the war. Indeed, Lana says that before the war began, Zack donated Jaxon's and Lily's old clothing and toys to relief organizations in Iraq. But one day in early September, insurgents blew up Rashid's family's shop— perhaps as payback for collaborating with Americans—killing Rashid and his entire family. "The boy was there one day," Larry remembers, "and the next day he wasn't. It was horrible. Zack became deeply depressed after the boy was killed."

Indeed, that fall Zack had grown so dispirited by Todd's injury and evacuation, the loss of Rachel, Lana's grave illness, and the loss of the Iraqi boy that he rarely left Saddam's vice presidential palace. "If Zack didn't have a mission he would sleep," Larry remembers. "He was happy-go-lucky and then he was just depressed."

SEVEN

CHAD EDWARDS

HOMECOMING

The interview for aspiring police officers lasts two minutes and goes something like this: Col. Hussein Mehdi, the dean of the training academy, scans the candidate from head to toe for signs that he is shifty. He asks a question to verify his résumé. If the applicant says he studied electrical engineering, for instance, Mehdi inquires about the properties of a light bulb. Then he gets to the heart of his probe: How do you feel about the "liberation war"?

—ARIANA EUNJUNG DHA,
"Flaws Showing in New Iraqi Forces; Pace of Police Recruiting Leads to Shortcuts," *Washington Post*, December 30, 2003

In November 2003, the 527th began its return to Giessen. Zack was among the first from the company to arrive back in Germany. The homecoming was bittersweet. Zack and the few 527th soldiers who had returned from Iraq feared that their dangerous and difficult slog in Abu

Ghraib had yielded little progress in the war. 527th soldiers like Zack, Jeremy, and Todd were all frustrated at the rising levels of violence perpetrated by insurgents around Baghdad and, more specifically, the slow pace of the recruiting and training of Iraqi police. "I was so pissed when I came home," Todd remembers. "Iraq was in the exact same place when we arrived, if not worse. I felt like it was all going to hell in a handbasket."

Though Lana was thrilled to have Zack back, he was "different," she remembers. "There was a disconnect. Part of him wasn't back. There was an emptiness. There were times during close and intimate moments when I felt like I had him back all the way. But those did not last long. It became harder and harder to find the man I had fallen in love with and the man I wanted to spend my life with."

Before the war, Zack had been talkative and gregarious, a soldier whom everyone in Giessen—527th soldiers and Giessen natives alike—wanted to befriend. But when he came back from Baghdad, Zack was quiet, withdrawn, and brooding. Zack's dark mood lifted a little by the end of the year—Lana's condition was improving and Zack began contemplating where he might like to be stationed with the army next. "Let's go to Hawaii!" Zack announced when he was in a rare light mood. Lana said that she'd go anywhere Zack wanted—she was just glad to have him back from Iraq. Jeremy's return to Giessen in December 2003 put Zack even more at ease. The good times that Zack and Jeremy shared in Giessen before they deployed to Iraq—hitting local bars like Babajaga's, jamming so loudly on their drums and guitars in the barracks that they drew noise complaints—were back. The pair were able to joke around after the December 13 capture of Saddam Hussein, with Zack telling Jeremy that he would have liked to have been there when U.S. forces had pulled Saddam from his tiny hole-in-the ground hiding place, and to have delivered a swift punch to his face.

But Lana and many of the military wives at Giessen sensed that even during the good times their husbands had been changed forever by the war. One military wife, who asked that she not be identified, says some of the soldiers of the 527th returned from Iraq "desensitized toward life

and scarily racist. They hated Arabs. They wished they were all dead."
She says that she could not reconcile the person her husband was when
he came back from Iraq with who he was before he'd gone. She filed for
divorce soon afterward. Lana feared that her relationship with Zack
would not last, but she was not yet contemplating separating from him.
She was beginning her recovery from the long, painful interferon therapy and she was happy that although Zack could sometimes be distant,
he still seemed to be thinking about their future.

Unbeknownst to Lana, however, Zack was thinking almost exclu-
sively of the past. Zack had always been opposed to the war, but after
returning from Iraq he'd grown angry and resentful about it, particularly
after the Iraq Survey Group, an organization comprised of nearly fourteen hundred military and intelligence specialists, declared in January
2004 that weapons of mass destruction could not be found in Iraq.
"Mom," Zack growled to Lori on the phone one day, "the war is a *joke.*"

Zack also struggled constantly with the loss of Rachel—why was she
taken and not him? Jeremy admits that he experienced very similar feelings of survivor guilt. "Why did so many others from the 527th—like
Rachel—get injured and killed when I didn't get hurt or even a scratch
on me?" he asks. And Zack was still furious with his superiors for refusing to allow him to return to Giessen to be with Lana when her condition was at its most tenuous. "Zack was over in Iraq knowing that he was
losing his family," Larry explains. "He wanted to go back to Giessen and
they just wouldn't let him. The guys who had family—particularly the
guys who had family back at the base—were torn. They wanted to do the
mission but they had the stress of leaving their family behind in a foreign country."

Though Zack's fellow military police officers told him that it was
unrealistic to expect that *anyone* from the company would be permitted
to be sent home permanently from Iraq—barring a death of a close relative,
perhaps—Zack insisted that he had been "messed over" by his superiors.
"Letting one soldier go home to his family," Zack seethed, "would have
been nothing." That Zack and Lana had appealed the decision up the

chain of command to the battalion commander—all to no avail—only infuriated Zack further. Jeremy remembers the leadership's attitude: "'Her recovery is going fine and we're not gonna spend money and logistics sending Bowen back to the rear.' They didn't want the numbers going down."

Even though he hadn't been injured during any engagement with the enemy in Iraq, Zack was struggling with the physical toll the war had taken on him. He told a doctor that he was experiencing frequent, severe headaches, an early indicator of the onset of PTSD. He was short of breath when he went out on patrols in Giessen. At night, Zack wheezed and coughed so much that he had trouble sleeping. He also had developed a severe, painfully itchy rash on his back; his right shoulder and lower back ached. As the spring of 2004 began, Zack was furious with the war for the emotional and physical toll it was taking on him So even though he was physically able to do basic exercises, like sit-ups, he began purposely failing his Army Physical Fitness Test (APFT). Zack's first failed APFT occurred on April 23 when he performed about forty-four sit-ups, below the "below average" number of fifty sit-ups in two minutes. Writing in a developmental counseling form that day, a 527th squad leader warned:

> SGT Bowen, your performance on your APFT that you took was well below standard . . . you are expected to not only meet the standard, but to exceed it. You had an extremely poor performance on your push-up event. . . . Your failure will now result in your removal from the OML [order of merit] list until you have successfully passed an APFT. You will have to attend a remedial PT session every day that you are on working status. This session will last a mandatory of 1 hour and will concentrate on the events that you are weakest in. I also encourage you to do more PT on your own that will help you out in the long run.

Zack attended the remedial PT sessions and Lana remembers that he worked intently on his sit-ups back at the barracks. "He let me know that he was having problems with his PT tests," Lana explains, "so I'd watch him at home as he did the push-ups. He had no trouble with them and

I thought that he was going to get past his problems with the APFTs fast." But unbeknownst to Lana, Zack purposefully failed his APFTs in May, April, and June. During a July 12 APFT, Zack again performed well below average on his sit-ups, bringing yet another warning, this time from a 527th MP Co. command sergeant major:

> ... you failed to meet the standard, thus you do not meet the requirements necessary to attend PLDC [Primary Leadership Development Course]. Your performance places you in a Category IV of the OML [the lowest category in the order of merit list]. You will remain in this category until you have met the standard. Failure to meet Army standards ... is detrimental to your career and could lead to separation from the Military.

The following day, the 527th MP Co. squad leader who conducted the first APFT back in April blasted Zack in a Developmental Counseling Form:

> How can you lead soldiers if you yourself cannot meet the standards. You will be assigned to my team as driver until you either pass a record APFT or you are transitioned to another position in the company.

The same day, in a separate Developmental Counseling Form, the squad leader outlined a strict new APFT regimen for Zack and warned him anew that failure to pass APFTs could result in a discharge from the military:

> SGT Bowen, This counseling is to inform you of your failure to progress and meet the Army standards on the Army Physical Fitness Test. You failed a record PT test on May 3, 2004 and then a diagnostic on May 19, 2004, June 8, 2004 and July 12, 2004. Over a period of 90 days you failed to show improvement and actually lost repetitions on your sit-ups. If you do not pass a record PT test by August 3rd, 2004, which is

your 90 day mark from the first record you took, it will be recommended to the chain of command that chapter paperwork be initiated on you. This is a tuly [*sic*] poor reflect [*sic*] on yourself and of the company. You are a non-commissioned officer and expected to exceed the standard. You are having trouble just meeting the standard. You will be assigned to conduct physical training twice a day, 6 days a week until the date of August 3rd, 2004 when your record will be given to you. If you are working shift, depending the shift you are working, you will conduct PT with two shifts a day. You will conduct PT 6 days a week with Sunday being your only day off. Even if you are not schedule [*sic*] to work on a day that falls in the 6 day cycle, you will come in and conduct PT with two shifts for that day. You will check in with the patrol supervisor and I will make sure that you showed up.

Just as his squad leader commanded, Zack took the APFTs six days per week. Yet he did not tell Lana about the new APFT regimen, nor, for that matter, did she know that he had failed the latest round of APFTs. "Zack was acting very strange and secretive," Lana remembers. "I knew that there was a change in his schedule but I didn't know exactly what was going on. Things started not adding up. Things were always being held back. Suddenly, there were always secrets."

By the early fall of 2004, the long series of failed APFTs had kickstarted Zack's separation from the military. Zack was removed from the military under "Chapter 13, AR 635-200: Unsatisfactory Performance," which is invoked when it is established that the soldier "would create serious disciplinary problems or a hazard to the military mission or to the soldier" and that rehabilitation would be inappropriate because the "soldier is resisting rehabilitation attempts."

The Chapter 13 separation resulted in a recommendation of an honorable discharge from Zack's company commander, Captain William A. Rodgers, which was appropriate because Zack had steadily risen through the ranks of the army and had received several medals and awards, among them the Driver and Mechanic Badge, a Kosovo Campaign

Medal, and a Presidential Unit Citation, which is granted to military units that have performed an extremely meritorious or heroic act, usually in the face of an armed enemy.

Yet on November 23, 2004, a First Armored Division colonel named Lou L. Marich recommended that Zack receive a general (under honorable conditions) discharge without providing any narrative to explain the discharge. Although the labels given to the two discharges may look similar to those unfamiliar with military lingo, this type of discharge is given if the negative aspects of the service member's conduct outweigh the positive. The difference in both status and benefits between an honorable discharge and a general (under honorable conditions) discharge is profound. Under a general (under honorable conditions) discharge, soldiers may lose benefits such as a home loan guarantee, life insurance, or disability and education benefits, which are evaluated on a case-by-case basis for those who receive this type of discharge. A general (under honorable conditions) discharge can further create serious obstacles for veterans in finding a civilian job, as it indicates that the vet had problems in the military. Indeed, when Zack signed his "Notification of Separation Under AR 635-200, Chapter 13, Unsatisfactory Performance" late that fall, he agreed to the following condition: "I may be ineligible for many or all benefits as a veteran under both Federal and State laws and that I may expect to encounter substantial prejudice in civilian life." Zack was not honest with Lana or any of his family members—even Lori—about the type of discharge he had received.

One afternoon during the late fall of 2004, after arriving home at the barracks in Giessen, Zack announced to Lana, "We're out of the military." When Lana pressed for details about the discharge, Zack refused to provide them, sparking a huge fight between them. "I was livid," Lana remembers. "We had started a life in the military so that Zack wouldn't have to bartend and I wouldn't have to strip. I told Zack, 'We're done.'"

Zack told his mother that he'd been discharged for medical reasons and he told Lana's father that he was *dishonorably* discharged from the military.

Zack's unwillingness to be forthcoming with Lana did cost him his marriage. Soon after Zack's blunt announcement and their subsequent fight, Lana packed up her belongings and flew back home to New Orleans, leaving Jaxon and Lily with Zack in Giessen. "I left the kids with Zack because they were in a good DOD [Department of Defense] school in Germany," Lana remembers, "and I wanted them to be with Zack as I tried to make a new life in New Orleans."

As Lana looked for a new job and a place to live, Zack was moved to a so-called transition point at the Giessen base. After some final processing, Zack was then discharged from the army. It was an extremely painful time for Zack—he had just endured an embarrassing separation from the military, his wife had left him, and he was struggling to raise two kids as a single parent.

Looming ahead was most likely the bartending grind in New Orleans, a life he believed he had left behind forever when he enlisted in the army way back in 2000. "He gave me a Nickelback CD just before he left," Jeremy remembers. "It was called *The Long Road.* Zack said, 'Well, man, you can have this. I'll get another when I get home.'" Zack was also vague when talking to Jeremy about the reasons for his discharge from the military and the type of discharge he received. "He told me that he was getting a medical discharge because he had big problems with his feet," Jeremy remembers. "I didn't think that made any sense. He did have health problems but he was capable of doing his PTs. I remember thinking, 'Somebody along the line failed him. Somebody did him wrong.'"

Jeremy was right to be suspicious of Zack's separation from the military. That Zack received a general (under honorable conditions) discharge instead of the recommended honorable discharge was unusual, inexplicable, and unfair given that Zack had served honorably in both Kosovo and Iraq and had caused no disciplinary problems. Indeed, during his more than four years of service, Zack received numerous medals, badges, and commendations. He had also quickly risen in the ranks from a private to a sergeant. The sole black mark on his military record was the set of failed APFTs in the spring, summer, and fall of 2004.

Christian Deichert, the military attorney who represented Zack in his discharge proceedings, told me that even he hadn't known that Zack had been given a general (under honorable conditions) discharge until I contacted him. He was also baffled that Zack was given this type of discharge after Zack's company commander had recommended an honorable discharge.

"I do not see a basis for the general discharge in this case other than the PT test failures themselves," Christian told me, "and there would have to be more to justify it for me. Based on the packet, I don't understand the characterization of service, and I don't agree with it." Christian added, "If Zackery had been entitled to a board hearing [soldiers who have served for six years or more are entitled to a board hearing and Zack had served about five years] and I represented him in the hearing, I would have laid out his record and argued that he deserved a chance to stay in and get his PT score back up. I would have argued that, if the board disagreed and decided he needed to be separated, he deserved an honorable discharge. On the other hand, if I represented the army in a separation board in this case, I would have had a hard time justifying a general discharge. Without more than the PT test failures, I would not have argued for one unless the chain of command recommended it, and if that were the case, I would have called them to testify to the board as to their reasoning." Christian did note, however, that while Zack was not automatically entitled to a board hearing, he could have appealed the general discharge by submitting "any matters to the separation authority," but he did not do so. "From that I have to conclude," Christian told me, "that he did not want to contest the chapter."

I also had Paul Sullivan, executive director of Veterans for Common Sense, examine Zack's entire military record. After reviewing it, Paul told me that he believed that the general (under honorable conditions) discharge was inappropriate given that Zack had served honorably in two war zones. "Instead of determining if Zack had any physical or psychological conditions, his chain of command appeared intent on an expedited discharge. His chain of command should have asked if there were psychological or physical reasons for his failure to pass the APFT, but they did not. There was no postdeployment medical exam. And even when a separation medical exam was completed, no one seems to have reviewed it with a critical eye. In short, all of the legal and medical due process safeguards designed to protect the interests of our soldiers failed miserably. This is a brutal irony given that Zack earned a Good Conduct Medal for being a responsible and diligent soldier without any record of offenses. There appears to be no prior adverse history—no court-martial, no AWOL, no demotions—nothing. Furthermore, Captain Rodgers recommended an honorable discharge, and this was reasonable based on Zack's prior performance, his promotions, and his awards. Every check in the military—his chain of command, the medical system, and the legal system—failed Zack, his wife, and his two young children. Everything that could have gone wrong went wrong during Zack's transition from combat soldier to civilian. The tragic result: Zack, a combat soldier with documented postdeployment mental health symptoms, was mercilessly kicked to the curb by the military. Our government can fix this travesty of justice by promptly granting an honorable discharge to Zack and by providing full VA benefits to Lana Bowen and her children."

EIGHT

DEREK S. BRIDGES

NEW ORLEANS

I guess the tables have turned on us. In Germany, Lana was stuck without a job, with two kids, a spouse with an inflexible schedule, little money and no friends. Here, it's me.

—ZACK, in a March 2005 e-mail to his mom, Lori

Lana had bad news for Zack when she picked him, Jaxon, and Lily up at the airport on a late December day in 2004. "I started seeing somebody," she told Zack. "An old friend. I got close to an old friend of mine." Zack sat in stony silence as Lana confessed to her new relationship. "I forgive you," he said a few moments later. "I don't need forgiveness," Lana replied angrily. "We're not gonna get back together." Zack and Lana had separated but not yet made any plans for divorce. Where, he wondered, would he and the kids live? Lana explained to Zack that the kids could live with her while he stayed in a hotel room and looked for someplace permanent. Zack nodded his head silently in agreement as they headed on I-10 East toward New Orleans.

Zack did not last long by himself in a New Orleans hotel: he was lonely, bored, and missing Jaxon and Lily. So at the outset of 2005, Lana suggested that they all move in together in an apartment in Terrytown, a New Orleans suburb on the west bank of the Mississippi River. To Lana, however, the living arrangement wasn't meant to be a reconciliation between her and Zack.

"I was just trying to make things easier for us and the kids," Lana remembers. "And I was okay with us living together and being friends." Zack didn't view the living arrangement the same way. "In his eyes," Lana explains, "we were gonna work it out." Zack also held out hope that he could find a job better than serving go cups to drunk French Quarter tourists. In the meantime, he was willing to care for Jaxon and Lily and handle all the domestic duties as Lana worked. In a March 30, 2005, e-mail to Lori—written in a rushed style and, strangely, in all lowercase letters—Zack excitedly detailed the challenges of balancing caring for the kids and a job search:

> salutations! yes, i am among the living (barely). i hope you don't mind the fact that i don't use capital letters or much punctuation in e-mails. . . . i just can't seen to find the time . . . to answer some of your questions. yes, i am letting my hair grow out (haircuts once a week for five years has taken its toll. it's coming along nicely, but in its frizzy faze [*sic*] so i'm left to the confines of hats for a couple more months). we have till next january on our lease here, so i don't foresee a move in the future. lana's re-taken a liking to this place and is trying to soak up as much of the civilized life as possible . . . i'm eating up all the time with the kids, i do all the shopping (i've even started clipping coupons), i prepare all the meals (i've always loved to cook), i do all the laundry and other househusband stuff and you know what? i don't mind it in the slightest! however, all that will come crashing down in the next few weeks as money grows tighter and everything is pretty much back on track. i'm thinking about driving a taxi (gasp!) for a while since the schedule is to work when you want and the kids don't fare well with only

an hour or two with a parent each day . . . i'm hoping to be able to get back into doing something with my music here soon. i love the guitar, but miss playing the drums (it's been about three years since i've been able to set up the kit and play with people). but i have been playing my crappy old guitar a lot lately. lily and jaxon get frustrated because they can't apply enough pressure to the strings to make a clean sound even on their kid's guitars. but that doesn't stop lily, she'll [go] long periods of time strumming open notes and singing at the top of her lungs for hours on end (very musical, that one). it drives lana crazy, but i encourage it and play along with my guitar while jax bangs on electric drum pads. i wonder why none of the neighbors seem to like our family? the kids are doing fantastic in school. jaxon continues to excel in reading and math, but has very sloppy handwriting, can't sit still, never stops talking, and lacks patience (i wonder where he gets it from??? curious). lily is the dreamer. it seems that she doesn't have the time in her busy life to deal with trivial things like paying attention in class and not being a moody little temper-ridden drama queen (wonder where she gets that from . . . points the finger at lana). however, she has decided that she will become a rock star actress doctor teacher when she grows up. well, i'd better get along before my computer crashes . . . i'll talk to you again soon.

love

z

The exuberance expressed in Zack's e-mail soon gave way to despair. Non-service-industry jobs are scarce in the tourism-driven New Orleans economy, and Zack was wary of returning to the French Quarter bar scene. In the spring of 2005, Zack found a job tending bar at a down-and-out watering hole on the one hundred block of the French Quarter's Chartres Street called Hog's Bar. Hog's was dimly lit and sparsely furnished, with a long wooden bar, video poker machines, a worn-looking 1970s-era chandelier hanging from the ceiling, and crumpled old dollar bills Scotch-taped to the mirror behind the bar. It was a favorite spot of transsexual strippers who danced at nearby clubs and had an uninspired selection of drinks, particularly for a New Orleans bar: bottled beer (nothing on draft) and cocktails mixed with warm, flat Coke or tonic water and no-name spirits. The bar's manager, Ted Mack, gave Zack the graveyard shift—2:00–10:00 a.m., which could be highly lucrative because Hog's was the afterwork hangout for strippers and transsexuals, who have cash in their pockets at 3:00 a.m., like to drink, and know how to tip well. Ted is a slim, middle-aged black man whose 1970s-styled looks (he has a short, graying Afro and sports tinted glasses and a gold crucifix around his neck) and cool yet assertive demeanor (managerial yet adept at navigating politics among employees) make him seem equal parts Al Green and Lester Freamon, the meticulous homicide detective from *The Wire*. Ted remembers Zack as a dependable worker popular with both women and the "girls" from the nearby clubs. "Zack didn't care if any of the girls at the bar liked him," he says, "and many of the girls took that as a challenge."

Amid the sea of admirers at Hog's—female, transsexual, and otherwise—one woman stood out for her total disinterest in Zack. Adrianne "Addie" Hall, a diminutive twenty-nine-year-old with a lithe dancer's body, wild eyes, and dirty blond hair, had a low opinion of Hog's and of Zack. When Zack wound down his shift at ten o'clock, he would hand over bartending duties to Addie. She tolerated Zack, but she fought constantly with the female bartenders with whom she worked during the day shift. Addie thought that the female bartenders at Hog's were slow and too easily charmed by Zack. Unlike her fellow bartenders and the drunk women who stumbled over from Bourbon Street to patronize Hog's, Zack struck her as a goofy, oversize frat boy with worn-out and embarrassing bar tricks, like playing magic tricks with quarters and playing cards.

But Zack was instantly attracted to Addie, who, he quickly found out, was a seamstress, poet, and dancer. Even though Zack had lived on and off in New Orleans since the mid-1990s, he had retained a highly idealized view of French Quarter bohemia—he worshipped the bartenders, bicycle deliverymen, and waiters who also happened to be aspiring play-wrights, actors, and musicians.

———

The French Quarter has been central to New Orleans life since the creation of the city in 1718 by Compagnie d'Occident ("the Company of the West"), a French trading company run by John Law, a Scottish economist and gambler with a keen eye for wildly speculative business ventures. Law's company founded New Orleans under the auspices of then Louisiana governor Jean-Baptiste Le Moyne de Bienville, and the city was named for the regent of France, Philippe II, Duc D'Orleans (Duke of Orleans). New Orleans was built on swampy land on the northeastern side of the Mississippi River in an area where the land takes a crescent shape (it is often referred to as the Crescent City). The French Quarter—or Vieux Carré (Old Square)—was the center of this new city. The French laid out a relatively simple street grid for the French Quarter: to the north, the neighborhood is bounded by Esplanade Avenue (across Esplanade is the Faubourg Marigny neighborhood, which would be established in the early nineteenth century); to the south is Canal Street (just past Canal is the Central Business District and then, farther upriver, Uptown); to the east is the Mississippi River, whose banks served as a natural levee for the new city; and to the west is North Rampart Street (across North Rampart Street is Faubourg Tremé—or simply Tremé—a predominantly African-American neighborhood established in the late eighteenth century by hat maker and real estate developer Claude Tremé).

Though the French had colonized Louisiana in 1714, New Orleans was still a backwater. When it was ruled by the French, New Orleans was even referred to as the "Isle D'Orleans." So Law, a born schemer, devised a plan to populate Louisiana—and New Orleans especially—with French criminals. "Prostitutes and female criminals (with the fleur-de-lis branded on their shoulders to mark them as under sentence for life) were rounded up for exile to Louisiana," wrote Ned Sublette in his New Orleans history *The World that Made New Orleans: From Spanish Silver to Congo Square*. According to Sublette, the French deportees to Louisiana included "tobacco smugglers, thieves, beggars, vagabonds, orphans, the unemployed, the incorrigible, the vicious, the depraved" as well as citizens who were wrongly implicated in a crime (back then, a quick way to dispose of an enemy was to falsely accuse him or her of a crime and then have that person shipped off to Louisiana). Law's scheme to populate New Orleans was at once insane and surprisingly effective, but it would quickly be overshadowed by his next great hustle: he wildly exaggerated the assets of his Company of the West and sent shares of the company skyrocketing in 1719. By 1721, however, the so-called Mississippi Bubble had burst; Law then fled France for Venice, where he indulged in his passion for gambling and died broke in 1729. It is no exaggeration to say that New Orleans was, as Sublette puts it, "founded as a gambler's bluff."

In 1763, New Orleans was ceded to the Spanish under the Treaty of Paris, which was brokered by Great Britain, France, Spain, and Portugal after a seven-year war between the empires. Under Spanish rule, all manner of critical services were established, from the creation of safety codes to the licensing of numerous professions. Even after a cataclysmic fire in 1788 that wiped out more than eight hundred buildings in New Orleans, the Spanish rulers persevered and created some of the city's most iconic architecture. Many of the Creole cottages and town houses—with their sweeping balconies, detailed ironwork, and brightly colored, almost psychedelic hues of pink and orange—date to Spanish rule. But Spanish governance of New Orleans did not last long: after briefly reverting back to French control in 1801, the city was sold to the United States in 1803 as part of the Louisiana Purchase. Thus began a turbulent century for the city, in which the British tried and failed to conquer it during the War of 1812 and the Union army briefly captured it during the Civil War. While New Orleans prospered financially in the early 1800s thanks to booming imports, including thousands of African slaves, the city was plagued with corruption and nearly subsumed with debt in the wake of the Civil War.

"The city," wrote historian Delia LaBarre, "was drowning in debt and often literally in floodwaters." New Orleans rebounded again in the early twentieth century thanks to a new pump system that improved drainage from floodwaters, and, as important, a cultural boom in jazz, literature, and—eventually—rock 'n' roll.

During the 1920s, ragtime bands played to enthusiastic crowds at Basin Street clubs just outside the French Quarter. A trumpeter named Louis Armstrong took it all in and in 1928 recorded a composition by New Orleans pianist and singer Spencer Williams called "Basin Street Blues," which Armstrong transformed into a swinging yet strangely mournful jazz standard. Ten years later, Thomas Lanier Williams III, of Columbus, Mississippi, reinvented himself as playwright Tennessee Williams after moving to Toulouse Street in the French Quarter. Williams's plays, including *A Streetcar Named Desire* and *Vieux Carré*, captured life in New Orleans in the mid-twentieth century: the former is set on Elysian Fields Avenue in the Faubourg Marigny, the latter at 722 Toulouse Street, Williams's original home in the French Quarter. In 1947, an African-American singer named Roy Brown entered the studio of music producer Cosimo Matassa on the corner of North Rampart and Dumaine streets at the outermost edge of the French Quarter and recorded a track called "Good Rocking Tonight," a wild mix of gospel and blues. "Good Rocking Tonight" may very well have been the first rock 'n' roll song; it also inspired a nineteen-year-old Elvis Presley to cover the song at Sun Studios in Memphis in 1954, famously ad-libbing "We're gonna rock, rock, rock!" on its chorus. Artists and musicians were drawn to the French Quarter, partly because the housing stock was cheap and surprisingly well preserved. Homes from the late 1700s and early 1800s were untouched because many of its residents were too poor to renovate them. "It was preservation by neglect," says John Magill, curator of the Historic New Orleans Collection.

The French Quarter was also such a powerful draw for artists because of New Orleans's long tradition of hedonism and hustling, stretching back to the days of the gambler John Law and the rogues he imported to Louisiana. And New Orleans's seemingly never settled identity—it is at once Spanish, French, African, Caribbean, and American—made the city attractive to artists looking to reinvent themselves. Indeed, New Orleans's multilayered history of European owners could make moving to the city feel like expatriating from the rest of America. "If you're in exile from your own culture," Tulane history professor Lawrence N. Powell once said, "this is a place where you can find some room to define who you are." The French Quarter bred a particularly peculiar brand of eccentric, such as Ruth Grace Moulon—aka "Ruthie the Duck Girl"—who wore evening dresses and roller-skated through the neighborhood as a small crew of ducks trailed behind her. Unlike the Beats in New York and San Francisco, who sought to transform politics and literature, the French Quarter eccentrics of the mid-twentieth century retreated to a surreal world of their own making. "She's not out of touch with reality," New Orleans–based photographer David Richmond said of Ruthie the Duck Girl when she passed away in 2008 at the age of seventy-four. "She's just not interested." Or as Blanche DuBois famously declared in *A Streetcar Named Desire*: "I don't want realism, I want magic."

When Zack met Addie during the late spring of 2005, he sensed that she might be the sort of French Quarter eccentric who floated outside reality and therefore thrived in the neighborhood. So that spring, Zack hung out at Hog's long after his late-night shift was over in order to get to know her better. In the beginning, Addie was reluctant to reveal anything significant about herself. But as the summer began, Zack started a slow courtship of Addie that included buying her shots of Jägermeister, and she soon opened up about her past.

Addie told Zack that she was raised in Durham, North Carolina, by a father who was a Vietnam vet and a homemaker mother. She attended Northern High School in Durham but did not graduate because she found sewing, dancing, and writing poetry much more interesting than her classwork. (Beneath a photo of Addie in the Northern High School yearbook there is a quote from her in which she enthuses, "I wear clothes that reflect my personality, and I also wear clothes for fun.") After dropping out of high school, Addie left home and traveled around the country. She lived an itinerant lifestyle on the road, crashing on the couches of friends and, when she was broke, even relying on help from strangers for basics like food and gas money. By the late 1990s, however, Addie settled down in Durham again, where she taught salsa and ballroom dancing at Nina's School of Dance. By 2002 Addie was feeling restless and contemplating yet another move. That year, after returning home from partying in New Orleans for several weeks during Carnival season, Addie simply packed her belongings into her car and headed to New Orleans accompanied by a platonic male friend named, coincidentally, Zack. Addie lived in the car—which she had parked on a quiet street in the French Quarter—for several weeks until she found her first apartment in New Orleans, on St. Peter Street.

The St. Peter Street apartment was a share with Dennis Monn, a New Orleans playwright who put on raucous and raunchy musicals/ burlesques, such as *The Palanquin Diaries: Confessions of a Mardi Gras Queen*, at a ramshackle theater called the Backyard Ballroom on St. Claude Avenue in the Ninth Ward. Addie and Dennis had met at a French Quarter bar soon after she arrived in New Orleans; the car she slept in was parked outside the bar where he worked. Dennis was immediately impressed by Addie's pop-culture savvy—she loved everything from Hal Ashby's early 1970s cult classic *Harold and Maude* to New Orleans soul queen Irma Thomas—and her considerable skills as a poet and seamstress. "She was so smart, it just killed me," Dennis remembers. "Her poetry was very, very good. And when it came to sewing she could make anything from anything." The two became fast friends, and when Dennis invited Addie to stay with him at his apartment on St. Peter Street she excitedly accepted his invitation. Addie was so enthused by the new living arrangement with Dennis that when she woke up in the morning after her first night of staying with him she eagerly whipped up a huge breakfast of scrambled eggs and screwdriver cocktails. "I'd given her a ten-dollar bill," Dennis remembers, "and she went to Matassa's Market and bought eggs, vodka, and orange juice. She made a feast in my sparse kitchen—all for ten dollars."

When Dennis found an apartment of his own in the Uptown section of New Orleans during the late spring of 2002, Addie landed a rental on Orleans Avenue in the French Quarter. Even though they lived apart, Dennis and Addie remained friends, and their shared tastes, such as their adoration for the work of film director John Waters, continued to strengthen their bond. In June 2002, when Waters flew to New Orleans to host a gallery opening for his show of video stills called Straight to Video, Dennis and Addie made sure to arrive early at the Arthur Roger Gallery in New Orleans's Warehouse District in order to meet him. That night, Addie happened to be carrying a copy of J. D. Salinger's *Catcher in the Rye*. When she met Waters, she thrust it toward him to sign. As Waters autographed the book, he quipped to Addie, "You know, this is the most popular book among inmates in the United States." Addie was thrilled by the encounter—she not only worshipped the Waters oeuvre, she had a wicked sense of humor as well. At her Orleans Avenue apartment, Addie kept a sewing mannequin that she would use to model some of her dress patterns. One afternoon, Addie decided to dress the mannequin in tourist clothing, a wig, and Mardi Gras beads and place it on the sidewalk outside her apartment. She then attached a "hand grenade"—a yellowish green cocktail, popular with Bourbon Street revelers, served in green, quart-size plastic containers shaped like a grenade—to the mannequin's hand and watched as inebriated tourists and French Quarter residents stopped and attempted to talk to the mannequin, believing it was a real person. Later that night, Addie posed the mannequin leaning face-first into an old, broken toilet that she had removed from her apartment; a drunk tourist actually thought that the mannequin was sick and began to rub its back in order to make "her" feel better.

"Addie was just wonderful to hang out with," Dennis remembers. "And I admired her in a way because she was a survivalist, a hustler. Her attitude was, 'What can I do to make my rent this month?'" Like many of her fellow French Quarter residents, Addie did what she needed to do to make ends meet: she waitressed, bartended, and worked as a maid at the French Quarter Wedding Chapel on Burgundy Street. Dennis got Addie the maid job after he landed a part-time gig there performing weddings. Addie's boss at the chapel was the Reverend Tony Talavera, a big, strapping, olive-skinned man with wild, unkempt gray hair and a salt-and-pepper mustache who had once convinced the New Orleans City Council to issue a proclamation recognizing the city as the "romance capital of the world." He remembers Addie as a tireless worker who cleaned his chapel, which often hosted up to a half dozen weddings per day. By the end of 2002, Dennis had grown so close to Addie that they spent Christmas together. "I'd found a Christmas tree by the side of the road and brought it by her Orleans Avenue apartment," Dennis remembers. "She cried when she saw it because it was the first Christmas tree she had in her life."

Addie's dark humor, wild creativity, and eagerness to fashion an existence away from some presumably more ordinary or otherwise undesirable past made her an ideal fit for the French Quarter bar and club scene. "Her world consisted of Addie and what she could see around her," Dennis remembers. "She didn't read the newspaper or watch TV; she didn't fucking care about anything." Addie was so industrious that she was able to transform her shabby studio and one-bedroom in the French Quarter into cozy apartments. "She could never afford a nice place," Dennis explains, "but she would paint and clean and even gut the places and try to make it at least comfortable for her. She often left the places in better condition than they were in when she moved in."

Addie, it seemed, could persevere through any hardships, from low-paying jobs to dumpy, roach-infested apartments. But when Addie drank heavily she became abusive to just about everyone around her, including close friends like Dennis. Addie was a true French Quarter eccentric. The *Times-Picayune*'s obituary description of Ruthie the Duck Girl fit Addie perfectly: "She could be sweet one minute and unleash a torrent of profanity the next."

———

One night, Addie was partying in the French Quarter with two offshore oil-rig workers whom she had met at a neighborhood bar. Addie was supposed to spend the night at Dennis's Uptown apartment later, and she brought the men along with her to the bar where he worked. The whole group was drunk, and to Dennis's surprise Addie was treating him dismissively. "I thought you were going to spend the night with me," Dennis told Addie. "Well," Addie replied nastily, gesturing toward Dennis for the oil-rig workers. "Why should I go home with this *faggot*? I ain't gonna get nothin' from him." Dennis is gay and he often uses the word "faggot," but he was offended by the nasty emphasis that Addie put on the epithet. "I call people 'faggot' all the time," Dennis explains, "but something about the way she was coming across was way too intense." Dennis tried to forget the incident at the bar as he, Addie, and the oil-rig workers packed into a cab and headed toward Dennis's apartment to wind down the night of partying. But as the cab drove Uptown with the four of them in it, he thought about just how badly Addie had treated him at the bar, and felt profoundly angry and hurt. "What's your fuckin' deal?" he shouted at Addie in the taxi. Dennis then ordered the cab to pull over to the side of the road, pulled his bicycle out of the trunk, and pedaled home by himself. Dennis didn't know what became of the oilmen or Addie that night—and he didn't care. "I didn't speak to Addie for three months afterward," he remembers.

Dennis and Addie reunited during the spring of 2003—the passage of time had healed some hurt feelings, but from then on Dennis knew to be wary of Addie when she was having one of what he dubbed her "spells," her dark, moody moments. More ominous, Dennis discovered that Addie kept an unloaded blue steel handgun in her apartment and would sometimes flash it at enemies during her spells.

Later that year, when Addie moved into a new apartment in the French Quarter at 1012 Governor Nicholls Street between Burgundy and North Rampart streets, Dennis worried that the spells were going to get a lot worse. The Governor Nicholls apartment was one-half of a poorly maintained Creole cottage on the outskirts of the French Quarter, and because Addie was low on cash she badly needed a roommate. "She was much better off mentally when she didn't have a roommate," Dennis explains, "but she needed a roommate this time. And I felt bad for Addie because the Governor Nicholls place was trashy."

Addie went through a series of roommates, none of whom lasted more than a few months. Then, in the early fall of 2004, she had Rob Van Meter—a coworker at Mona Lisa, an Italian restaurant in the French Quarter where she worked doing deliveries—move in with her. Like Dennis, Rob understood Addie's personality from the get-go—he loved that she could be nurturing (she'd make oatmeal breakfasts for Rob at Mona Lisa) yet also bold and confrontational with friends, coworkers, and customers alike. "She would deliver food to people and then cuss them out," Rob told me. "She'd say, 'I risked my life to come down here for a dollar tip?' She had no problem giving people the finger or starting fights. That's why I liked her. I guess I'm kind of like that a little bit." Because Rob was looking for a place when he met Addie—he and his boyfriend had bought a condo Uptown and were waiting to close on the contract—he moved in with Addie out of necessity and didn't expect to be in the apartment longer than a few months. Soon after unpacking his belongings, however, Rob knew he had made a mistake. "It was an evil apartment," Rob remembers. "It was one of the few houses on Governor Nicholls that hadn't been renovated. It hadn't been touched at all; it was just disgusting. There was no stove, no kitchen, no heating or air-conditioning. So Addie would cook on an electric skillet and keep the food in a dorm-type fridge." Rob also discovered that the apartment had an awful history. "The previous tenants' lives had gone to shit," Rob explains. "I was told by a neighbor, '*Everyone* hits bottom here.'"

Rob attempted to make the best of the situation, but spending so much time with Addie made him view her moodiness and confrontation-prone personality in a very different and less sympathetic light. Once, he had found Addie's outbursts—and even her bar fights at French Quarter watering holes like Cosimo's, just around the corner from the Governor Nicholls apartment—amusing and even admirable because Addie seemed so willing to stick up for herself. But living with Addie meant that he was sure to be put in her crosshairs. "When she drank she would get this evil look in her eye and she would just be nasty," Rob explains. "She'd say, *'You're a faggot—you like to get fucked in the ass, huh?'*" Rob, like Dennis, uses the epithet liberally. But also like Dennis, Rob felt that there was an uncomfortable, angry edge to the way that Addie employed the word. Sometimes, it didn't seem like Addie was joking when she called Rob a "faggot," or, as Dennis remembers, "the joke got really old."

Addie's volatility was made more frightening by some of the company she kept. She would often hang out with cocaine dealers and sleazy out-of-towners partying in the French Quarter. One night, Addie brought a coke dealer back to Governor Nicholls and, in exchange for a few bumps, allowed him to cut and package his goods in the apartment. When the dealer finished bagging up his product he gave Addie a minuscule bag of coke as a thanks, sending her into a rage. She then turned to Rob and suggested that they beat up the dealer and steal his stash. "Do you want to fuckin' roll him?" Addie shouted at Rob. "Let's fuckin' roll him! You wanna kick his ass?" Rob was stunned and speechless by the idea that Addie could think he'd want to ambush a drug dealer, especially in New Orleans, arguably the most street-justice-adjudicated city in America. "What are you talking about?" he stammered. The coke dealer made a hasty exit with his stash intact—but Dennis was shaken for days by the incident. "That was the first time," Rob remembers, "where I thought, 'Whoa, she *is* crazy.'"

Dennis was concerned about Addie's behavior, too. She was constantly in and out of relationships with rough guys who worked service industry jobs in the French Quarter. Many of the men Addie dated were physically abusive with her; when she caught one boyfriend in his apartment masturbating to a gay porno video, he beat her so badly that at the end of the fight she was left with a broken shoulder. "Her arm and shoulder were in a full cast," Dennis remembers. "Her face was completely black-and-blue. He beat the fuck out of her."

Most worrying, Addie's spells were becoming increasingly violent. By the end of 2004, Addie was involved in bar fights; one fight ended with her cracking a beer bottle over the head of a patron at a French Quarter bar. Chastened by the attempted robbery of the drug dealer and Addie's volatile behavior, Rob began to distance himself from her. It was best, Rob thought, to treat Addie like a roommate and not a friend, lest he fall victim to one of her spells.

Yet that's exactly what happened one night that fall, when Rob lay awake in his bed and heard Addie and a friend open the door to the apartment, put their keys and wallets down on the coffee table in the living room, and then snort line after line of cocaine. As Addie got more and more coked up, she began talking nastily, and loudly, about Rob, not realizing that he was still awake in the next room. "He's giving me rent money week to week," Addie groused. The complaint seemed baseless to Rob, as he and Addie had agreed that he would give her rent money on a weekly basis. "Are you serious?" the friend replied to Addie conspiratorially. "He's got money. He just bought me drinks tonight." Addie was outraged. "What!" she screamed. "That *motherfucker*. Who does he think he is?"

Rob actually didn't have much money left after his paycheck, even though he had moved from a daytime manager position at Mona Lisa to working as a pastry chef at Emeril's. It was a better job, sure, but it was still sweaty, low-paying kitchen work. "It was so nasty and mean-spirited and just fucking creepy of her to do that to me," Rob remembers. Just before dawn that morning, Rob packed his bags and, at about 7:30 a.m., as Addie lay passed out on the living room couch, he left the apartment for good even though there were utility bills in his name. "I grabbed everything I could," Rob remembers, "and just ran."

About two weeks after Rob fled the Governor Nicholls apartment, he called Entergy and had the unit's utilities turned off. Rob then went to get the rest of his belongings from the apartment but Addie would not let him in because she was furious with him for having shut off the utilities. Early one morning a few weeks later, Rob went back over to the Governor Nicholls apartment; finding a side window open, he shimmied through it quietly so as not to disturb anyone inside. But as Rob pulled himself into the apartment he lost his balance and fell inside, landing on top of Addie's new roommate, who was sleeping on a mattress under the window. "I want my fucking stuff," Rob shouted as the shocked roommate squirmed out from underneath him. Fortunately, the roommate was understanding and held Addie off in another room as Rob collected his belongings. Unfortunately for Rob, however, he forgot to take his pay stubs from his job at Emeril's—so Addie, ever the hustler, had the power turned back on in his name.

NINE

DEREK S. BRIDGES

HOLDING OUT

"Why are they making us leave? Did they evacuate Iraq? Why didn't they just give us a job? Say, 'Here, dude, if you're going to stay, get busy'?"

—SQUIRREL, in a September 19, 2005, interview with *Time* magazine

As 2005 began, Addie continued to alienate friends and roommates with her abusive behavior, yet those who knew her best—like Dennis—remained close with her. They understood that friendship with Addie could be wonderful and strange—you just had to get out of her way when she went into one of her spells. Fortunately for Addie, one new friend seemed to understand both her dark moods and her creativity. Capricho DeVellas, a big, broad shouldered, barrel-chested deliveryman with a booming laugh who was born in New Zealand but moved to New Orleans as a teenager with his family, met Addie during the summer of 2004 when she was out on her bicycle doing deliveries for Mona Lisa and was instantly taken with her. "I would see her out on the street and she would be doing arabesques on her bicycle," Capricho remembers. "She seemed absolutely amazing and fun. So I went up to her and said, 'Would you like to get some coffee?'" Addie took Capricho up on the offer and in the days afterward they rode their bikes around the French Quarter and the Marigny together, stopping at bars and coffee shops. Soon afterward, they began informally dating and, unsurprisingly, Addie's spells began to surface. But where others had been mystified by the dark moods, Capricho sensed that the spells were a defense mechanism sprung from some kind of abuse.

"She would mentally turn any man that she was with into an abuser," Capricho explains. "She would see him as the enemy. Women who experience abuse often turn men that they are with into the figure of abuse." Addie's behavior seemed so familiar to Capricho because he had just ended a relationship with a woman had been sexually abused as a child. "I had been with another woman who had been damaged in the same way," Capricho explains, "and she could tear people apart just like Addie could."

Sure enough, after a late night of drinking Addie told Capricho that she had been sexually abused as a child. The abuse, Addie claimed, became so extreme that it once landed her in the hospital with a urinary tract infection before her thirteenth birthday.

Soon after that intense late night of conversation, Addie and Capricho agreed to break off their romantic relationship but remain friends. "There was no way we could survive a relationship because of the damage she had received," Capricho explains. "But I also knew that I never wanted to lose contact with her."

With Rob having moved out of the Governor Nicholls apartment and Addie struggling to preserve her remaining few friendships, Addie and Capricho became closer than ever. Addie even liked to say that her closest friends were members of her "tribe." So, soon after Addie and Capricho decided to keep their relationship platonic, she lovingly invoked his childhood nickname "Caps" and told him, "You're part of my tribe."

Addie taught Capricho ballroom and salsa dancing, sewed his ripped jeans, and, because he was such an attentive listener, constantly read her poetry to him. "You know someone is a good poet," Capricho explains, "when they can move you to the core. That's what Addie could do." But by the late spring of 2005, tensions between the pair resurfaced after Capricho began seeing another woman seriously. At first, Addie told Capricho that she was happy he'd found a new girlfriend, but then she would stubbornly refuse to acknowledge the girlfriend, making for awkward moments when Addie would stand silently fuming in her presence. Capricho then decided it would be best to pull back from his friendship with Addie, though he hoped that they could one day become friends again, as he still loved and admired her.

————

"Caps!" It was early in the afternoon of August 23, 2005, and Addie was standing on the corner of Frenchmen and Royal streets in the Marigny, trying to get the attention of Capricho, her arms wrapped around an extraordinarily tall, blond-haired man. When Capricho rode his delivery bike over to Addie, she warmly embraced him and then wrapped her arms again around the blond guy, whom she introduced as her new boyfriend, Zack.

To Capricho, Addie and Zack made for a strange-looking couple: she was thin with a reedlike body and just over five feet tall, while Zack was big and burly and stood at nearly six foot ten. The couple also had not been dating long. They had met while working together at Hog's Bar earlier that summer and began dating in late July after Zack had won over a skeptical Addie by regularly keeping her company long after his night shift at Hog's had ended. Indeed, Zack was such a constant presence around Addie when she was slinging drinks at Hog's during the daytime hours that bar manager Ted Mack banned Zack from the bar when he wasn't on shift. But that afternoon, Capricho was struck by how Zack visibly adored Addie, as well as by the positive effect it seemed the relationship could have on Addie's usually stormy demeanor—unlike with other past boyfriends whom Capricho had met or knew of. Though, like himself, Zack was gregarious, easygoing, and likable, Capricho surmised that Zack would soon join Addie's tribe.

Any deepening friendships between Zack, Addie, and Capricho would have to wait. On Saturday, August 27, a powerful Category 3 hurricane—Katrina—swirled in the Gulf of Mexico, and storm models showed that New Orleans was about to take a direct hit. At around five o'clock that afternoon, New Orleans mayor C. Ray Nagin urged the city's citizens to leave the city, though he stopped short of calling for a mandatory evacuation.

That night, Lana placed a panicked call to Zack. "What are you going to do about the hurricane?" she asked. "Well," Zack replied calmly, seemingly unfazed by the coming storm, "I'm gonna stay here with Addie." Lana was furious at Zack's thoughtlessness; he didn't even acknowledge that she was caring for the kids alone at the West Bank apartment. "Just come over here," she begged Zack, "and be with the kids." Zack insisted that he was going to ride out the storm over at the Governor Nicholls apartment with Addie. "Bring Addie," Lana said. "I don't care." Zack was silent for a moment and he seemed to consider the offer. But then he offered another flat, emotionless no. Lana couldn't believe that Zack was ignoring her and the kids' plight. She also thought it was ridiculous that Zack was uncomfortable with the idea of bringing Addie over to the West Bank apartment. "I had nothing against her," Lana explains. "I gave him to her. I could have had him back anytime I wanted." Lana also was struck by Zack's callousness that day; he ended the call by saying, "Ya'll are gonna be fine," so she furiously slammed down the phone. "Of course we weren't going to be fine," Lana remembers. "Nobody was."

———

Early the next morning—Sunday, August 28—Katrina was upgraded to a Category 4 hurricane and then, a few hours later, to a Category 5. Later that night, Mayor Nagin received an urgent call from National Hurricane Center director Max Mayfield. The storm, Nagin was told, was going to be the "worst of the worst" and the entire city needed to be evacuated. At about ten o'clock on Sunday morning, Nagin ordered a mandatory evacuation of New Orleans.

That afternoon, thousands of cars—eighteen thousand per hour by some estimates—streamed out of the metropolitan New Orleans area, though thousands of poor New Orleanians who did not have access to cars or couldn't afford gas stayed behind. Zack and Addie, meanwhile, hunkered down at the Governor Nicholls apartment with an abundant supply of liquor, beer, and bags of ice commandeered from Hog's Bar, while Lana kept close watch over Jaxon and Lily and stocked her West Bank apartment after a last-minute trip to the grocery store with essentials such as canned food and bottled water. Capricho, meanwhile, spent the remaining hours before the storm hit boarding up windows in the Elysian Fields Avenue home of his girlfriend's father, who had already evacuated the city. But by nightfall Capricho had yet to complete the job, and, as hundred-mile-per-hour winds blew through New Orleans late that night, he feared that he and his girlfriend were going to be sucked out the home's windows.

At approximately six o'clock the next morning—Monday, August 29—Katrina made landfall near Buras, Louisiana, clocking 145-mile-per-hour winds. At eight o'clock, Mayor Nagin reported that water had begun flowing over the levee in the black working-class Lower Ninth Ward neighborhood. Later that morning, in the middle-class Lakeview neighborhood, a large section of the Seventeenth Street Canal levee was breached. Levee failures sent several feet of water into both areas. Yet Lakeview and the Lower Ninth Ward were not the only neighborhoods affected by the failure of the man-made floodwalls and levees system meant to protect New Orleans from floodwaters: in all, there were a staggering fifty-three levee breaks. What transpired on that late August day, then, was not a "natural disaster"; Raymond Seed, a professor of civil engineering at the University of California, Berkeley, later called the levee failures "one of the two most costly failures of engineered systems in history (rivaled only by the Chernobyl meltdown)."

Yet New Orleans neighborhoods built on higher ground—such as the French Quarter—were not flooded. And because communications were scarce thanks to mass power outages, some New Orleanians were not fully aware of the disaster that had befallen their fellow citizens. On Tuesday, August 30, Capricho and his girlfriend were sitting on the front porch of her parents' Elysian Fields Avenue home, happily basking in the surprisingly cloudless, lucid, blue posthurricane sky over New Orleans, when "all of the sudden we started seeing these families walking up Elysian Fields from the Lower Ninth Ward," Capricho remembers. "They were carrying pillows, bundles of bedding. One little kid was holding a Monopoly board." The Lower Ninth Ward, they realized then, was underwater.

"It was time to get the hell out," Capricho remembers. He and his girlfriend loaded a car with their belongings and headed toward the Huey P. Long Bridge, which spans the Mississippi River, connecting New Orleans to nearby Jefferson Parish. From there, they hoped to travel to the Florida Panhandle—which is about two hundred miles from New Orleans—and wait out the storm's wake at a beachside hotel. Yet they feared that the Huey P. Long Bridge would be blocked by deputies from the Jefferson Parish Sheriff's Office who insisted that New Orleanians stay out of the area because they did not have supplies to meet even the needs of their own citizens. Indeed, cops from Jefferson Parish town Gretna *did* block hundreds of New Orleanians—many of them poor and black—from crossing the bridge even after they had been told by the NOPD that buses were waiting in Jefferson Parish to evacuate them to safety. But instead of climbing aboard buses, New Orleanians who attempted to cross the Crescent City Connection were met with Gretna cops who fired warning shots over their heads. The Gretna police were later the target of state and federal investigations as well as lawsuits filed in federal court claiming that the department violated the constitutional rights of evacuees. Capricho and his girlfriend—who are both white—made it across the bridge without interference from cops and sped toward safety at the Florida Panhandle.

The levee breaks destroyed much of New Orleans: lost in the floodwaters were 200,000 houses, 81,000 businesses, 175 schools, and 6 major hospitals. But the high ground of the French Quarter—the original center of the city—was left mostly unscathed: destruction was manifest in visible, and survivable, elements like caved-in chimneys, uprooted oak trees in the courtyard of the St. Louis Cathedral, and blown-off roof tiles scattered through the neighborhood's streets.

Because the French Quarter was in relatively good shape and Zack and Addie believed that they had endured the worst by remaining in the city during the storm itself, they refused to even consider evacuating New Orleans. Their decision to stay put pre- *and* post-Katrina put the couple in a tiny minority of the city's residents. Those who had the means to evacuate before the storm did so and the few who remained when the levees broke evacuated shortly afterward due to a lack of food and drinking water, an absence of electrical power, and homes that had taken on several feet of water.

Instead of evacuating a nearly emptied-out New Orleans, Zack and Addie happily embraced survivalism back at the Governor Nicholls apartment, fashioning paper plates into flyswatters and using tree limbs for campfires. During the day, Zack and Addie would clear Governor Nicholls Street of trash and felled tree limbs. When they completed their cleanup tasks in the late afternoon they'd down cocktails served on ice that Zack had stashed away from Hog's Bar. At night, the couple would put a rickety white painted wooden table and a few folding chairs on the street in front of their apartment and serve dinners of canned beans or canned soup to their fellow holdouts over an open bonfire—often started by lighting old mattresses.

One of their favorite dinner guests was Jim Gibeault, a New Orleans landlord. In one well-known photo of Zack, Addie, and Jim, the trio is seated on Governor Nicholls around a wooden table covered with beer bottles, cans of beans, and a jar of honey. A shirtless Zack is opening a can of beans as Addie—who is dressed in a bikini top and shorts—sits and chats with Jim, who with his long, flowing white beard and happy eyes resembles Santa Claus. When their dinner guests went home, Zack and Addie lit candles and listened to *Trouble*, the 2004 debut from singer-songwriter Ray LaMontagne, on a battery-powered boom box. Its title track quickly filled the soundtrack to their relationship. "I've been saved," LaMontagne sings on the song's chorus, "by a woman." Yet *Trouble* also hinted at problems to come—the CD's cover art features an illustration of a devil courting a young woman wearing a blindfold. In the early morning hours, when the French Quarter was completely quiet and still, Zack and Addie would make love right in the middle of the street.

The immediate aftermath of the levee breaks—mass power outages, eerily abandoned streets, and a silence that descended over the entire city even during the daytime hours—had a cleansing effect on Zack and Addie. The disaster seemed to have washed away their pasts—his tour in Iraq, her sexual abuse—and created a world of their own in which they could fall in love. On the rare occasions when Zack and Addie left the perimeter of the Governor Nicholls apartment, they biked down the French Quarter's streets holding hands as they pedaled.

While out biking in the French Quarter one afternoon, Zack and Addie met Jack Jones, a retired oil-rig worker born and bred in rural Cameron Parish and a French Quarter resident since 1977. Like Zack and Addie, Jack had refused to evacuate during the storm, and that day, he suggested that they come by his Chartres Street condo in the French Quarter to smoke a joint. Zack and Addie accepted his invitation and because of Jack's ragged looks—he had a scraggly five o'clock shadow, a dirty baseball cap, bleached-out blue jeans, and cowboy boots—they assumed they'd be toking up in one of the worn-out, 1970s-era condo conversions that dotted the French Quarter. But when they arrived at Jack's apartment—which had soaring ceilings, dark wood floors, and extraordinary provisions—they found that he was a survivalist without peer in New Orleans.

His Cameron Parish upbringing had prepared him well for life in the flood zone. "My advice to anyone who lives in New Orleans," Jack explains in his thick Louisiana drawl, "is this: *you live in a fucking swamp.*" So in the weeks before Katrina made landfall Jack had hundreds of gallons of drinking water, dozens of cans of food, cases of bleach (which he used to treat water for bathing), and a working satellite phone, which was regularly utilized by reporters who had decamped to a nearby bar, Molly's at the Market. On his sprawling balcony, Jack set up an outdoor kitchen centered around a mammoth grill. In his courtyard, Jack built an outdoor shower. Jack's Chartres Street condo was so stocked with luxuries that, in the wake of the storm, reporters from national publications like *Time* magazine filed their stories from there.

Jack, unsurprisingly, became a source of great quotes to journalists from the local media as well as the Associated Press. "They may have to shoot me to get me out of here," Jack told the AP. "I'm much better off here than anyplace they might take me." Zack and Addie were so thrilled by Jack's ability to create such amenities amid the apocalypse that they asked him if they could crash at his place. Jack hesitated. He had seen Addie around the French Quarter and heard about her legendary temper. "She was a firecracker," Jack remembers. "I'd heard that she was a great person but when she started drinking she would open fire on people. Somebody would say something she didn't like and she would cuss him out or threaten to whup their ass." But because Zack and Addie seemed so eager to stay at the Chartres Street condo, Jack agreed to take them in on the condition that they assist him with his day-to-day duties like cleaning Chartres Street of debris and bleaching the bathwater. For the next few days, Zack and Addie slept on Jack's balcony at night and during the day helped him gather supplies and clean water. "It was hard work but they enjoyed the lifestyle of not having to go *to* work," Jack remembers. "It was right up their alley."

Zack and Addie were not alone in enjoying the survivalist life in the post-Katrina French Quarter. The near total lack of local, state, and federal government assistance to hurricane-battered New Orleanians was nearly as debilitating as the levee breaks. Supplies of food and water were low to nonexistent at the Superdome and the Ernest N. Morial Convention Center (both in New Orleans's Central Business District, just blocks from the French Quarter), where tens of thousands of New Orleanians waited for days for help. Looters roamed the streets. FEMA, days after Katrina made landfall, had yet to establish command and control, meaning that aid and critical supplies such as food and drinkable water were not flowing to the area. So those who remained in the city, particularly in the small, close-knit French Quarter—a neighborhood, ordinarily, of about four thousand permanent residents and many other visitors, where only a few dozen remained—banded together in order to survive.

"We didn't see cops for about six days," Jack remembers, "and when the cops would come by, they'd ask if we had weapons because they were being overrun." A profound sense of unity and pride was forged from these ugly and desperate circumstances.

On September 4, 2005, the few who remained in the French Quarter were appropriately described as "tribes" by an Associated Press reporter. Indeed, the AP piece—"French Quarter Holdouts Create Survivor 'Tribes'"—went on to describe how the neighborhood holdouts boasted of their ability to overcome the lack of essentials such as electricity and hot water, and of their pride in their fellow residents for tapping into the best of themselves when so many in the city appeared to be doing just the opposite. "Some people became animals," one French Quarter resident told the AP while sipping a warm beer. "We became more civilized."

Zack and Addie, unsurprisingly, were thrilled to participate in this refined brand of post-Katrina tribalism. Even before the storm, Addie had been searching for some kind of tribe of her own, and Zack had longed to rediscover the strong sense of brotherhood he had experienced with his fellow 527th MP Co. soldiers, such as Todd, Jeremy, and Rachel.

"It's actually been kind of nice," Zack told a reporter from the *Mobile Register* one morning as he stood on the sidewalk in front of the Governor Nicholls apartment, picking up felled tree limbs. "And I'm getting healthier, eating right and toning up." Zack was equally enthusiastic when talking with his brother, Jed, who called one night to check on him from Iraq, where he was serving his first tour in Saddam Hussein's hometown of Tikrit. "Everything's fine," Zack told Jed. "We're living the good life down here. I've got a camp stove and lots of cans of beans. And I broke into a bunch of bars and stole all the booze." Zack sounded a similar note when talking with the *Mobile Register*. "We're bartenders," Zack said, "so we're well stocked."

When the couple ran out of booze, they would frequent the two French Quarter bars that remained open around-the-clock in the wake of the storm: Molly's at the Market on Decatur Street and Johnny White's Bar on Bourbon Street. In the French Quarter, where many establishments never close, bars are more than places to grab a drink or meet with friends: they are second homes. It's not unusual to walk into a neighborhood bar and see a French Quarter resident having a few drinks with his dog, settling in for dinner by having food delivered to the bar from a nearby restaurant, or simply beginning the morning with a shot of Jameson's or a pint of Blue Moon beer. Both Molly's at the Market and Johnny White's are archetypal French Quarter bars. Molly's is an Irish bar established in 1974 that serves up potent drinks (like a Bloody Mary with a shot of Guinness) to a small crew of regulars like Jack Jones. Johnny White's, which opened in the early 1990s, is a sparse sports bar with about six bar stools, a jukebox, and two televisions, usually blaring a Saints game; it counts its patrons' dogs as "regulars."

One night at Johnny White's, Zack and Addie began chatting with bartender Greg Rogers, known by everyone as Squirrel. Squirrel had seen both Zack and Addie working at Hog's Bar but had never been formally introduced to them. "I know you," Squirrel told Addie that night. "I think your name starts with an A." Addie shook Squirrel's hand. "I'm Addie," she said, and then introduced Zack. After a few rounds of drinks, the couple invited Squirrel back to the Governor Nicholls apartment for more cocktails, but he passed on the offer because he was working long shifts. Squirrel then told the couple that if they needed drugs—coke, pot, anything—he'd be happy to take care of them.

The next night, Squirrel ran into Zack and Addie on Royal Street and they said they'd like to take him up on his offer. But before Squirrel could hand them a twenty-dollar bag of coke, he got a call from a manager at Johnny White's that he was needed back at the bar. So he suggested Zack and Addie follow him there. As they turned the corner onto Orleans Avenue, they were approached by a group of NOPD officers. And as the cops strode across the street toward the three of them, Squirrel inconspicuously dropped the bag of coke by the tire of a parked car. Zack flashed his military ID, Addie her driver's license, and Squirrel said simply, "I'm a bartender," which in the Katrina-wracked city put one on par with EMTs, firefighters, and even the Coast Guard, who had rescued or evacuated more than 33,500 people in Katrina's aftermath. The cops let the whole group go. Before Squirrel split off from Zack and Addie, he gestured toward the bag of drugs on the ground, which the cops had failed to notice. When the NOPD left the scene, Zack discreetly picked up the bag of coke and he and Addie headed toward Governor Nicholls. The incident made Squirrel curious about his new friends. He was shocked that Zack—who since returning to New Orleans had let his hair grow out in a wild, blondish brown mane—had a military ID. And, as a veteran of the war in Afghanistan, in which he had served as a navy corpsman, Squirrel wondered whether Zack had ever been to war.

The kid-gloves treatment that Squirrel, Zack, and Addie received from the NOPD that night was a good example of the French Quarter holdouts' semi-VIP status. Many of the holdouts, including Squirrel and Zack and Addie, even became momentary media celebrities, profiled by reporters in publications ranging from *Time* magazine to the *Mobile Register* to the *New York Times*. A *Mobile Register* story about Zack and Addie characterized the couple as restlessly inventive, disaster-era do-it-yourselfers. The piece concluded on a cheery note with both Zack and Addie proclaiming their willingness to stick with New Orleans for as long as the city needed to recover. "Until then," the reporter wrote, "they'll be on Governor Nicholls Street, eating lots of canned food, pouring drinks, cuddling cats, sweeping streets and, of course, swatting flies." But it was a front-page *New York Times* piece—appropriately head-lined "Holdouts on Dry Ground Say 'Why Leave Now?'"—that brought the couple the most attention. The article described Addie's dedication to keeping the spirit of the city alive even in the wake of the greatest disaster in its history:

> In the French Quarter, Addie Hall and Zackery Bowen found an unusual way to make sure that police officers regularly patrolled their house. Ms. Hall, 28, a bartender, flashed her breasts at the police vehicles that passed by, ensuring a regular flow of traffic.

The *Times* piece was even approvingly linked by Manhattan media gossip website Gawker. "JOE FRANCIS," proclaimed Gawker's editors, referring to the *Girls Gone Wild* impresario, "WOULD BE SO PROUD." Squirrel, meanwhile, merited a mention in prominent *Times* man David Carr's profile of Johnny White's patrons, such as Marguerite Smith, who played guitar in a New Orleans band called Jake and the Mistakes:

> Smith said she was an Apache and a Catholic, that she was 44, and had nine children and 15 grandchildren: "All gutter punks and bikers," she said. "See what a good mother I am?" Gesturing to the dim club with tiny televisions on the bar, she added, "Just ask my son Squirrel, he's tending bar in there."
>
> "She is not my mother," said the bartender, Greg Rogers, known to some as Squirrel. "She is one of those street people who thinks that she is mother to everyone. But she is a good person."
>
> She certainly appeared to be. Holding a lighter against the darkness, she provided three strummed chords to an otherwise silent city. And in spite of the Diaspora of musicians, she was not alone making her music. She may play for herself, but she also plays for those who remain.
>
> "I can read a crowd and I play accordingly," she said, adding that she had performed as a member of Jake and the Mistakes. "I am the chief mistake."

Just outside the high and mostly dry French Quarter, away from the glare of the media and the revelry at bars like Johnny White's, there was danger and deep despair. When Zack and Addie took bike trips into the Bywater and the Marigny, they often rode by a corpse stuffed in a shopping cart—left there to rot for days. A trip that Zack and Addie made one night to a locally owned supermarket called Robert's, on the corner of Elysian Fields and St. Claude avenues, nearly turned into a disaster. Like many of their fellow holdouts, Zack and Addie had taken food and supplies from Robert's in the days after the storm. "They'd gone to Robert's several times to 'accumulate supplies,'" Jack Jones remembers, using a euphemism for looting, "but on this one night, Addie went into Robert's alone while Zack waited outside. It was pitch-dark inside the store and when Addie was in one of the aisles a man grabbed her and tried to rape her." Addie had fought her attacker off, and when she and Zack returned to Jack's condo later that night, she assured them that she would be okay, that she would be able to put the incident behind her. But Addie was shaken, all the more so because she'd suffered from violent sexual abuse as a child. Suddenly, the horrors of poststorm life—which she had so bravely and even joyously confronted—began to profoundly affect her.

Another trauma arrived for Addie soon afterward. Early in the afternoon of Friday, September 2, Jack managed to score several pounds of hamburger meat from a National Guardsman. Obtaining the meat was a huge coup: he, Zack, and Addie had been subsisting on canned food and ramen noodles. But as Jack fired up the massive grill on the balcony of his condo and placed the thick hamburger patties on top of it to cook, hundreds of buzzing, clacking, metallic-green flies descended on top of the meal. The scene did not resemble a Sunday barbecue where a few flies buzz around the grill: post-Katrina flies were fat and shiny and traveled in thick clouds of hundreds. "When they landed on the sidewalk," Jack remembers, "the entire sidewalk would turn green." Coming right after the attempted rape, the horrific scene of the flies swarming over raw meat sent Addie reeling. "She broke down right there and started crying," Jack remembers.

The next day brought another unhappy—even traumatic—sight for Zack. On Saturday, September 3, the army's Eighty-second Airborne Division arrived in New Orleans via Fort Bragg, North Carolina, and fanned out across the city to perform search-and-rescue missions and assist Louisiana National Guard troops in keeping the peace. That night, as Jack, Zack, and Addie relaxed on the balcony of Jack's condo, they all watched in awe as members of the Eighty-second Airborne—many of whom had just served tours in Iraq and Afghanistan—marched down Chartres Street sporting full combat gear and maroon berets. "There must have been more than a hundred of 'em, all coming down the street from Jackson Square," Jack remembers, "Zack looked down and all he saw was red berets. They yelled up to us, 'Ya'll all right?' We were fine. We were just out there cooking and watching TV and partying."

Zack, however, was not feeling fine: the sight of the Eighty-second Airborne on the street below him reminded him of his failures in the military. Indeed, seeing so many soldiers in a near-combat environment can be a significant emotional trigger for PTSD. Worse, the always freewheeling, now anarchic, atmosphere of his refuge in the French Quarter had been suddenly transformed into a police state. "That weekend felt like a lawman's Mardi Gras," Dan Baum wrote in the *New Yorker*. "The dry slice of New Orleans filled not only with federal and state troops but with well-meaning deputy sheriffs and policemen from as far away as Oregon and Michigan—cops whose activities were uncoordinated, who knew nothing of the city, and who were pumped on rumors of violence. They tumbled out of their cars in boxy bulletproof vests, pointing their M-4 carbines every which way, as though expecting incoming rounds. Adding to the Dodge City atmosphere were such private soldiers as those of Blackwater, U.S.A., who lurked on the broad steps of several mansions, draped in automatic weapons . . . the phrase on the lips of the guest enforcers was 'martial law.'" To many city, state, and federal officials, the worst of Katrina's fallout had subsided because New Orleans was, if still far from functioning or providing for its citizens, at least firmly under law enforcement's control. New Orleans's homeland security director,

Terry Ebbert, proclaimed that the crisis was over. But the poststorm Shangri-la of the French Quarter holdouts—in which they, not the Eighty-second Airborne, not the Louisiana National Guard, and certainly not the NOPD, had fed and protected one another—was in ruins. For the holdouts, the crisis had only just begun.

———

By the evening of Sunday, September 4, the Superdome had been fully evacuated of its nearly twenty thousand evacuees, many of whom were moved to the Astrodome in Houston. The local media were reporting that the streets of New Orleans were, as the *Times-Picayune* put it, "getting safer by the minute." But French Quarter holdouts like Jack, Zack, and Addie were bridling under the iron-fisted approach of the law enforcement arrivistes. On Tuesday, September 6, Mayor Nagin signed a "Promulgation of Emergency Order" that directed the New Orleans police, the city's fire department, and the U.S. military to "compel the evacuation of all persons from the city of New Orleans, regardless of whether such persons are on private property or do not desire to leave." Many of the holdouts—including Zack and Addie—openly defied Nagin's emergency order. The holdouts argued that they had survived the worst of the storm and there was no reason to leave New Orleans simply because of the say-so of city government and law enforcement officials who had already failed them so profoundly. The holdouts also felt that they had performed a community service of sorts to New Orleans by remaining in the city and performing poststorm services that ranged from cleaning the streets to protecting homes and businesses from looters.

"They can't do this," Addie told reporters from the *St. Petersburg Times* on Friday, September 9. "I'm an American citizen. They're saying I have no rights." Addie's fellow holdouts, many of whom sported homemade T-shirts bearing the acronym RFQ (Restore the French Quarter), also decried Nagin's evacuation order as authoritarian and un-American. At Kajun's Pub, a dive bar on a run-down strip of St. Claude Avenue in the Marigny, owner Joann Guidos recounted to the *New Yorker* that when

NOPD warned, "If you don't leave, you'll be shot," she replied defiantly: "Never in this country." But while forced evacuations continued in New Orleans throughout the weekend of September 10, many in local law enforcement and even the military were sympathetic to the holdouts. "We're keeping in mind that these people are still Americans," U.S. Army Captain John Sherrill told the *St. Petersburg Times*, "and they still have the same inalienable rights as any American."

The defiant stance the holdouts staked out that week successfully repelled law enforcement's efforts to remove them from New Orleans. But within a few days the holdouts would be besieged by what some of them viewed as yet another invading force: New Orleans residents returning home after evacuating the city before Katrina made landfall. Nearly everyone who had the means to evacuate New Orleans prior to the storm did so; although heartbreaking images of New Orleanians waving for help on their rooftops had quickly become iconic, the governor of Louisiana had evacuated 90 percent of the region's vulnerable population. Most of the few who stayed had remained not by choice but by necessity. For example, the city government had no plans to evacuate the more than one hundred thousand residents of New Orleans who did not have access to a car. And those who did evacuate did so to save their lives, not because they had given up on New Orleans. But some of the more militant holdouts—Zack and Addie among them—looked disdainfully upon the evacuees who began trickling back into New Orleans after Mayor Nagin officially announced residents could return home on Monday, September 19. Zack and Addie sneered at these residents of the city as though they were army deserters.

"They hated it when people started coming back," Jack Jones remembers. "They hated everybody from the Katrina sightseers to people who hadn't survived the hurricane and were making their way home." Jack sensed that behind Zack and Addie's expressed resentment of the evacuees lay a fear that their return symbolized a change back to what passed for ordinary in New Orleans. "They liked the lifestyle we had during the hurricane," Jack explains. "They liked camping out. They liked not having to work. They liked not having the responsibility of paying bills. They didn't like the change back to normalcy."

New Orleans was beginning its recovery that fall, but Zack and Addie were far from alone in feeling pessimistic. In early November, the city's population stood somewhere between 60,000 and 80,000, far, far below its prestorm size of 455,000. Racial tensions were simmering, stirred by ugly pronouncements from Louisiana politicians. "We finally cleaned up public housing in New Orleans," Louisiana congressman Richard H. Baker told the *Wall Street Journal*. "We couldn't do it, but God did." Former city council president Peggy Wilson, meanwhile, declared that the city should keep out "welfare queens."

By the end of September, Zack and Addie were desperately trying to hold on to their utopia: Zack made his temporary stays at Addie's Governor Nicholls apartment permanent and the couple adopted several neighborhood stray kittens. They also opened their home to several of their closest friends who were struggling from post-Katrina depression, including Capricho DeVellas. Carpricho was suffering from what he would later call a "nervous breakdown," brought on by the destruction of his beloved city and the dissolution of his relationship with the woman with whom he rode out the storm.

At the beginning of October, Capricho stayed at Zack and Addie's Governor Nicholls apartment for about four days, with the couple cooking him meals and Addie even giving him foot massages. "I called it 'the Zack and Addie Spa,'" Capricho remembers. "They brought me back from wherever I was. It was at that point that I considered Zack family." Soon after Capricho moved back into his own apartment, Zack and Addie hosted a barbecue in the courtyard of the Governor Nicholls apartment, in which they regaled friends with stories of how they'd rode out Katrina's aftermath together. "I wish this love," Addie announced to the large group of friends gathered outside their apartment that day, "for every human being on the planet."

Even though Capricho had grown closer to both Zack and Addie during his days-long stay at their "spa," he was astonished then by how deeply in love they appeared to be. "I stood in the courtyard that afternoon and was just amazed," Capricho remembers. "They were absolutely, completely in love." Similarly, Zack's mom, Lori, remembers a phone call right after Katrina in which Zack said "that Addie was his soul mate, that he'd never been in love before, and that this was it."

But by the end of October, ordinary life had begun forcing its way into Zack and Addie's post-Katrina bubble: they returned to their jobs and Lana began demanding that Zack resume his parental responsibilities. Lana was furious about what she, Jaxon, and Lily had been forced to endure without any assistance from Zack during Katrina and its wake: a stay at a shelter on the West Bank, followed by a hurried evacuation to Sugarland, Texas, which was six hours away, where she worked as a waitress at a local Applebee's to support herself and the kids. Zack had not provided Lana and the kids with any money during this time and, worst of all, he did not return any of the messages that she had left on his cell phone during and after the storm—leaving Lana to believe that he had not survived.

So when Lana finally returned to New Orleans in late October and found out where Zack was staying, she staged a dramatic confrontation that she hoped would force him to support her and the kids. "I rented a van and drove out to damn Governor Nicholls with a baseball bat in my hand," Lana remembers. "I wasn't gonna knock him out. I was just going to knock on his door with it." But when Lana banged on the door of the apartment with the bat, Zack was not there. Only Addie was inside; she chose not to answer the door. When Zack received word from Addie of Lana's dramatic visit, he quickly arranged a face-to-face meeting with her. "Can we meet?" Zack asked meekly during a phone call. "Sure we can," Lana replied coldly. "Can you bring the kids?" Zack said. "Oh no," Lana cried angrily, "I will not bring the kids. I haven't made them any promises to them about us. They're hoping that I'll get back with their daddy." Lana then instructed Zack to meet her the following day at a bar on South Peters Street in New Orleans's Central Business District.

When Lana arrived at the bar, she instantly felt a tangible sense of hostility and resentment coming from Zack. Without even first saying hello, Zack seethed to her, "Addie doesn't ever want to see you again." "No problem," Lana replied coolly. "I want to see the kids," Zack insisted. "You need to pay child support," Lana answered. "What, I have to *pay* to see my kids?" Zack shouted back at Lana. "No, you can see your kids," Lana explained, "as long as we make some arrangements. If you're going to take the kids with Addie I need to meet her." Zack refused to agree to Lana's proposal; after all, Zack explained, he had yet to meet the man whom Lana had been dating ever since the last days of his military service in Giessen. "You want to meet him," Lana said, gesturing toward the opposite end of the bar, "he's over there." Zack then refused to look in the direction of Lana's boyfriend, and bellowed, "I have no desire to meet the man who took my wife!"

Lana was shocked by the intensity of Zack's anger—he had always been the more levelheaded half of the couple, even when they argued—but she held her ground. "If Addie is going to be their stepmother," Lana insisted, "I have to meet her. Listen, Zack, this is not about me being mad at you and Addie being together. She can have you." Lana then found herself overwhelmed with bitterness and anger toward Zack for abandoning her during Katrina and for turning what should have been a straightforward agreement about the kids into a heated debate. *"I'm real, real done with you,"* she practically snarled. The finality of Lana's remarks about their relationship forced Zack to back off; he nodded in agreement and the pair went their separate ways, with Lana leaving the bar with her boyfriend.

In the days after the meeting, Zack arranged to come by Lana's West Bank apartment and pick up the remainder of his belongings, which had been stored there since his return from Giessen. Because he did not own a car, Zack had Jack Jones drive him out to the West Bank. But when they arrived there late that afternoon, they discovered that most of Zack's possessions had been looted during the storm. "When we got there, everything was in disarray," Jack remembers. "It looked like the entire place had been looted. Even Zack's drum set was looted. But when Zack found some of his clothes and the special boots that the military had made for him, we loaded up the car and left."

Arriving back at the Governor Nicholls apartment that afternoon, Zack explained to Addie that she would have to meet Lana face-to-face and that the kids would be staying with them on a biweekly basis. Because their relationship was still so new and both were still adjusting to post-Katrina life in New Orleans, Zack was nervous about how Addie would take the news. But to his surprise, Addie was thrilled at the notion of becoming a stepmom of sorts; she even recruited Jack to drive her out to Wal-Mart to buy children's clothes for Jaxon and Lily. "I think I'll have Zack's baby," Addie proudly announced to Jack that day outside Wal-Mart. Jack was skeptical that Addie could handle parenthood. "Addie was just not that type of girl," Jack explains. "She had a lot of ghosts."

Jack's instincts about the manner in which Addie would handle Zack's kids turned out to be correct. When Lana met Zack at the Blue Bayou Water Park in Baton Rouge to hand over Jaxon and Lily for their first visit, Addie sulked in their rental car and refused to meet Lana at all. "She stayed in the car the entire time," Lana remembers. "She didn't want to have anything to do with me." Back at the Governor Nicholls apartment, Addie barely interacted with Jaxon and Lily, choosing instead to go off on long bar crawls in the French Quarter; then she'd come home drunk and shut the bedroom door to be alone with Zack. "The kids told me that Addie didn't like them," Lana explains. "They said that she came home drunk, said hello, and then went to sleep with Daddy."

By the end of November, Addie's coldness toward Jaxon and Lily turned into outright hostility: whenever Zack took the kids for the weekend, she forced Zack to rent a hotel room. Zack reluctantly agreed to take Jaxon and Lily to a hotel and, in order to make himself more comfortable, stayed at the Hotel Richelieu, which is located on the same block as Jack's Chartres Street condo. To the couple's closest friends, like Capricho, this odd, uncomfortable arrangement was an ominous sign that Zack and Addie's relationship would collapse now that the intensity and immediacy of hand-to-mouth living during Katrina and its wake was gone. "Everything changed when real life started coming back in," Capricho remembers. "They were living in a bubble. She wanted him to be a creation only for her. It was the same with him: he fell in love with the goddess of the French Quarter. But that was not reality—and reality started forcing its way in."

———

With the visits from Jaxon and Lily exposing rifts in their relationship, Zack and Addie began looking to reconnect with the holdouts with whom they had shared such strong bonds during the aftermath of the hurricane. On Christmas Day in 2005, Zack, Addie, and Squirrel all decided to invite friends over to celebrate the holiday together at Squirrel's Esplanade Avenue apartment. The celebration would even be Katrina-themed: guests were instructed to make and bring tree orna-ments related to life during the storm. Zack and Addie showed up at Squirrel's apartment bearing a small life-preserver-shaped ornament. Zack also brought a big stack of board games—Risk and Scrabble among them—because Squirrel was still recovering from a car accident that he'd been involved in just after Katrina. By the end of a long Christmas Day, which the group of former holdouts spent drinking and reminiscing about the storm, Squirrel made plans to spend New Year's Eve with Zack and Addie. On New Year's Eve, the trio went to Kajun's Pub, the bar where owner Joann Guidos had made her brave stand against the NOPD when they tried to remove her. Just before sunrise, as the New Year's revelry at Kajun's was winding down, Squirrel revealed some good news to Zack and Addie: he'd found an apartment on Burgundy Street, right around the corner from their Governor Nicholls apartment. "We're gonna be so close," Squirrel told the couple, "that we're gonna be able to holler over to each other."

Reuniting with Squirrel that Christmas and New Year's was one promising development among many for Zack and Addie that indicated 2006 could be the year they finally found their groove in the French

Quarter in spite of their problems. Addie got a job working behind the bar at the Spotted Cat, a jazz club on Frenchmen Street in the Marigny. The Spotted Cat was a small, cramped space with few seats, but it swang nearly nonstop due in part to a booking policy that brought in several local bands, like the New Orleans Jazz Vipers, nearly every night. Addie quickly became a favorite bartender among the jazz bands that played there because she was honest in paying out the tips that customers had left for them. "She never stole our tips," remembers Amzie Adams, an artist, photographer, and musician whose band, Spirit Walker, played the Spotted Cat regularly. "But she always seemed preoccupied. She would be dealing with you in the moment and as soon as the moment was gone she would drift off."

Zack, meanwhile, found a job delivering groceries at Matassa's Market on Dauphine Street in the Lower French Quarter. Small and with aisles so crowded with boxes of food stacked on the floor that customers have to step over them, Matassa's is the corner-store equivalent of the Spotted Cat. And like the Spotted Cat, it's a New Orleans institution. Owners John and Louis are the sons of Cosimo Matassa, the former recording engineer who recorded—beginning in the 1940s and continuing into the 1970s—proto–rock 'n' roll singles such as Roy Brown's "Good Rocking Tonight," Little Richard's "Rip It Up," Fats Domino's "My Blue Heaven," and Professor Longhair's "Tipitina" in his New Orleans recording studios.

The market's storied history is augmented by the deep French Quarter tradition of bicycle delivery culture. It's not unusual to go see a local band and then realize that the lead singer is also the guy who brought over an order of red beans and rice earlier that day. French Quarter residents utilize deliverymen and -women, to bring them everything from food to cigarettes to illegal drugs. The bicycle deliveryman is such a central part of French Quarter culture that when the Preservation Hall Jazz Band shot a video for its song "Complicated Life," it had the vocalist on the song, Clint Maedgen, play a deliveryman from Decatur Street restaurant Fiorella's Café, where Capricho DeVellas worked in Katrina's aftermath. In the video, the camera tracks Maedgen as he croons "You got to get away from, the complicated life, son" while riding his bike—its basket holding a brown paper bag filled with food from Fiorella's—throughout the French Quarter and on the Moonwalk along the Mississippi River.

Especially as he had recently been working the dull, lonely graveyard shift at Hog's, Zack relished being part of the neighborhood's vibrant bicycle delivery community. Just about everyone in the neighborhood came to know Zack, and he savored the notion that he was fully living in a French Quarter bohemia. With the job at Matassa's, Zack finally felt that he had found equal footing with Addie, who, with her sewing, dancing, and poetry, was his goddess of the French Quarter. Lana remembers that after Zack was hired at Matassa's, his self-confidence, which had been low since Katrina had receded, was restored. "Because of that job, *everybody* knew Zack," Lana explains. "He thought that he was the king of Bourbon Street, the king of the French Quarter."

But living among those whose work and socializing was circumscribed completely by the neighborhood—people known sometimes as "Quarter rats," but whom Addie more affectionately dubbed "Quartericans"—brought with it temptations that were especially hard to resist in the first few months after Katrina, when salves of any kind were a necessity. Though delivery jobs do not make workers rich, the tips during the high tourist season in New Orleans—JazzFest, Mardi Gras, the French Quarter Festival—can make cash *too* plentiful, providing a temptation to go out and spend it all in French Quarter bars and nightclubs.

In the early spring of 2006, Zack and Addie went on marathon drinking and drug sprees, which often ended with Addie lashing out at Zack and her friends during her notorious spells. One night, Zack and Addie were hanging out with Capricho at the North Rampart Street gay bar Starlight by the Park, where Zack occasionally bartended to make some extra cash. There, they played a debauched drinking game called Suicide Kings. Whenever the king of hearts card—known as the suicide king because the king is holding a knife to his head—is pulled, the person pulling the card chooses what the other players must drink. That night, Zack drew the suicide king several times in a row and demanded that Capricho and Addie drain the entire contents of a pitcher of a beer. Unsurprisingly, the effect of the alcohol on Addie was much more intense than on the much larger Capricho. Bleary-eyed and dizzy, Addie began insulting both Zack and Capricho. When they began to return the taunting, Addie angrily got up from her bar stool and dramatically strode out the front door.

Worried that Addie might be easy prey for the armed robbers who prowled the Lower Quarter, Zack and Capricho headed after her into the night. As they searched for Addie well into morning, Zack and Capricho exchanged frustrated text messages. At one point, Capricho had grown so weary of the search for Addie that he texted Zack, "GOD, SHE'S BEING SUCH A BITCH." A few minutes later, a reply came from Zack's cell phone: "I READ YOUR MESSAGE." It was Addie. Zack had found Addie wandering near lower Decatur Street alone and she had drunkenly commandeered his cell phone and sent the message to Capricho. As Capricho pondered his response, Addie texted him again from Zack's cell phone, this time with an even nastier message: "YOUR ENTIRE LIFE IS A WASTE." Exhausted by the all-night search and Addie's insults, Capricho called her and explained that certain types of bad behavior would have to stop. "When you get drunk you start acting like a tyrant," Capricho told Addie that morning. "If you act like this again I'm going to walk away. I don't need this in my life."

A few hours later, Capricho received a call from Zack. "I'm outta here," Zack announced. "I'm hopping a train to Oregon to see my dad." Zack told Capricho that after he caught up with Addie on Decatur Street they'd returned to the Governor Nicholls apartment only to have a knock-down fight. Zack declared that he was unwilling to take Addie's abuse any longer and that he needed a long—perhaps permanent—break from both her and New Orleans. Soon after hanging up the phone, Capricho received a frenzied call from Addie. She told him that the late-night drunken fight with Zack had become physical: the couple had been so inebriated that neither of them remembered when they woke up what had happened. "Addie had woken up with bruises on her arm," Capricho remembers. "Something torrential happened with Zack—she just didn't know what."

Though their split was acrimonious, Zack was so miserable without Addie on the four-day train trip to Portland, Oregon, to see his father, Jack, that he regaled his fellow Amtrak passengers with stories about his French Quarter goddess. Nonetheless, when Zack arrived in Portland he declared to his entire family—brother Jed and mom Lori included—that he was finished with New Orleans and was going to start a new life in the Northwest. Jed eagerly seized on Zack's newfound willingness to leave the French Quarter bar scene behind him.

"I told Zack, 'Why don't you go over to Iraq again and work as a contractor, maybe join Blackwater,'" Jed remembers. "But Zack said, 'I'll never go back to that place again.'" Unbeknownst to Jed, after just a few weeks in Portland, Zack was already making plans to return to New Orleans.

In a phone call to Lori, Zack explained that he was heading back to New Orleans because he felt guilty about leaving Jaxon and Lily yet again. "I gotta go and make it up to the kids," Zack told Lori. To Lori, Zack sounded despondent about his impending return to New Orleans and the multiple failures that had marked his life, from the military discharge to the marriage that had just fallen apart. "Every time I talked to Zack he was sorry," Lori explains. "It was 'I'm sorry I did this.' 'I'm sorry I did that.' 'I made a bad decision.' 'I made a bad choice.' He was apologizing all the time for everything."

Zack hadn't told Lana that he was heading to Portland, and when she found out that he'd left New Orleans, she got on the phone and demanded that he return to the city. "I was tired of making up lies to the kids about Daddy," Lana remembers. "Right after Katrina I told them, 'Daddy's not here because he's helping the people of New Orleans.' 'Daddy's working for the Red Cross.' 'Daddy's building the levees!' I just made shit up and I couldn't do it anymore."

Addie was also miserable without Zack. While Zack was in Portland, she rarely left the Governor Nicholls apartment, with regular visits only from Capricho, who brought her Stevie Wonder CDs and Ben & Jerry's Chunky Monkey ice cream in attempts to lift her spirits. During one of Capricho's visits, Addie confessed to him that she had attempted suicide twice in the past. Capricho begged Addie to hang on—he told her that Zack would miss her and New Orleans far too much to remain away for long. "Caps, I'm not gonna kill myself," Addie said. "I learned my lesson. I had somebody try and kill themselves in front of me and right then I knew that I was not going to do that ever again." Even though Capricho knew that Zack and Addie's relationship was combustible, he felt that their time apart would allow anger to subside and better memories to come forward, that they could then get back together and perhaps even thrive as a couple. He remembered how happy and connected with each other they had seemed in Katrina's wake. "I wanted them to work it out and be together because they were so much in love," Capricho explains, "and having lost a relationship after Katrina, I wanted to see something work out for someone else. So I bought Zack a plane ticket home to New Orleans."

TEN

THOMAS NEFF

THE SUICIDE KING

If I commit suicide, it will not be to destroy myself but to put myself back together again.

—ANTONIN ARTAUD, "On Suicide"

Zack and Addie had a brief and blissful reunion when he flew back from Portland to New Orleans in the early spring of 2006. The couple didn't leave the Governor Nicholls apartment for three days. But as strong as their love could be for each other, their anger could be just as strong. That spring, Zack and Addie fell right back into their now familiar behaviors: they would head out drinking and Addie would spiral into one of her spells, which would inevitably conclude with her verbally abusing Zack. "You cannot sit there and take that," Capricho told Zack that spring. "You can't allow her to hurt you. Don't give her that outlet. Don't become that enemy for her. Just leave." Zack would nod his head in agreement with Capricho's advice and then mumble listlessly, "Yeah, yeah, you're right." But because Capricho was also friends with Addie, he did not want to seem to be taking sides, and by the end of the spring he resolved to stop intervening in the relationship entirely.

Unfortunately, as the summer began, Addie's spells became so unrelentingly dark and vicious that Capricho could not avoid confronting her. On July 1, 2006—Capricho's twenty-eighth birthday—he planned to spend the night with Zack and Addie at bars all around the French Quarter and Marigny. But as Capricho got dressed at home for the evening, he received a nasty text message from Addie: "Don't bother coming by. I don't want to be the last-ditch stop on your free drink escapade." Upon reading the message, Capricho thought to himself, *Ah, she's on a downtwist.* Capricho was right—Zack and Addie had separated yet again—so he and Zack headed out for a night on the town on their own.

Capricho and Zack's first stop was Oswald's, a French Quarter bar then owned by comic, magician, and former *Night Court* sitcom star Harry Anderson. That night, Anderson happened to be hanging out at the bar and he was so charmed by Zack that he gave him a hat from his immense collection. (On *Night Court*, Anderson's character often wore a fedora.)

"Out of respect for Harry, Zack wore the hat on a hot, humid midsummer night in New Orleans," Capricho remembers, "and as soon as we left Zack took it off and said, 'Jesus, give me a Coors Light.'" The pair then hit a Bourbon Street strip club called Big Daddy's, but the night didn't turn out as planned. Zack confessed that he was too depressed by his breakup with Addie to celebrate Capricho's birthday, so he asked Capricho if he could crash at his apartment on Burgundy Street in the Marigny. Capricho eagerly took Zack in—he reasoned that it was better to help give Zack and Addie a break rather than continue to fruitlessly counsel Zack about his relationship. But after a few days, Addie showed up at Capricho's apartment and demanded to have Zack back. "I'm going home," Zack said meekly to Capricho, and then shut the front door behind him. "At this point I began to realize that this was turning into an unhealthy relationship," Capricho remembers, "so when I was around either of them alone I would say, 'You need to take some time apart and get yourselves together.'"

Neither Zack nor Addie heeded his advice. That summer, their fighting turned into seemingly daily breakups followed by teary reconciliations. Addie would throw Zack out of the Governor Nicholls apartment and he would spend the night at the run-down Empress Hotel on Ursulines Street in Tremé. Or he'd crash at Squirrel's apartment on Burgundy Street in the French Quarter. "Zack moved all his stuff into my apartment," Squirrel remembers, "and he made a little place for himself to sleep in one corner. He'd work all day, grab a twelve-pack of beer on the way home, and then we'd smoke, drink a few beers, and smoke a joint together."

Early one morning, after a long night of drinking and drugging with Squirrel, Zack confessed that he was still haunted by his tour in Iraq, only to have Squirrel scold him for being stuck in the past. "Dude," Squirrel lectured Zack, "you were just an MP in Iraq. I was a medical corpsman in Afghanistan. I had to literally *sew* people back together. What the fuck did you do that was so horrible?" Zack refused to talk about his tour in Iraq and Squirrel noticed that Zack's eyes welled up with tears. "I was just too wasted to hear Zack's story," Squirrel says. "I should have let him get it all out. I was insensitive."

In between stays at Squirrel's apartment and the Empress, Addie would take Zack back. Then he would haul his belongings back to the Governor Nicholls apartment on a Matassa's delivery bicycle that had an enormous metal basket designed to carry huge loads of groceries. Zack used the bike so often to transport his possessions that his coworkers dubbed it "Zack's moving truck." "She would kick him out and then chase him down and tell him that she loved him," Jack Jones recalls. "Or he would kick her out and then when she would return home she would kick *him* out." That summer, Zack and Addie's lives existed on parallel and intersecting tracks of vicious fights and reconciliations, and marathon drinking and drug sprees. "First it was breaking up and getting back together every two days," Capricho remembers, "then it was every eighteen hours. This was insanity."

By the end of the summer, Zack and Addie's downward spiral had become apparent even to total strangers. After yet another fight with Addie, Zack told Inez Quintanilla, a bartender at legendary French Quarter bar Lafitte's, that "women are blood suckers and money whores." When Inez responded, "Dude, you got issues," Zack shot back, "We all got issues. If you been through what I been through, maybe you would feel the same way."

When Zack came to pick up Addie at the Spotted Cat one night that summer, a pair of patrons, New Orleans–based visual artist Michael Fedor and his brother Joe, a literature teacher visiting from New Jersey, sensed an ominous, dark energy between the couple. "We were at the bar trading verses of poetry back and forth with Addie," Michael remembers. "After a few hours the crowd started to thin out and the music died down. We were about to get up and leave but Addie said [speaking of another customer], 'Please stay a little longer; this guy is creeping me out.' I just didn't sense it from the guy but we stayed because we liked Addie. Then the guy left and Addie's boyfriend [Zack] arrived. We were expecting an Adonis-type guy. But when he arrived, he walked very purposefully along the edge of the room. He was like a spider crawling along the wall. I remember thinking, 'This is the guy you should be worried about.'"

By mid-August, Zack and Addie's fights attracted the attention of law enforcement. In the early morning hours of August 14, Addie fought with Zack at the Governor Nicholls apartment and then angrily stalked off, carrying her trusted blue steel handgun. Armed and nearly delirious with rage, Addie then got into a shouting match with a man on a French Quarter street. "What the fuck is wrong with you?" Addie shouted at the man as she trained her handgun on him, according to a police report. When the man called the cops, Addie fled to the Governor Nicholls apartment, where she changed out of her jeans and into a nightgown. It was a lame attempt to fool the NOPD into thinking that she had been sleeping while the incident took place. Sure enough, when cops arrived at the Governor Nicholls apartment with the man whom Addie had threatened, they found the gun, along with a bag of marijuana and two pipes. The man identified Addie as the woman who pulled a gun on him. Addie was arrested and taken to Orleans Parish Prison (OPP), where she was booked with aggravated assault with a firearm, first-offense possession of marijuana, and possession of drug paraphernalia. "Addie got arrested for pulling a gun on some guy," Zack told Capricho at work at Matassa's the next day. Though Capricho was somewhat surprised by the arrest, the incident was "Addie just being Addie." Capricho was, however, shocked when Zack said that he would not help bail Addie out of OPP. "He had lots of money," Capricho remembers, "he'd been working seven days a week at Matassa's." Addie eventually convinced several friends to pool together money for the bond—about two thousand dollars—and she was freed from OPP in mid-August. "She got herself out," Capricho explains, "and they got back together."

The good feelings of reuniting with Zack did not last long. Early in the morning of September 28, a little more than a month after Addie's arrest, the couple got into a screaming match at the Governor Nicholls apartment. At around five in the morning, Addie physically pushed Zack out the door and slammed it behind him. Furious, Zack stood on the stoop in front of the apartment and loudly banged on the front door in hopes that Addie would let him back in. But she refused to open the door, and by then Zack and Addie's sleepless neighbors on Governor Nicholls were angry enough with the couple to call 911. When cops arrived on the scene a few minutes later, they found Zack sulking on the front stoop. As Zack rose to greet the officers, he discreetly pulled a bag of marijuana out of his front jeans pocket and tossed it onto the street. The cops, however, saw the bag of pot sail to the sidewalk. They hauled Zack to OPP, where he was booked with first-offense possession of marijuana. After he spent two days in OPP, Addie put up five hundred dollars in bond money and Zack was bailed out of jail. During the taxi ride back to the Governor Nicholls apartment, Zack lamented to Addie that he was put behind bars for possessing marijuana with a street value of three dollars.

The arrests, the short prison stints, and the nonstop fighting were all evidence that Zack and Addie's relationship had descended into total madness. The madness was fueled, in part, by free drugs from Squirrel. After the couple loaned Squirrel nine hundred dollars when he was short on rent money during the summer of 2006, he granted the couple unfettered access to his stash of cocaine at his Burgundy Street apartment. At first Zack and Addie would take one or two twenty-dollar bags of coke, but as their fights grew in intensity, so did their appetite for drugs. "I was giving them four hundred dollars per week worth of drugs," Squirrel remembers. Yet even as Zack and Addie continued to take hundreds of dollars' worth of coke from Squirrel, Addie still considered his debts to the couple unpaid. When Squirrel attempted to settle his debt with Zack and Addie by offering them a final complimentary half ounce of coke (worth an approximate street value of six hundred dollars), Addie threatened him: "Squirrel, what do we have to do to get you to pay us? Do I have to punch you in the head?" Squirrel backed down and told Addie that both she and Zack could continue to pilfer his stash free of charge for as long as they wished. At French Quarter bar Cosimo's later that night, Zack took Squirrel aside and meekly apologized for Addie's behavior. "I knew that Zack hadn't meant me any harm," Squirrel remembers. "She was the one doing all the screaming and talking."

Mired in an increasingly loveless, abusive relationship, Zack began looking for sexual and emotional contentment elsewhere. Earlier that year, Zack had begun partying at a gay leather bar, the Phoenix, on Elysian Fields Avenue in the Marigny. Zack had hung out at gay bars with gay friends before; he had even bartended at the North Rampart gay bar Starlight by the Park. But at the Phoenix Zack did more than simply have a few drinks. There, Zack befriended a local real estate agent and, late that summer, the two began dating. Zack tried to keep the relationship a secret from even close friends like Capricho and Squirrel, but Zack's boyfriend happened to be a client of Squirrel's. Back at Squirrel's Burgundy Street apartment one night, Squirrel confronted Zack about his sexuality. "Zack had just come from work at Matassa's with a twelve-pack of Pabst Blue Ribbon," Squirrel remembers, "and we were sitting in the house drinking beers and watching a movie. I asked him about his boyfriend. And he says, 'Squirrel, you know I'm kinda bi?' I said, 'What's kinda? Your definition of "kinda" is what?'" Zack explained that in the past he would have men perform oral sex on him, and that with his relationship with Addie falling apart, he was finding himself open to having a relationship with a man. Zack insisted that Squirrel keep the relationship—and these sexual proclivities—from Addie. Unsurprisingly, in the tiny post-Katrina French Quarter, news of Zack's boyfriend soon reached her anyway.

Furious at Zack's infidelity, Addie began to taunt Zack with antigay epithets. One afternoon early that fall, Addie rode her bike by Matassa's and shouted at Zack in front of his friends, "It would be nice to have sex with a straight man one of these days!" On another occasion, Addie stole Zack's cell phone, called all the women in his phone book, and told them he had AIDS. She then deleted all of the phone numbers from the SIM card on his cell phone.

Addie was furious with Zack, least of all for his cheating on her. Her rage was further fueled by mounting financial problems: she had long struggled from paycheck to paycheck, but the drinking and drug sprees were leaving her broke. Dennis Monn remembers seeing Addie early that fall at French Quarter deli Verti Marte, paying for groceries with quarters she had scrounged up around the house. "I knew she was low so I gave her money," Dennis remembers. And the always shabby Governor Nicholls apartment had fallen into total disrepair that fall. In early September, a toilet in the apartment had stopped working entirely. When Addie asked her landlord to fix the toilet, he refused, so she called in a plumber, whom she paid out of her own pocket. Addie then threatened to deduct the cost of the plumber from her next month's rent, infuriating her landlord, who threatened to file an eviction notice against her.

(Landlord-tenant law is highly unfavorable to tenants in Louisiana, and he would have been successful in getting Addie thrown out of the apartment.) With a likely eviction, and unacceptable living conditions, Addie knew that she had to move out of the Governor Nicholls apartment fast—yet she did not have nearly enough cash for the first month's rent and a one-month deposit on a new place. So she turned to Zack for financial help.

That fall, Zack was working two jobs—delivering groceries for Matassa's and tending bar at Buffa's, a ramshackle watering hole on Esplanade Avenue in the Marigny—so Addie knew that he had ample cash for a down payment on a new rental apartment. Weary of life at the Governor Nicholls apartment and of his temporary stays at Squirrel's apartment and the Empress Hotel, Zack agreed to front Addie the money for a new lease, and to move back in with her once they found a new place. Perhaps in a new environment, Zack reasoned, the fierce battles that had marred much of the couple's time together at the Governor Nicholls apartment would finally come to an end.

———

Early in the afternoon of October 2, 2006, Zack and Addie went apartment hunting in the French Quarter. After just a few hours of searching, the couple found a "For Rent" sign posted on the wrought-iron gate outside 826 North Rampart Street, a building owned by onetime New Orleans mayoral candidate Leo Watermeier. The first floor of the building—a two-story Creole cottage built in 1829—houses the Cultural Center of Priestess Miriam Chamani's Voodoo Spiritual Temple, which is crowded with African masks, voodoo dolls, and mojo bags for sale. Behind 826 North Rampart is a lush courtyard and a complex of small studio and one-bedroom apartments, also owned by Leo. But on that October day, the open rental was for a small one-bedroom apartment on the second floor of the Creole cottage with an attractive, direct view of the sprawling, thirty-two-acre Louis Armstrong Park across the street. The apartment had been vacated less than twenty-four hours when Zack and Addie showed up.

Zack and Addie told Leo that their landlord at the Governor Nicholls apartment had doubled their rent in the wake of Katrina—a lie, because they didn't want Leo to know the real story about the plumbing-costs conflict—and that Leo's $750 per month one-bedroom was well within their budget, as both were working full-time. Because Zack and Addie had enough cash for the first month's rent plus a one-month deposit—a rarity in the post-Katrina city—Leo handed over the keys to them without so much as drawing up a lease.

But on the morning of October 4, Addie unexpectedly showed up, alone, at Leo's office at 812 North Rampart, demanding a six-month lease in her name only. To placate Addie, Leo hastily prepared the document in his own handwriting on a piece of yellow legal paper, which they both signed. "Five minutes later, I get a phone call from Zack," Leo remembers. "He says, 'Did you just sign a six-month lease with Addie?' I said, 'Yeah.' He said, 'Oh man, I'm screwed; she's kicking me out and the lease is in her name.' I said, 'Well, I had no intention of the lease not being for you; I thought it was for the two of you. Don't get mad at me.' Then he hung up." Leo rushed over to the apartment and to his surprise found Zack and Addie standing in the stairwell. Leo remembers, "She said, 'I caught him cheating on me! With a man!'" Leo was a little taken aback that his new tenants would reveal such intimate details about themselves. "I don't want to get involved in drama," Leo said to Zack and Addie. "I'm gonna look after your place," Addie told Leo. "I'm gonna be a good tenant."

After Leo left the couple, their fighting continued, well into the afternoon. Zack was furious with Addie for kicking him out of the apartment—he'd just paid two months' rent, after all—and, more important, he had recently promised Lana that he would take Jaxon and Lily the next weekend. "No matter what else happened," Lana's father, Carl Shupack, explains, "those kids gave Zack a reason to live. So losing that apartment absolutely destroyed him. He just couldn't handle it. I know that he was thinking, 'Where am I going to take my kids now?'" Squirrel understood Zack's fury with Addie for signing the lease in her name. "She muscled in," Squirrel explains, "put her name on the lease, and fucked him over. It was his money. He found the place."

Most of Zack and Addie's friends had become so befuddled by the couple's constant dramas that they had stopped talking to them entirely, and, as a result, some weren't aware that they'd moved from the Governor Nicholls Street apartment to 826 North Rampart. When Capricho showed up at the Governor Nicholls apartment one afternoon in early October, he found the door unlocked and stacks of old newspapers and broken furniture inside. "I was like, 'Where the fuck is Addie?'" Capricho remembers. "'Where the hell has she gone?'"

As Zack and Addie's argument continued well into the night of October 4, Zack grew increasingly despondent about not just his poisonous relationship with Addie but his entire life, which seemed to him now a long accumulation of shames and failures: dropping out of high school for no good reason, and then decamping to New Orleans to party with his dad; having kids at far too young an age; enduring the loss of friends in Iraq; the general discharge that jeopardized his benefits and ended his military career; the dissolution of his marriage with Lana soon afterward; irresponsibly failing to care for Jaxon and Lily during and after Hurricane Katrina; the return to the endless succession of low-level jobs in New Orleans, the place he believed he'd left behind when he enlisted in the army. Finally, because Addie had signed the lease to 826 North Rampart in her name, Zack, in his despair, was confronted by the prospect of homelessness: he couldn't go back to Lana and live with her at the West Bank apartment, and the notion of carting his belongings to the run-down Empress and then making up an excuse to Lana as to why he couldn't take the kids again embarrassed him. In fact, unbeknownst to Lana and even Addie, when Zack was moving between the Governor Nicholls apartment and the Empress, he actually *had* been homeless for a while. When Zack didn't have the money for a night at the Empress, he would sleep on a tattered couch on the third floor of an abandoned Greek revival mansion on the corner of Esplanade Avenue and Bourbon Street.

As midnight neared, Zack and Addie's fighting turned physical. About an hour later, according to Zack's extensive suicide note, Zack clasped his hands around Addie's neck and strangled her to death.

━━━

"She had stolen this apartment (ask Leo Watermeier, he'll explain that one)," Zack wrote in Addie's journal on the morning of Thursday, October 5, just hours after killing her, "tried to kick me out, then would not shut the fuck up so I very calmly strangled her. It was very quick."

Yet Zack's fury was not dampened with Addie's passing—he was overcome with rage that their relationship had spiraled so far downward, angry and saddened that she was gone from his life, apparently still both lusting after and hating her, and, finally, furious with himself for killing her and confused about what to do next. "After sexually defiling the body a few times," Zack wrote, "I was posed with the question of how to dispose of the corpse." But before he could focus on how to effectively clean up the crime scene, Zack passed out in his bed in a drunken stupor, waking at about six o'clock, in time for the morning shift at Matassa's, where he encountered a concerned Capricho.

"Zack was unshaven and quiet and smoking a cigarette," Capricho remembers, "so I said, 'What happened?' He looked at me and said, 'Me and Addie split, man. We had a real falling-out. She packed her bags, took some of my money, and went back home to North Carolina.'"

Capricho wondered if Zack had killed Addie—he says that Zack was dark and downcast in the days before the murder and that he simply had "gotten a bad vibe" from him—but he dismissed the idea because it was "not something you can even comprehend a friend doing." Also, Zack's story about Addie's departure seemed plausible because Addie had threatened to leave the French Quarter several times in the past. "This is something that Addie had threatened to do many, many times," Capricho remembers. "She said, 'I'm just gonna get the fuck out of the French

Quarter. I'm gonna go to Bali or Morocco and start over.' It wasn't too hard to comprehend that she would do something like that. And she did everything spur-of-the-moment; she was all about doing rash things."

Later that day, after work at Matassa's, Zack walked over to Chartres Street to visit Jack Jones at his condo. "He found comfort with me here because we had gone through so much during the storm," Jack remembers. When Zack arrived at Jack's apartment that afternoon, he was unusually warm and friendly with Jack. Out of the blue, Zack suggested that the pair take off on a trip to the Far East; Zack had cash on hand from working at Matassa's and Buffa's seven days a week and he couldn't imagine a better traveling partner than Jack. "Man, how would you want to hang out with me in Asia?" Zack asked. "I would," Jack replied, "but I've got responsibilities, like my home and my dog. What about you? What would you do with your stuff?" Zack stammered that he would put his belongings—most of which were still packed in boxes and sitting in the courtyard behind 826 North Rampart—in a storage facility. "He seemed preoccupied, stressed, something wasn't normal with him," Jack remembers. Jack then asked about Addie's whereabouts, as he was used to seeing the two of them together. Zack explained that he had broken up with Addie and, as a result, she'd packed up and moved back to Durham. The explanation seemed somewhat plausible to Jack because Addie had stopped by his apartment a few days earlier and announced that she was moving back to North Carolina. "She asked to borrow six hundred dollars because she wanted to go back home to Durham," Jack remembers. "I wouldn't give it to her because she was drinking and doing drugs. Instead, I offered her to stay at my place. But she refused." But Jack also knew how much Addie loved New Orleans and found it hard to believe that she would abandon the city entirely. "I knew her too well to quit worrying about her," Jack remembers. "It didn't sit good with me."

Capricho's and Jack's questions about Addie dogged Zack. It was becoming clear to Zack that any and all suspicions about Addie's absence would lead directly back to the North Rampart apartment. So, when Zack arrived back at the apartment just after nine o'clock that Thursday night, he began to slowly and methodically clean up the crime scene. First, he dragged Addie's corpse into the tiny bathroom and started to methodically dismember her. "I came home, moved the body to the tub, got a saw and hacked off her feet, hands and head," Zack wrote in Addie's journal. "Put her head in the oven (after giving it an awful haircut) put her hands and feet in the water on the range." As Zack worked through the night, he kept the light on in the bathroom, which made uneasy one of Leo Watermeier's tenants in the back building, jazz singer John Boutté.

A native of New Orleans's Seventh Ward who had played coronet and trumpet in high school, John began singing gospel and blues music while serving as a commissioned officer with the army in Korea. When he returned to New Orleans, John—who is short and reed-thin with caramel-hued skin and intense brown eyes—struck out on his own with a singing style rooted in the redemptive soul of Sam Cooke. With his raspy, tender croon and purposeful, intelligent manner, John had become one of the most significant post-Katrina voices in New Orleans. When John played the New Orleans Jazz and Heritage Festival during the late spring of 2006—just a few months before Zack and Addie moved into 826 North Rampart—he performed a cover of Randy Newman's "Louisiana 1927" that captured the mix of anger, defiance, sadness, and pride that New Orleanians had felt in the months and years after Katrina. John changed Newman's lyric about "what the river has done" to "what the levee has done," and the crowd shouted their approval as though they were attending a religious revival.

John is an observant man who seems deeply tapped into the city's post-Katrina mood, and when Zack and Addie moved into 826 North Rampart he instantly sensed that something was not right with the couple. John had heard that Zack served in the army but didn't believe this because of Zack's slouchy gait. "He just didn't have that military bearing," John remembers. Then there was the bathroom light that Thursday night that remained on for hours on end. "The light in the bathroom was on for so, so long," John remembers. "It never went off."

John had lived in Leo's buildings for years—first at 826 North Rampart, where he occupied the one-bedroom apartment that Zack and Addie had eventually taken, and then in his small studio in the back building, 832 North Rampart. John hadn't felt comfortable in any of the apartments—he felt that Leo didn't vet the tenants thoroughly, a charge that Leo angrily denies—and he had such an ominous feeling about the one-bedroom at 826 North Rampart that he'd actually had a priest come by and bless it when he was living there in 2004.

"This is an old city with old spirits," John explains. "Don't tempt them." So even though John could never have imagined what Zack was doing in the bathroom of the apartment he had once rented, he was overcome with fear and foreboding that night. Just before sunrise on Friday morning, he thought that someone was standing outside his window—but when he checked, no one was there. Later, John was so convinced that a shadowy figure was on the back building's balcony that he had a friend come by to see if anybody was there. (His friend saw no one.) John also remembers seeing "shadows dancing" by a huge oak tree in the courtyard that night. To many other people, the light in Zack's bathroom would have been dismissed as carelessness, if noticed at all, but as John explains, "In order to play music, you have to be tuned in in certain ways."

Zack's bathroom light remained on even after he became too exhausted to continue working on Addie's body and went to bed. "I got drunk(er)," Zack wrote in Addie's journal, "and some hours later turned off the stove, filled the tub with water and passed out." Zack planned to spend the next few days continuing the task of disposing of Addie—"I was to be off all weekend so I had plenty of time to work," he wrote—but "due to laziness spent most of that time coked up in various bars with different girls."

After waking up Sunday afternoon, Zack remembered that he'd agreed to take Jaxon and Lily for the weekend, so he called Lana and asked her to bring the kids by Matassa's. Realizing that Lana would be furious with him for again missing out on his time to take the kids, he offered to give Lana six hundred dollars in cash that he owed her in child support if she showed up at Matassa's that afternoon. Lana agreed to meet him there, and when she and Jaxon and Lily arrived at Matassa's, Zack was in a happy, generous mood. "Ya'll go run inside," Zack told the kids, "and get all the Cokes and candy you want." While Jaxon and Lily scoured the aisles of the grocery store for candy and gum, Zack handed Lana the six hundred dollars and told her, "Why don't you let me fix up the place this weekend and have the kids come next weekend?" Lana was skeptical of Zack's offer—wouldn't Addie intervene and force Zack and the kids into a hotel? "No," Zack said forcefully, "Addie's not gonna stay at the apartment this weekend." Lana was surprised that Addie would allow Zack to have the North Rampart apartment all to himself, but she agreed to let him have Jaxon and Lily regardless. When the kids rushed out of Matassa's with fistfuls of candy, Lana told them that they would be spending the next weekend with Daddy, and they cheerily piled into the car and headed back to West Bank.

Zack then returned to 826 North Rampart, where he continued his work on Addie. "Sunday night," Zack wrote, "I sawed off the rest of the legs and arms and put them in roasting pans, stuck them in the oven, and passed out. I came to seven hours later with an awful smell emanating from the kitchen. I turned off the oven and went to work Monday. This would be the last day I'd work."

Early that evening, as Zack completed his shift at Matassa's, and Addie's dismembered body lay in pots and pans on the stove and in the oven, John Boutté and a physician friend decided to have an al fresco dinner out by the big oak tree in the courtyard behind 826 North Rampart. "We were sitting out there in the backyard eating our hors d'oeuvres," John remembers, "and Doc noticed a funny odor. But we didn't think anything of it—everything smells in New Orleans."

Later that night, three days after he had killed her, when Zack returned home from work at Matassa's, the sight of Addie's rotting, dismembered corpse struck and overcame him with horror and self-hatred. "I scared myself not by the action of strangling the woman I've loved for one and a half years . . . but by my entire lack of remorse," Zack wrote in Addie's journal. "[So I] decided to quit my job and spend the 1500 in cash I had being happy and kill myself."

Zack then attempted to plunge entirely into an oblivion of drug and drink, guzzling bottles of Jameson, snorting thick rails of cocaine, and throwing down hundreds of dollars for lap dances in French Quarter strip clubs.

On Sunday, October 8, Zack spent the evening at the Hustler Club on Bourbon Street; he managed to so charm one stripper that she took him to her home in the New Orleans suburb of Metairie for two days of wild sex and drugs. When Zack returned to New Orleans that Tuesday— October 10—he hit the strip clubs again and ran into Squirrel just outside Rick's Cabaret at 315 Bourbon Street.

"Where's Addie?" Squirrel asked. "She tried to rip me off for a bunch of money and then she split," Zack answered. "She split?" Squirrel replied, perplexed. "And ripped you off? That don't make sense." Unlike Capricho and Jack Jones, Squirrel never believed that Addie would make good on her threats to leave the French Quarter. Addie, after all, was a dedicated "Quarterican." Furthermore, while Squirrel had no trouble believing that Addie would screw Zack out of a lease, it was difficult to grasp that she would actually rob Zack and, if she was indeed finally delivering on her threat to leave the Quarter, make off with the proceeds to go home to North Carolina, instead of to one of the more glamorous locales, like Morocco, that she often mentioned. Squirrel's insistent questions about Addie caused Zack to abruptly end the conversation with a friendly clap on the back. Zack then headed off to a party at the Hustler Club down the block at 225 Bourbon. As he showered strippers with one-dollar bills, Zack realized that it was October 10—the eighth anniversary of his wedding with Lana.

In a cocaine-and-whiskey haze, Zack stumbled to a pay phone and called Lana at her West Bank home. It was just after midnight when Zack made the call. "Let's have a drink!" Zack shouted to Lana when she picked up the phone, seemingly not at all aware of how late it was. "I don't think that's appropriate anymore," Lana replied sternly. Zack was angry and hurt that his offer was dismissed outright by Lana. "You're still my wife," he blurted out. "We're not divorced." Lana calmly explained that they were each in a relationship and that even a casual drink on their anniversary would rightly be seen as suspect by their mates. "You got a girl," Lana told Zack that night. "I got a man. I don't think we should be celebrating our marriage."

With Lana refusing all of his entreaties, Zack then desperately promised her more child support money. "I've got money for winter coats for the kids," he told Lana. "It's four hundred dollars; why don't you come get the money?" Then Zack made a remark that soured Lana on him for the rest of the night. "I wanna party," he said from the Hustler Club pay phone, "with my favorite stripper."

Furious, Lana told Zack that she was going to bed—and then hung up the phone. The short and unsuccessful conversation with Lana sent Zack plummeting back to earth; his night was over.

The next day, Wednesday, October 11, Capricho arrived at work for the evening shift at Matassa's only to have his boss, Louis Matassa, warn him that "Zack's gone off the radar. He's disappeared. He's not answering his phone. He hasn't shown up for work in two days." Capricho immediately panicked because the last time he had seen Zack he had seemed so despondent about the dissolution of his relationship with Addie. "I knew how much his relationship with Addie meant to him," Capricho remembers, "so my initial reaction was that he killed himself. On my first delivery out I called him: 'Zack, give me a call back, no questions asked. I just want to know if you're all right. If you want to be left alone, I'm not gonna tell anybody that you called me. Just know that I'm here for you.'" About a half hour later, Zack called Capricho back and said, "You're the only person who called and was actually concerned about me."

Capricho's call seemed to lift Zack's spirits and he promised his good friend a night on the town in return for his kindness. "I'll be by Matassa's in two hours," Zack told him. "You and me are going out and I'm buying all your drinks."

By the time Zack showed up at Matassa's that night, he was already seriously inebriated, having downed a fifth of Jameson. "I needed a vacation, man," Zack said of his sudden absence from work. "I just couldn't deal." The pair then took a cab to the Hustler Club, where Zack bought Capricho several rounds of drinks and a lap dance from a stripper dressed as a policewoman. "Zack was buying shots and lap dances, and because it was a strip club, this was a *lot* of money," Capricho remembers. But Capricho thought that the stripper's policewoman act was cheesy, and the constant rounds of shots Zack was buying were rendering him incapable of enjoying either the drinks or the strippers. "I was not turned on by anything that night even one bit," Capricho says. "Zack was flirting with two of these women and all I could think about was my girlfriend."

Just after four o'clock in the morning, when Capricho told Zack that he was going home, Zack pulled him aside and whispered, "I'm not who everybody thinks I am. I have a persona that I present."

Addie had expressed a similar sentiment about Zack to Capricho the very last time he had seen her, at the Governor Nicholls apartment— "Zack isn't the nice guy that you think he is"—so Capricho was momentarily struck by Zack's comment. But that night, Capricho was too drunk and too tired to stop to consider at length any larger meanings of the remark. "You mean that you present a certain persona when you're bartending," Capricho told Zack, "and that's how you get your customers to come back." Zack hesitated for a moment and then said blandly, "Yeah, like that." With dawn creeping up on them, Capricho decided to head home to the Marigny, get some rest, and put his worries about Zack aside. He had a full day of work at Matassa's ahead, and he had to begin preparing for a housewarming party he was going to host later that week.

On Saturday afternoon, just hours before his house party was set to begin, the bartender that Capricho had hired for the night failed to show up at his apartment. So he called Zack to ask if he could help out behind the bar, even though he had seemed alternately—and unusually— sulky, boisterous, and strange at the Hustler Club a few nights earlier. To

Capricho's surprise, however, Zack cheerfully offered: "Hey, man, you got yourself a bartender." That night at Capricho's apartment, Zack kept the manic party rolling, slinging drink after drink for the revelers until sunrise. After the last guest went home, Capricho and Zack sat in the living room and took turns commandeering the CD player, playing albums by Soundgarden, Tool, and Pearl Jam, and Ray LaMontagne's *Trouble*, the album Zack and Addie had fallen in love to soon after they first met during the late summer of 2005, with its title-track chorus—"I've been saved by a woman"—that had once seemed tailor-made for Zack and Addie's redemptive relationship. At about five o'clock in the morning, Capricho and Zack called it a night: they were exhausted and Capricho had to be at Matassa's for an early shift in about one hour. Zack, meanwhile, told Capricho that he was going to get up early the next morning and start planning a trip to the Cayman Islands to put the memories of his broken relationship with Addie far behind him. The trip seemed plausible because Zack had boasted to another friend that he was packing for a "divine, two-week trip to Grand Cayman."

So Zack rose from the couch, shook Capricho's hand tightly, clapped him on the back, swung open the apartment's front door, and announced, "I'm going on vacation, see you later."

That morning, Capricho stumbled over to work at Matassa's while Zack returned to 826 North Rampart to Addie's now rotting corpse (it had been more than a week since her murder). "I didn't hear anything from Zack Sunday, Monday, Tuesday," Capricho remembers, "but I didn't think anything of it because I was working so much and cleaning my apartment after the party."

Zack, meanwhile, was setting the stage for a dramatic exit from this world. He inflicted twenty-eight cigarette burns all over his body, one for each year of his life. In the suicide note that he furiously scrawled into the pages of Addie's diary, he recalled his final, heady days partying with Capricho ("good food, good drugs, good strippers . . . Had a fantastic time living out my days"), quoted Metallica's song "St. Anger" ("Fuck it all and fucking no regrets"), chronicled Addie's slaying and the botched disposal of her body in excruciating detail, and then, finally, offered a terse laundry list of his life's failures:

Friends
Jobs
Military
Marriage
Love

At the bottom of the note, Zack provided a challenge of sorts to the cops—and perhaps the journalists—who would investigate the crime. "It's just about time now," Zack wrote. "The only numbers left are friends and family members. *So go to work.*" The note complete, Zack spray-painted Lana's phone number on the wall above the bathtub and, in a reference to Addie, wrote "I LOVE HER" on the living room wall. Finally, early in the afternoon on Tuesday, October 17, Zack stopped by Squirrel's apartment on Burgundy Street to see if he could roust him from his sleep for what would be—unknown to Squirrel—one last night of partying. When Squirrel refused to get out of bed, Zack walked to the Omni Royal at 621 St. Louis Street, coolly strode through its lobby, rode the elevator to the La Riviera rooftop pool bar, spent a long afternoon having drinks by the pool, and at 8:30 p.m. jumped off the roof.

ELEVEN

CRAIG MORSE

THE WAKE

The hospitals aren't re-opening. It's like they don't want us to have health care. This is entropy—but it's entropy on purpose.

—AMZIE ADAMS

At approximately ten o'clock that evening, NOPD detectives working from the instructions in the note that Zack had tucked into his shirt pocket drove over to 826 North Rampart to search for Addie's body. With Leo Watermeier's assistance, the cops pushed open the heavy iron front gate leading to the courtyard cluttered with Zack's and Addie's belongings—including Addie's bike, with a MAKE LEVEES NOT WAR sticker affixed to its frame—and rushed upstairs to the one-bedroom apartment rented by the couple.

"The apartment was a mess," NOPD detective Tom Morovich remembers. "There was moving boxes and junk and crap just everywhere; and there were beer cans all over the coffee table to the point where you couldn't see the table. It looked like the people who lived there had just moved in but hadn't unpacked." With the apartment in such disarray, Tom and his fellow NOPD detectives were further surprised that there appeared to be no blood anywhere on the apartment's floor—nor was there any smell from Addie's corpse, which had been stored in the kitchen for nearly two weeks, as they would quickly find out from one of Zack's notes, which specified the exact date—October 5—of the murder. "Then we noticed that the window air-conditioning unit was on and set real low," Tom remembers, "so it was very cool—that's what helped hide the smell."

Moving toward the kitchen, Tom saw Zack's messages on the walls in black spray paint—"I'M A TOTAL FAILURE," "PLEASE HELP ME STOP THE PAIN," "I LOVE HER," "PLEASE CALL MY WIFE"—and, finally, a wide arrow sprayed in silver paint that pointed toward the oven. "Her head was in the pot," Tom explains, "and her torso was wrapped up in a garbage bag in the refrigerator. At one point the cops had to exit the apartment because detectives from the homicide department didn't want anything contaminated." The decision to leave the apartment was also driven by the cops' need to take a mental breather. "I couldn't conceive of what had happened there," Tom remembers. "In ten years in law enforcement I had never seen anything that disturbing."

With the cops waiting on the wide, grassy neutral ground in front of 826 North Rampart, workers from the coroner's office—led by chief investigator John Gagliano—burst through the iron gates and ran upstairs to Zack and Addie's apartment. The activities of the coroner's office were noticed by John Boutté, who had once worked for the coroner. "When I got up to go to the bathroom, I saw Gagliano walking out of the building with a plastic container," John remembers. "I was fucking *floored*." John then thought back to the smell emanating from 826 North Rampart and became sickened.

Early the next morning, Wednesday, October 18, Lana received a call from the coroner's office. "'Are you Zack Bowen's wife?" the caller said. "Yeah," Lana answered impassively. "Why?" There was a pause. "He's dead."

Lana couldn't comprehend what she had just been told. "What do you mean?" she asked. "He jumped off a building," the caller continued. "He killed his girlfriend."

Lana hung up the phone and then called a friend who, having seen news regarding an unnamed man who had killed himself and had been linked to a murder, made the connection that this was most likely Zack and gave Lana the most basic—and least gory—details about the crime. "Once I found out about the Omni Royal I knew everything I needed to know," Lana remembers. "We used to take the kids swimming there. I felt like Zack made a personal decision to hurt me and the kids."

Later that afternoon, the coroner's office released Zack's and Addie's names to the media. "I would imagine that he was in some serious mental anguish and pain," NOPD chief of detectives Anthony Cannatella told reporters that day. "I couldn't fathom to think what caused him to do it." Cannatella also noted that even though Zack had killed, dismembered, and then stored Addie in the kitchen, there was no sign of cannibalism at the crime scene, as some media outlets had already reported. Lana's friends, meanwhile, besieged her with phone calls urging her not to turn on the TV. Lana took their advice, as the news of Zack's suicide—let alone the horrible details surrounding his murder of Addie—had so shocked and stunned her already.

Because Zack had written in Addie's journal that he was employed at Matassa's—he even copied down the address of the grocery store for the cops—his bosses there learned of his fate in person from NOPD homicide detectives just as the NOPD revealed details of the murder-suicide to reporters for the first time that Wednesday afternoon. When Capricho came back to Matassa's from a delivery at around five o'clock that night, his boss, Louis Matassa, pulled him aside and said, "Caps, come over here. I got bad news.'"

Capricho thought that he was about to be fired—Zack had recently told him that Louis was going to send him packing for being "too arrogant and too slow." Sensing Capricho's discomfort, Louis said, "It's not about you." For a moment, Capricho's mood stabilized, but then he thought about Zack and Addie's broken relationship and Zack's strange, sudden announcement of a vacation to the Cayman Islands. "I knew something was horribly fucking wrong," Capricho remembers.

"Zack jumped off the Omni Royal hotel," Louis continued, "and he left a suicide note in his pocket that led them to Addie's body, which he cut up." Capricho couldn't find the words to respond. "I was floored," Capricho remembers. "It's just not something that is reachable. There are times when you can put yourself in someone else's shoes. But then there are some things that are so beyond our grasp of what we are capable of or what we understand ourselves to be capable of, we cannot go to that length. That's what this is. It is surreally untouchable. It stays where it is."

That afternoon, the first stories naming Zack and Addie specifically as the couple involved in the murder-suicide appeared on local TV news stations like WWL; these stories were then picked up by national outlets such as the Associated Press and Fox News. By then, Lana had gathered the strength to call Lori to deliver the news about Zack. Lori, in turn, called Jed, who only days earlier had returned from a tour in Iraq to his wife, Tonya, and their home in Jasper, Georgia. "I was at work and my cell phone rang but I missed the call," Tonya told me. "When I checked my voice mail there was a message from Lori: 'Please call us.'" The grave tone of Lori's voice frightened Tonya and she frantically called Jed, who was working at the cigar store the couple ran together in Jasper.

"My brother killed his girlfriend," Jed told Tonya, having already heard from his mother, "and he's committed suicide."

Jed and Tonya then agreed to meet back at their home. When Jed arrived, Tonya said, "It's gotta have made the news by now." Jed went into the living room, turned on his computer, and then went online. "Holy shit," he shouted. Tonya ran into the living room and stared at the headlines on the computer screen. "Ohhhhh," she sighed, "fuck me."

———

Back in New Orleans the next morning—Thursday, October 19—the *Times-Picayune* hit newsstands with a huge front-page story about Zack and Addie bearing the headline "BOYFRIEND CUT UP CORPSE, COOKED IT." This encouraged more dark jokes all over town, just as the *New York Post*'s classic 1983 headline "HEADLESS BODY IN A TOPLESS BAR" encouraged New Yorkers to make light.

As Rob Van Meter, Addie's former roommate at the Governor Nicholls apartment, arrived at his job as the personal chef to Dr. Brobson Lutz and his partner, Dr. Kenneth Combs, one of his coworkers taunted him: "We found a new chef on the block. There's a chef who's better than you." Rob had just begun working that fall for Lutz and Combs, so he felt vulnerable and believed his coworker was telling him the truth.

"Look in the paper," the coworker continued, "some girl on our block got killed and cooked." (The Lutz-Combs home on Dumaine Street, which they purchased from Tennessee Williams in the early 1980s just before his death, was right around the corner from Zack and Addie's apartment at 826 North Rampart.)

If Rob's coworker had realized that Rob had known Addie—let alone lived with her—he likely wouldn't have made the joke. When Rob turned to his coworker's copy of the *Times-Picayune* that Thursday morning, he was overcome. He thought back to sleeping side by side with Addie in the dingy Governor Nicholls apartment, and the horrifying image of her dismembered body being pulled out of an oven hit him hard. "I was hysterical," Rob remembers. "I couldn't leave the bed for a day and a half. As much as I sometimes hated her, thinking about her being cut to pieces was too much."

On Wednesday night, Dennis Monn—perhaps Addie's closest friend in New Orleans—had seen the TV news coverage of the murder-suicide, but in most of the reports Addie was identified simply as a Jane Doe. After watching one news report on the evening news about a dismembered Jane Doe, Dennis remembers thinking, "God, that's probably Addie given her history." But then he caught himself. Addie had always been in abusive relationships, but the notion that she would end up as a dismembered Jane Doe was simply too outrageous. "I felt sick for a second," Dennis remembers. "How could I think that?"

But when Dennis went to work at a temp job at a public high school in New Orleans's Central Business District on Thursday, he saw a copy of the *Times-Picayune* and all of his darkest fears about Addie were confirmed. "I have to go home," Dennis told his boss that morning, "and I don't really want to talk about why." Because Dennis couldn't pull himself together enough to explain his feelings, his boss said sternly, "Well, Mr. Monn, you can't just leave." Flustered and feeling emotionally overwhelmed, Dennis blurted out: "The girl who got her head cut off—that was my former roommate." Dennis's boss asked for no further explanation; he was allowed to go home. Dennis was so shattered that he spent the next two days at his Mandeville Street apartment mourning the loss of Addie.

While Rob hadn't had any significant contact with Addie in years, Dennis had seen her just weeks prior to her murder. In mid-September, during a break from packing up her belongings at Governor Nicholls, Addie rode on her bike over to Dennis's apartment and delivered a long string of bad news. She was being forced to leave the Governor Nicholls apartment under the threat of eviction; she and Zack were breaking up; and then, most ominous, she hinted that she "had things" on Zack that proved he was dangerous. "Everyone loves him," Addie told Dennis, "but he's fucking crazy. Everyone thinks he's the nice, clean-cut guy; he's not." Dennis pressed Addie for details about Zack. "He's fucked up from being in the war," Addie continued. "He mentioned something about witnessing a child being murdered. It's really fucked him up and I can't deal with it."

As Dennis was preparing to head out of town to attend a music festival in rural Tennessee, he offered Addie the use of his apartment. She declined the offer and went home. That was the last time Dennis saw her.

The front-page *Times-Picayune* story sent Zack and Addie's friends in New Orleans reeling. In Jasper, Tonya and Jed had to handle an array of practical concerns in the midst of their shock: they wanted to get and relate to Lori as much information as possible about Zack from the coroner's office, and they had to figure out what to do with Jaxon and Lily, as Lana was completely overwhelmed by phone calls from reporters—all of whom she refused to speak with—and by the task of removing Zack's belongings from the North Rampart apartment, which had become a crime scene. First, Tonya called the NOPD. "We can't tell you anything," one detective told Tonya, "you're not next of kin." Undeterred, Tonya then phoned the coroner's office. "We can't release anything," Tonya was told, "but we can tell you that we do have a body here and it is Zackery Bowen." Because Tonya wasn't getting anywhere with law enforcement, she turned her attentions to Jaxon and Lily. "Put the kids on the plane," Tonya told Lana, "and send them to us." Jed booked an early evening flight for the kids from New Orleans to Atlanta (Jasper is about sixty miles from Atlanta). A severe afternoon thunderstorm in New Orleans delayed Jaxon and Lily's arrival until midnight.

That night, as Tonya waited for her niece and nephew to arrive at Atlanta's Hartsfield Airport, she imagined how reassuring it would be to reunite with them. But when Jaxon and Lily straggled off the jetway, Tonya was unnerved by how much they had come to resemble their parents. "It was like Zack and Lana were walking off the plane," Tonya remembers.

On the long ride back to Jasper, Tonya tried to feel more comfortable with the kids, but when they arrived at home a call from Lana rattled her once again. "Will you keep the kids?" Lana asked. "Will you enroll them in school?" Tonya caught her breath; she was overwhelmed with Jed's recent return from Iraq and the sudden, dramatic death of her brother-in-law. "We're all basket cases right now," Tonya told Lana forcefully. "So, no, Lana, I don't think we can do it. You're the mother. *Step up.*" Lana admits that she asked Tonya and Jed to care for Jaxon and Lily but says that she did so because she was simply overcome with anguish and loneliness, and felt that she could not care for them. "They shouldn't have had to take me and the kids on," Lana told me, "but I had no one."

Reeling, Lana left her West Bank apartment one night after drinking and went on a long, aimless drive through Louisiana and Texas, and was pulled over by the police and arrested for drunk driving.

Fortunately for her and the kids, Lana did not face jail time—only probation—and when she returned to New Orleans she was ready to care for Jaxon and Lily again. But the horrors of that fall were far from over for Lana. She struggled with guilt about Zack's fate, especially because in mid-September—about two weeks before Zack murdered Addie—she had taken Zack out to dinner and broken the news to him that after their long separation she finally wanted a divorce. Lana's plan was for a "quickie divorce" from Zack in October; she would then marry her boyfriend in November on a cruise. Meanwhile, Jaxon and Lily would fly out with Zack to Lori's for Thanksgiving and Christmas, in order to minimize their direct exposure to the divorce that fall. Over dinner, Zack agreed to the idea but Lana remembers that he "felt a little indignant. Finally it was the end." Now, Lana continued to struggle with what she should tell the kids about their father's death.

In a sensible effort to get professional help, Lana took Jaxon and Lily to a New Orleans psychiatrist, who recommended that they be told *all* of the details about the murder-suicide. Lana thought that this was a terrible idea—but she reasoned that "a psychiatrist has to know better than me, right?"

So Lana told Jaxon, who was then eight, and Lily, then six, what Zack had done to Addie—including her dismemberment—and what Zack had done to himself afterward. That fall, Jaxon became quiet and reflective, while an anguished Lily made crayon drawings of Zack leaping off the roof of the Omni Royal and was panic-stricken with a constantly upset stomach. "It almost killed my daughter," Lana remembers. "Bad advice, huh?"

It seemed that there was nowhere to hide from the horrors that fall: when Lana took Lily to see a gastroenterologist, the doctor pulled Lana aside and asked, "Did he eat her?"

The pervasive media coverage of the murder-suicide, much of it citing and further spreading the false rumors that Zack had feasted on Addie—the myth even reached the UK with the *Daily Mirror* story "Man Cooks and Eats Girlfriend" and the *Independent*'s "Murder Most Mysterious:

The House of Horrors in New Orleans"—kept reviving the nightmare for Lana, Jed, Tonya, and Lori throughout the fall of 2006. That the family was beset by tensions between Lana and Jed, and that Jed was still recovering from a miserable tour in Iraq in which he'd serviced helicopters at Camp Speicher in Saddam's hometown of Tikrit, made efforts to begin healing even more difficult. So, to keep matters simple and avoid media coverage, the Bowens decided against a funeral for Zack, opting to have him cremated instead, with Lana keeping the ashes in New Orleans. Addie's remains sat unclaimed for months at the Orleans Parish coroner's office and were finally taken by family members late that winter.

Zack's cremation did not bring Lana any peace. When Lana looked at the urn that held Zack's ashes, she felt an impossible desire to reconcile turbulent and conflicting feelings about her dead husband. Lana was furious with Zack for destroying Addie's life and, if she found it impossible to heal from the tragedy, her own—and for casting an irreversible shadow over the lives of Jaxon and Lily. "He ruined my fucking life and he ruined his children's lives," Lana says angrily. "They will never be whole." She was also resentful of Zack for choosing an exit from this world that was paved with drink, hard drugs, strippers, and good-byes only—it seemed—to friends like Squirrel and Capricho. Zack's long party ended for him when he leapt off the roof of the Omni Royal, but Lana, Jaxon, and Lily would be dealing with the tragic mess he had made for the rest of their lives.

At the same time, Lana felt grateful that Zack had mustered the courage to end his own life after he took Addie's. "Thank God he did it," she says. "If he was alive I couldn't even imagine what my kids and I would be going through. I probably would have left the country." Lana was not celebrating Zack's passing—she was simply relieved that the family would not have to endure a long, very public murder trial, and, more important, that Zack's conscience had been so shaken by his brutal murder of Addie that he meted out the ultimate justice to himself. Yet she also missed Zack and harbored fond feelings for parts of their marriage. He had done his very best to be a good husband—prior to Iraq, he had never shirked his responsibilities in caring for Jaxon and Lily, even when he was a teenage father. She remembered that the decision to join the military had been driven by Zack's vow to care for his new family, at any cost. Indeed, upon enlisting in the army Zack took out $250,000 in Service Members Group Life Insurance (SGLI), a VA program that provides low-cost group life insurance to members of the uniformed services. The maximum amount of coverage is $400,000, so Zack's decision to arrange for a six-figure sum—which I revealed to Lana when I obtained his entire military record—proved again to Lana that Zack had been intensely devoted to both her and the well-being of his family. It is also a rare insurance plan in that it pays out in cases of suicide. (Lana is currently working with a New Orleans attorney to find out if Zack converted the SGLI insurance to VGLI—Veterans Group Life Insurance—upon his separation from the military.)

Finally, there was Iraq. To Lana it was no coincidence that her relationship with Zack had fallen apart after he returned from the war, and that it was after Iraq when Zack's profound sense of responsibility for Jaxon and Lily seemed to evaporate like mist on the waterfront. Lana had people more prominent than him to be mad at, and she had events larger than both of their own lives to blame.

Lana was so torn between rage at and empathy for Zack that she struggled, successfully, against impulses to dispose of his ashes entirely, and disrespectfully. "I wanted to set them on fire in my backyard or flush them down the toilet," Lana admits. "That was my biggest struggle: trying to see the person he was instead of the monster he became."

———

Lana wasn't alone in sifting through her feelings about Zack and Addie, this couple who for many New Orleanians had been plucked from obscurity, heralded as post-Katrina holdouts and now fallen precipitously, to become even more famous as the city's most gruesome murder-suicide in memory. When I arrived in New Orleans right before Halloween 2006 for my fifth wedding anniversary, opinions about the couple varied wildly. To many New Orleanians, they were French Quarter freaks meant to be forgotten. "To know them," wrote Tara Jill Ciccarone on the website nolafugees.com, which provides reportage and *Onion*-like satire of the post-Katrina city, "you'd have to know a side of the city most try to ignore."

To more sympathetic New Orleanians—like Ciccarone—Zack and Addie were symbols and symptoms of a city collapsing psychologically from the stresses of the storm and the nonexistent recovery. "They were my age," Ciccarone wrote, "around the cusp of thirty in a post-Katrina New Orleans that is still sapping us, still fucking with us. We are at the mercy of a sort of disturbance in the force, and we've been there for so long, we're accustomed to it. New Orleans was never like the rest of America, which is easy to forget, but now, especially after a year, there seems to be a tendency to accept madness as norm, fragments as wholes."

By the end of October, the murder-suicide had so dominated discussion on the local news and in the blogosphere that the Associated Press ran a piece headlined "Dismemberment Murder Rivets New Orleans." And New Orleans's mischievous sense of morbidity—as evidenced by a popular bumper sticker reading "New Orleans: We Put the Fun in Funeral" and the jazz funeral itself, which begins with a solemn dirge and becomes joyful—together with the lurid details of Zack and Addie's death, so horrible that it was difficult to assimilate them in a sober way, especially in the city's hardened post-Katrina emotional terrain, worked to turn their deaths into grim, local farce.

During that Halloween, the New Orleans residents and visitors alike who packed Frenchmen Street in the Marigny—the block where Addie had tended bar at the Spotted Cat—sported homemade T-shirts that read "NOTHIN' SAYS LOVIN' LIKE MY GIRLFRIEND IN THE OVEN." Proprietors of popular French Quarter ghost tours, meanwhile, added 826 North Rampart Street to their itineraries. As guides passed the apartment with their tourist charges in tow, they would relate the horrid tale of "Bowen the Butcher." One cemetery guide, sixty-four-year-old Midge Jones, told the Associated Press that he would be interested in renting Zack and Addie's apartment. "As long as it is cleaned up and painted, and [has] a new gas stove," he said, "I've got no problem with it."

———

Though I had followed the media coverage of the murder-suicide when I was down in New Orleans for my wedding anniversary, I was much more concerned with New Orleans itself; back then, there was a tangible sense of depression, exacerbated, because of the halting recovery, by a fear that the city might never come back.

Adding to the misery was the skyrocketing murder rate, which brought the sixty members of the Louisiana State Police and three hundred National Guardsmen to the city's streets. On Halloween night, a gunman walked into Club Decatur on Decatur Street in the French Quarter and shot three men and two women. All five victims survived the incident and the next morning Club Decatur employees could be seen impassively hosing blood from the sidewalk. "People don't realize this isn't a normal community yet," NOPD superintendent Warren Riley told *USA Today* that fall. "There are people out there on the edge."

As my wife and I wound down our anniversary trip early that November, I began thinking more seriously about Zack and his life lived on the edge in Kosovo, Baghdad, and, finally, New Orleans—and, of course, what had pushed him over.

So, on a whim one morning, I walked from the Soniat House to Fiorella's Café on Decatur Street, where I'd heard Capricho was working as a deliveryman. After sitting down at a table and ordering a lunch of rice and beans, I asked my waitress if Capricho was working that day. "*Caps!*" she shouted toward the kitchen, and a few moments later, Capricho came out to greet me. After a brief introduction, Capricho agreed to meet with me and talk about Zack that afternoon at his Burgundy Street apartment, the same apartment that Zack had tended bar in for the last time about two weeks earlier. When I arrived at Capricho's one-bedroom apartment—which neighbored a coffee shop called Marigny Perks, where Capricho worked part-time behind the cash register—its shutters were tightly closed and it was eerily dark. Flyers for Capricho's housewarming party featuring cocktail maestro Zack cluttered the floor, as did old copies of *New York* magazine, beer cans, and dirty ashtrays piled high with stubbed-out cigarettes. After spending only a few minutes with Capricho I could tell that he was deeply depressed and panic-stricken. He was mourning the loss of both his close friend Zack and his onetime girlfriend Addie. He let out big, anguished sighs between every sentence as he described his difficulties in coming to grips with the murder-suicide.

"I haven't been able to sleep," Capricho told me. "I've been drinking quite a bit. I am not having a good time with this. I quit Matassa's—they wanted me to stay, they told me I could come back. But at the moment I can't deal with the ghosts in the aisles." Capricho also confirmed my fears about how depressed many New Orleanians remained nearly fifteen months after Katrina. "When you live in New Orleans you live in a dream," Capricho said then, "but with Katrina too much reality struck home. The feeling of a community based upon joy and revelry and mystery and danger and debauchery was gone." Capricho explained that the depressive state of post-Katrina New Orleans was particularly difficult for Zack and Addie to manage because the storm had once been a powerfully cleansing moment for them. "Katrina was horrible for many," Capricho told me, "but it was magical for Zack and Addie. It allowed these kids who were damaged to stave off reality, to fall in love without interference."

The next morning, in advance of a late-afternoon flight back to New York, I met Leo Watermeier for the first time. We talked for hours in the courtyard behind Zack and Addie's apartment. "I was in New York for 9-11 and the mood changed very quickly afterward," Leo told me. "Each day it got better. But that's not what happened here. The mood hasn't turned. The future is up in the air."

As Leo and I talked, I found it difficult to concentrate on our conversation as we were surrounded by Zack's and Addie's belongings, which sat unclaimed in the leafy courtyard of their North Rampart apartment—Zack's delivery bike, the dolly he used to cart his possessions to and from the Hotel Empress, Addie's toaster oven and coffee machine. It was a scene so sad that even the most careful and respectful reporting can only hope to pay tribute: two lives that had once been such powerful symbols of New Orleans's seemingly indomitable spirit reduced to this sad still-life in an abandoned landscape.

As I left 826 North Rampart, I ran into Priestess Miriam Chamani, the proprietor of the Voodoo Spiritual Temple below Zack and Addie's apartment, who was unlocking the heavy wrought-iron gate that leads to the courtyard. When Leo introduced us, she heartily embraced me. I was surprised by the warmth of her greeting, because in the wake of the murder-suicide Priestess Miriam had been subjected to lots of unfair treatment and speculation, like cruel and stupid comments on the *Times-Picayune* website that had accused her of using voodoo to drive Zack to murder Addie. A separate Associated Press article had dismissed the notion that voodoo had played a part in the murder-suicide, but nonetheless made repeated, winking references to voodoo culture in New Orleans. "There is no suggestion the slaying had anything to do with voodoo, but some guides are already dropping the story into the yarns they spin as they take visitors on tours of the Quarter, a place of Gothic spires, curlicued wrought-iron balconies, and shop windows cluttered with voodoo candles and bottles of exotic potions."

Connecting Zack and Addie's fate to New Orleans's voodoo culture was absurd on its face: the couple had no real interactions with Priestess Miriam, and voodoo priestesses are spiritual guides who conduct healing rituals, not inspire homicides. And after talking with Priestess Miriam, I was reminded of how lousy and offensive it was, although I suppose tempting if one is going to treat the French Quarter—the heart and a jewel of the city and of America—only as a playground in which to cavort and a spectacle at which to gawk, and its inhabitants only as servants, or as actors in that spectacle, and not as full human beings with fears and desires that we can understand. Princess Miriam is a sweet, smiling woman who speaks sparingly, but always has wise things to say. Just before heading back to the Soniat House to finish packing for the trip home, I asked Priestess Miriam if Zack and Addie, or the astronomic murder rate, or the crawling pace of the recovery would force her from New Orleans. "If you are a healer like me," she told me, "there is no place to run."

TWELVE

CRAIG MORSE

MURDER CITY

During the last ten years three hundred and three persons have been murdered in New Orleans or vicinity. And yet only FIVE of the murderers have been hung. Only five—although eleven were actually sentenced to death. Consequently the chance of being hung for committing a murder in this community is as five to three hundred and three. Almost as little danger of being hung for having committed murder as of being run over by a railroad train or cut in two by a buzz saw or brained by a brick falling from a chimney. . . . If the dead are not indignant . . . they ought to be.

—LAFCADIO HEARN, September 8, 1880

Friends: As you all think about the carnage in New Orleans this weekend (7 dead through 3 pm Sunday) and for the past two years (Almost 400 people have been killed in a city of 250,000 in the past two years)—nothing outside of Baghdad is close—I hope that this tragedy

forces everyone to think outside of the "box" to work together to get
this under control, before everyone loses it.

> —Tulane criminologist PETER SCHARF in an
> April 2008 e-mail to city officials

By the end of my trip to New Orleans in the late fall of 2006, I convinced a longtime friend and onetime editor at *GQ*—who had just taken
over the reins at *Penthouse*, charged by its publishers with placing serious
features into the magazine—to assign a feature about Zack to me. Thanks
to Capricho's cooperation, I was able to finish the *Penthouse* piece about
Zack quickly. A few weeks later, in early 2007, I was back in New Orleans
on a short business trip. That week, I tracked down Capricho and, over
beers at a Decatur Street bar, gave him an early copy of *Penthouse* with
my Zack story.

"I can't handle this right now," Capricho told me, shoving the magazine into his backpack. "Maybe I'll be able to read it later." Capricho,
obviously, was still mourning the loss of Zack and Addie, and when I
returned to New York in March I found that I could not shake their
story off either. So I began the process of tracking down Zack's fellow
soldiers from the 527th MP Co. But military culture's devotion to obe-
dience and loyalty can often mean that soldiers are unwilling to speak to
civilians—even close friends and relatives—about their combat experiences,
and I was rebuffed by the few troops whom I was able to contact. Unbeknownst to me at the time, several soldiers from the 527th—including
Jeremy and Todd—had purchased the issue of *Penthouse* with my Zack
story. They appreciated that I had attempted to humanize their friend,
who had been so demonized elsewhere. By the late spring, vehement
refusals to participate in a book about Zack were piling up in my e-mail
inbox. The soldiers of the 527th assumed that I was out to smear both
Zack and the military, as evidenced by one angry e-mail that I received
that spring:

Sir I will tell you now that if there is anything bad stated about Zack . . .
you don't want to know what I will tell you to do with it. He was a friend
and I will have nothing to do with anything that degrades his name or
the name of the military. A lot of us came out of the war with problems
and that is no excuse for his actions but it does help to make sense of it
all. Sir I will again state I will have nothing to do with anything that
looks down on the Military or on Zack or any other Soldier who has
done the service asked of them by this great country.

Despite the steady stream of rejections to my interview requests, I
pressed forward with my investigation. Beyond the bluster and go-fuck-
yourself replies from 527th soldiers, which I could handle, I discovered
that there was a real, deep, abiding love for Zack.

I also sensed, again and again, through correspondence and also
reading and investigating, that some of the mental health problems Zack
faced when he returned from Iraq were not his alone. One 527th soldier
told me that he could relate to Zack's downward spiral of PTSD and
drinking and drug abuse: "He was in a phase I call 'washout.' I went
through it for a while and finally had to go see a doctor. My saving grace
was my platoon sergeant. He pushed me into getting an appointment."

As I struggled to earn the trust of the soldiers from the 527th MP Co.
that spring, the extent of the PTSD epidemic among Iraq and Afghanistan veterans was just beginning to become clear.

In May, the Defense Department's Task Force on Mental Health
reported that more than one-third of currently serving troops and living veterans from all conflicts were suffering from problems such as
traumatic brain injury and PTSD. The Defense Department warned that
the number of troops and veterans suffering from mental health problems such as PTSD was expected to worsen substantially thanks to
longer, and repeated, tours of duty in Iraq and Afghanistan and that
"the system of care for psychological health that has evolved in recent
decades is not sufficient to meet the needs of today's forces and their

beneficiaries, and will not be sufficient to meet the needs in the future."

—————

Late that spring, after filing a Freedom of Information Act request with the army for Zack's military record and securing my first interview with a 527th soldier—Sergeant Charles Shepard—I decided to move to New Orleans in order to dig deeper into Zack's case. By this point, criminologists and journalists were publicly pointing out strong parallels between post-Saddam Baghdad and post-Katrina New Orleans, and these went beyond the enormous, evident governmental failures and into specifics having to do with crime and security.

"We used to think we had a green zone, like in Baghdad, where you were safe," Tulane criminologist Peter Scharf told NPR, "but the reality is that probably there is no green zone. You're not safe here." New Orleans was even earning nicknames like "Baghdad on the Mississippi" (*Time*) and "Baghdad on the Bayou" (*City Journal*).

Of course, with the murder rate in New Orleans making national news, my decision to relocate to the city with my wife was not popular among our friends and family. Even Capricho was wary of me starting a new life in New Orleans in the middle of the summer, a traditionally high crime season and a vulnerable time for the locals, when the city's teenagers are hot and restless and a scarcity of tourists stumbling down Bourbon Street puts service-economy workers in the criminals' crosshairs.

"It's going to be a trial by fire, man," Capricho warned in early July, explaining that the summer of 2007 promised to be worse than most. A rash of robberies had shaken the French Quarter that spring, many perpetrated by a sadistic mugger who prowled the neighborhood in his car looking for female marks, then beat them senseless and took their cash. I blithely dismissed Capricho's concerns: I'd written about street crime for nearly a decade, had moved to New York just as the crack era crested in the early 1990s, and even endured death threats after the publication of my first book, *Queens Reigns Supreme*, a chronicle of the rise of hip-hop culture and the crack epidemic in Queens.

Nothing could have prepared me for the lawlessness I encountered when I first arrived in New Orleans in late July 2007. Soon after we moved into our apartment in the Lower Quarter—the residential end of the French Quarter, with small restaurants, gay bars, coffee shops, Creole cottages and town homes, and the Governor Nicholls Street home of Brad Pitt and Angelina Jolie—the neighborhood was hit by a rash of violent crimes. On August 10, a group made up of two men, three women, and a fourteen-year-old boy committed three armed robberies in the Lower Quarter in under ninety minutes. Later that month, my wife went out to do errands on North Peters Street around three in the afternoon and found herself watching helplessly as a waitress coming off her shift was robbed and savagely beaten on the sidewalk just steps away from her. She came home shaken. North Peters is one the busiest streets in the French Quarter, home to such citified outposts of modern consumption and entertainment as Urban Outfitters and a Hard Rock Café, which made the daytime mugging all the more unnerving.

In August, a staggering twenty-six people were murdered in New Orleans, the highest per capita murder rate for the month in a decade. The city's population, debated over by city officials and demographers, stood at around 288,000, down from the pre-Katrina estimate of around 455,0000. Twenty murders in one month is a number more often seen in America's largest cities, not in such medium-size towns. The fewer the living, the more they are affected by the news of the dead. The murders are also taking a profound emotional toll on remaining Katrina survivors such as Jack Jones who, ironically, have suffered the greatest losses after the storm.

"I know of about twelve or thirteen people who have either been killed or committed suicide since the hurricane," Jack says. So while Katrina took approximately fifteen hundred lives, the post-Katrina murder epidemic—which as of January 2009 had already claimed nearly six hundred lives—is shaping up to be a second, prolonged drowning for New Orleans.

The extent of the murder epidemic became clear to me when Capricho lost yet another coworker to violence just weeks before I moved to New Orleans.

The murder of Fiorella's manager Chris Roberts on June 17, 2007, did not generate national headlines, and it received only sparse coverage in New Orleans. But it illustrates the city's plight—and the surprising connections between murder cases here—more vividly than any set of statistics. On December 22, 2006, Chris, a thirty-three-year-old motorcycle mechanic, his girlfriend, Jeanette Kelly, and their young daughters, Aoife (Gaelic for "Eva") and Siobhan, piled into a truck and began the 441-mile drive home to New Orleans from Huntsville, Alabama, where they had been living in post-Katrina exile. In Huntsville, Chris had built wiring harnesses—the nervous system for motorcycles—for a boutique motorcycle outfit called the Confederate Motor Company. Chris was loved by his bosses, building motorcycles was his life's passion, and Confederate's bikes were purchased by the likes of Brad Pitt and Tom Cruise. But Chris and Jeanette had fallen in love in New Orleans and wanted to participate in the city's post-Katrina recovery. So Chris submitted his letter of resignation to Confederate in early December 2006, even though he had no real job prospects in New Orleans. "After much difficult consideration," Chris wrote in his resignation letter, "my family has made the decision to return to New Orleans on the 22nd of December for personal reasons. I will always be proud to have been a part of something so exceptional."

Though their friends in New Orleans warned them repeatedly of the city's post-Katrina perils—"Everyone told us not to go back because of safety issues," Jeanette remembers—the family let out a loud cheer as they crossed the Louisiana state line on that cold late December day. It didn't take long, however, for Jeanette and Chris to realize just how dangerous New Orleans had become since Katrina.

On December 28, 2006, Dinerral Shavers, the twenty-five-year-old snare drummer for New Orleans's iconic Hot 8 Brass Band, was shot and killed after picking up his teenage stepson and his son's friend on Dumaine Street in the Sixth Ward (the killer was apparently gunning for Dinerral's stepson but hit Dinerral instead).

Then, on January 4, 2007, independent filmmaker Helen Hill was murdered in front of her husband and two-year-old son during what was apparently a botched home invasion in the couple's double-shotgun home in the Marigny. Helen's husband, Paul Gailiunas, a physician at a health clinic for low-income residents, was awakened by his wife's screams just after 5:00 a.m. He rushed into the living room with his son in his arms to find Helen struggling with an intruder. Before he could intervene, the attacker shot and killed her. Then, as Paul ran for cover, the gunman shot him in his left forearm, right hand, and cheek. Paul survived and, miraculously, the child escaped from the barrage physically unscathed.

Helen's killing marked the sixth murder in New Orleans in a twenty-four-hour period. A January 5 *Times-Picayune* headline announced— "Killings Bring the City to Its Bloodied Knees." The half dozen killings, so soon after the slaying of Dinerral, brought thousands of angry New Orleanians to the streets in front of city hall on January 11, calling for an end to the violence.

Further stoking the outrage was the awareness that both Helen and Dinerral were especially passionate New Orleanians who had staked their lives on the city's recovery. Dinerral had successfully completed a months-long bid to be accepted into the Musicians' Village, a community of seventy-two single-family homes for local musicians in the Upper Ninth Ward built by the New Orleans Area Habitat for Humanity (NOAHH). Helen had convinced her husband, Paul, to return to New Orleans after a long post-Katrina exile in South Carolina by having friends fill out postcards addressed to Paul that listed a "good reason to come back to New Orleans." Chris Roberts and Jeanette Kelly attended the January 11 anticrime march. Though the couple was concerned about their safety in New Orleans, they decided to stay because they were so committed to the city's recovery and were in the midst of preparing for major career changes. Chris sought to attend Delgado Community College in New Orleans to study electrical engineering, while Jeanette, who worked as a freelance graphic artist, hoped to go to school to become a psychiatrist.

In the meantime, Chris waited tables at Fiorella's—working alongside Capricho, who was employed as deliveryman—while Jeanette took on freelance graphic design gigs whenever she could get them. Though Chris had preferred working for a motorcycle company like Confederate, and freelance jobs were scarce for Jeanette, the couple was nonetheless thrilled to be back in New Orleans. As the spring of 2007 arrived, Chris was feeling optimistic—he was promoted to a manager position at Fiorella's and his first Father's Day was just weeks away (he'd had Aoife with Jeanette; her older daughter, Siobhan, is from a previous marriage). But on June 17—Father's Day, at around 8:00 p.m.—Chris was sitting in his ground-floor apartment on Esplanade Avenue and North Prieur Street in the Esplanade Ridge neighborhood when he heard what sounded like gravel crunching under wheels. He had just purchased a new Suzuki motorcycle and he feared that a thief was stealing the bike by trying to quietly push it down the street. So Chris jumped up from where he was sitting and rushed out his apartment door to the building's entryway, where he encountered a robber who was indeed pushing the Suzuki away with the motor off. The robber fired one bullet into Chris's head and another into his heart. Then the attacker pedaled away on his bicycle, leaving Chris to die at the scene. The Suzuki was left behind, most likely because its ignition system was too complex for someone unfamiliar with motorcycles to turn on.

Two weeks earlier, Jeanette's hairdresser—Robin Malta—had been murdered. Robin, forty-three, was a prominent member of the New Orleans gay community: he owned a popular Decatur Street hair salon and had once served as the grand marshal of the city's annual gay pride event, Southern Decadence. Robin had been bludgeoned to death in his home on Port Street in the Marigny. The high-profile and beloved victim, the brutality of the slaying (Robin was struck in the head with the metal leg of an ironing board more than a dozen times), and its strange aftermath (the NOPD later recovered Robin's gold 1997 Nissan Maxima burned and abandoned on a desolate side street) made it one of the most notorious murder cases of 2007.

"I have to get out of here," Jeanette said to herself. So in July, Jeanette and her kids flew to Detroit, the city where she had been raised and that she left for New Orleans in the mid-1990s when Detroit had grown too dangerous.

—————

When my wife and I returned to New Orleans in the summer of 2007, just as Jeanette left for Detroit, I was stunned to hear that Capricho had lost yet another coworker in the post-Katrina murder epidemic. I would also soon discover that a central figure in Zack's life was connected to yet another major homicide in this new New Orleans. On an unusually chilly early fall day in 2007, I received a terse text message from Capricho: "Squirrel is back." After a months-long stay in his small Michigan hometown in an attempt to emotionally recover from the deaths of Zack and Addie, Squirrel had at last returned to New Orleans. As soon as I received the text, I called Capricho. He urged me to come by Matassa's immediately because Squirrel was only going to be in the French Quarter for a few minutes. Capricho explained that because Squirrel was trying to leave the drug game—he was working in construction in New Orleans— he hoped to make his visits to the French Quarter as brief as possible. So if I missed Squirrel at Matassa's that afternoon, it would be months before I could catch up with him again.

Eager to finally meet Squirrel in person, I hopped on my bike and pedaled quickly the two blocks over to Matassa's. When I arrived, Squirrel was impatiently pacing on the sidewalk outside Matassa's, chain-smoking cigarettes. He was wearing faded jeans, a blue 1970s-style T-shirt with the words "FRENCH QUARTER" imprinted on the front, and a short string of puka shell beads so tight around his neck that it fit like a choker. Squirrel was pale and wan—he looked like he hadn't slept in days—so I invited him back to my apartment for a drink. I sat Squirrel down at my dining room table and poured him a big plastic tumbler full of straight vodka—embarrassingly, Absolut New Orleans, because that was all I had in the cupboard at the time—and he began to open up about his life since returning to New Orleans that fall.

"The Squirrel," he said with a long sigh, speaking about himself in the third person, "was just nabbed for murder." Squirrel is undoubtedly a rough guy, always up for a bar fight or a confrontation with a customer who owes him a drug debt. But the news that he was arrested in a murder case was surprising. "Yeah, murder," Squirrel snapped at me, sensing my unease. "The Malta thing."

Squirrel wasn't aware that I'd been talking with some of Robin Malta's friends and clients—nor was he likely aware that Robin had been quoted in an old *Times-Picayune* story about Zack and Addie. ("That guy must've just lost it," Robin said of Zack to a *Times-Picayune* reporter on October 20, 2006. "Something must've just cracked in his head. To be so nonchalant about the whole thing. It's just crazy.")

Reeling from all these strange connections between the murder cases, I let Squirrel tell me about his experience as a suspect in Robin's slaying. "It all started about a week ago," Squirrel begins. "I was drinking at Buffa's. I'd been there about four hours and I'd had three beers. I decided to step outside to smoke a joint with a friend. Then I walk out the door and all of the sudden—bam—it's the cops."

The NOPD officers said little as they pushed him into a squad car—"We're taking you in," they muttered—but when Squirrel arrived at the Eighth District police station on Royal Street in the French Quarter, he quickly realized that he'd been implicated in the Malta case. "Did you ever sell Malta drugs?" one detective asked. "If he had come into a bar and bought drugs from me," Squirrel replied calmly, "I wouldn't remember it."

Another detective stepped in and alleged that Squirrel's hair had been found at the murder scene on Port Street. "How do you know it's my hair?" Squirrel said he shouted at the detectives. "You can take samples of my hair, my blood, anything you want, right now." There was a long silence until one of the detectives said, "We know you did it," sending Squirrel into a rage. "You won't be able to place me on the scene," Squirrel sputtered at the cops. "You won't be able to place me anywhere near it. So fuck you. You ain't got shit. You have people saying I did it. You really need to talk to those people who you got that information from and find out what type of people they are. Maybe it's someone who didn't like me. Maybe it's someone I upset. Maybe I took money out of their pocket because I sold better drugs than them. Listen, charge me with this. I'm hungry. I want a cigarette. This is bullshit. Take me to jail and then I'll see you in court."

Squirrel's insistence that the NOPD charge him with the murder or release him worked: he was released soon afterward. But the nightmare of being a suspect in the Malta case was far from over for Squirrel, even though a New Orleans man named Mark Ott would later be charged in the killing. Word spread through the French Quarter that Squirrel had been picked up in the case. Because Robin was much beloved in the French Quarter and the Marigny, Squirrel had become persona non grata in both neighborhoods. "I was eighty-sixed from all the bars because of the Malta thing," Squirrel explains. "From Aunt Tiki's to the Abbey on lower Decatur, everyone is talking about it."

The experience at the Eighth District police station and the rejection by his friends in the neighborhood left Squirrel so bitter and depressed that he sank back to drinking and drugs and, just days before we met outside Matassa's, he ended up sleeping for several nights in a dog park in the French Quarter (hence his disheveled look when we met). "First the storm," Squirrel said angrily, "then Zack and Addie and now . . . this." He took an enormous swig of vodka and his eyes got a wild, angry look. "The Malta thing, it's just not my MO," he continued. "You see, I have the fear, the fear of God. Of all the things you might do in your life, murder is the only thing you're not gonna get forgiven for."

Fear of God or—perhaps more important—fear of law enforcement is in short supply in post-Katrina New Orleans. Though New Orleans has never been a peaceful city—in 1994, it reigned as the murder capital of the United States—its murder rate has skyrocketed since Katrina, claiming nearly six hundred lives by the beginning of 2009. In 2006, after racking up 162 homicides, New Orleans eclipsed high-crime cities like Baltimore and Philadelphia to claim the undesired crown of the murder capital of the United States. By the end of 2007, the total number of homicides in New Orleans—including Robin Malta's, the eighty-eighth murder of the year—had jumped to 209. The number of murders in New Orleans fell slightly in New Orleans in 2008—to a total of 179 for the year—but the per capita murder rate remained so high that during the fall of 2008 the city made *Foreign Policy*'s list "Murder Capitals of the World."

Even the most conservative estimates put the city's murder rate for 2007 and 2008 at more than 60 per 100,000 population. By way of comparison, Philadelphia—aka "Killadelphia"—had about 27 murders per 100,000 population in 2007. Baltimore—home of *The Wire* and wracked by some of the highest heroin addiction rates in the country, a deeply entrenched drug trade, and a stubbornly high homicide rate—recorded 44 homicides per 100,000 population in 2007 and 37 per 100,000 population in 2008.

The chaos and violence on New Orleans streets and the dysfunction of its criminal justice system post-Katrina have their unfortunate precedents. Since its birth in the early 1700s, New Orleans has been a violent and unjust place. The crack wars of the late 1980s and early 1990s were particularly brutal in New Orleans. In 1994, at the height of the city's crack era, 425 slayings were recorded, setting a local homicide record that still stands. The traditionally high crime rates can be attributed in part to a long ailing public education system, high poverty rates, and even the lack of basic infrastructure.

"If you look at the state of the state, we are virtually last in everything that is good, and first in everything that is bad," wrote C. B. Forgotson, the former chief counsel for the Louisiana state legislature. Yet during the 1990s, under the stewardship of police chief Richard Pennington, who emphasized community policing and a cleanup of corruption in the NOPD, the murder rate declined significantly from over 80 per 100,000 to just under 40 per 100,000 by the end of the decade.

In 2004 the murder rate in New Orleans started rising again, ushering in what Tulane criminologist Peter Scharf calls the "Second Wave Epidemic." The Second Wave Epidemic was driven in part by the bulldozing of the St. Thomas housing projects in 2001, which dispersed small-time hustlers across the city, who then battled for turf with entrenched dealers in surrounding neighborhoods. The spike in murders was also driven by successful federal prosecutions of the city's kingpins prior to the storm.

"Pre-Katrina, the feds targeted a select group of people who controlled a large part of the drug trade in New Orleans," explains New Orleans criminal defense attorney Rick Teissier. "They thought that if you picked off the lieutenants and got to the top of the cartels then you would solve the problem. But what ended up happening is what happened when Pablo Escobar was killed. They created a whole new beast—microcartels fighting over the action."

Katrina's arrival in late August 2005 took nearly fifteen hundred lives, destroyed billions of dollars in property, and created a diaspora of thousands of New Orleanians that was deepest in a swath of the country that spread from Houston to Atlanta and trickled out far beyond those cities. But in the storm's immediate aftermath, there had been a strange calm on the streets. Indeed, there were no murders at all in New Orleans until November 2005. "When we came back there was elation," explains Amzie Adams, the Marigny-based visual artist and musician whose band was paid by Addie when they played at the Spotted Cat. "We had survived. We came back to our city. For the first three months there were no murders. So right after the storm my band played in roving parades throughout the city. We rolled through the neighborhoods you couldn't even walk in before Katrina. And here we were walking though 'em, playing music, even dancing. We'd play and yell, 'Fuck Bush!' and people would come out of their homes screaming, 'Yeah!' There was a feeling of elation then—maybe the good people will come back and the bad people will stay away. It seemed like we were right when there were no murders during the first three months after the storm. We thought, 'Man, this is hope. There's a chance here.'"

But unbeknownst to most New Orleanians and even the city's law enforcement, New Orleans hustlers who had evacuated the city were making new, wholesale drug connections in big cities like Houston and Atlanta. When these drug business players returned home to New Orleans during the spring of 2006, they battled it out with more locally established players. The first sign that New Orleans was set to return to the murderous days of the mid-1990s occurred on June 17, 2006, when five teenagers were killed in a hail of gunfire on a street corner in the rough Central City neighborhood. Later that fall, as I visited New Orleans just after Zack killed Addie, there was yet another quintuple shooting, this time at Club Decatur in the French Quarter. Along the way, the criminal justice system in New Orleans—never a model of probity or even competence—continued its downward spiral: during the summer of 2007, District Attorney Eddie Jordan dropped charges against the suspect in the quintuple June 2006 Central City murders as well as the charges against David Bonds, the accused killer of Dinerral Shavers. When Jordan dropped both cases, he cited uncooperative witnesses, but after a public outcry charges were reinstated against the suspects in the cases.

Killings have become so commonplace that the Second Wave Epidemic touches just about every corner of New Orleans, from the devastated Lower Ninth Ward to the bohemian Marigny and Bywater to the tonier neighborhoods uptown. "Murder in New Orleans is becoming more democratic," criminologist Scharf says acidly. "Now even white people have a chance to get killed." Post-Katrina, it's not unusual to meet New Orleanians mourning simultaneously several friends who have been killed or who have killed themselves. Jeanette Kelly lost her boy-friend and her hairdresser to murder in a single month. Amzie Adams played back-to-back good-byes for two slain friends, Addie Hall and Helen Hill—a jazz funeral at the Spotted Cat for Addie, and a second line parade for Helen. The term "second line" once referred to those who came out to dance and listen to the music played by the main partici-pants of a jazz funeral—the "first line." Now, a second line is a parade in itself that can be held in honor of the dead, or simply for one of New Orleans's many social aid and pleasure clubs, such as the Treme Side-walk Steppers. Indeed, second lines are common in historically African-American neighborhoods like Tremé.

"I've been to a bunch of funerals since the storm," Amzie explains. "I'm almost not gonna go to them anymore. A second line is better; the dead are relieved of their sorrow. We're gonna live for them. But Helen wanted to be here. So I feel marked. I came back like they did. I'm just as much of a mark as they are. . . . People are still dying from the storm. Helen Hill and Addie Hall did not drown in the flood or die in a 115-degree attic, but they got that knife of psychic indifference stuck in 'em."

In the song "Two Black Suits" by local rockers the Happy Talk Band, lead singer Luke Allen sings wryly of having two separate suits on hand for the steady stream of funerals in post-Katrina New Orleans: "one of linen and one of wool / for summer and winter funerals." In the song, Luke also catalogs friends and acquaintances he's lost since the storm, including Bucky James, a bartender at the Spotted Cat who worked with Addie. Just a few weeks after Addie's murder, Bucky hung himself. Soon after his suicide, a friend of Bucky's named Rod Amis wrote on his blog, "I'm starting to dread . . . telephone calls because, more often than not, they are about someone I knew in New Orleans who is now dead."

————

I learned quickly that in post-Katrina New Orleans, you can never let your guard down. Along with my friends in the Quarter and the Marigny, I obsessively checked blogs like NOcrimeline.com and citizencrimewatch.org, which provide a far more realistic view of street crime than the city's sole paper, the *Times-Picayune*. ("VIOLENCE CLAIMS MORE VICTIMS" read a typically tepid headline after a week's worth of shootings culminated in three deaths.)

By September, safety concerns had caused me to alter my day-to-day lifestyle in multiple ways: I no longer carried a wallet, preferring instead to stick a single credit card and a few dollars in the front pocket of my jeans. After dark, I walked down the middle of the street to avoid muggers crouched behind parked cars. And I rarely allowed my wife to venture out alone at night, an antiquated rule that I became entirely comfortable enforcing.

By the early fall, I was weary of chancing the dark, empty streets of the French Quarter at night and was depressed by the realization that the wave of homicides was further endangering the already tenuous post-Katrina recovery. So, on an unusually humid early October afternoon, punctuated by heavy, crackling thunderstorms, I drove out to visit Tom Morovich—the first NOPD detective to arrive at the bodies of both Zack and Addie—at his one-bedroom condo in the New Orleans suburb of Gretna to get some perspective on the murder rate and perhaps even some advice on how to navigate the streets of New Orleans safely. In most big cities, cops rarely talk to journalists, but since Katrina the rank and file of the besieged NOPD have reached out to members of the media, often in direct defiance of their superiors. The cops seem sometimes to want to talk to reporters out of a deep sense of loneliness, as both the public and even the city government have shunned them since the storm.

When Tom pulled open his front door, he greeted me as though I were a buddy from the NOPD. Over several rounds of sports drinks— Tom was preparing for an eleven o'clock night shift, so he couldn't consume any alcohol—we talked for hours in his living room about everything from the stunning failings of the Orleans Parish district attorney's office (which had secured a conviction in just one of 161 murders in 2006) to

Zack and Addie, a case that Tom admitted he could not shake off more than a year after the fact.

As we talked, Tom's TV was turned on to local news coverage of the funeral of Harry Lee, the old-fashioned sheriff of nearby Jefferson Parish well known for his hard-charging law enforcement style and unapologetic defenses of racial profiling, who had just died at age seventy-five after a long bout with leukemia. ("If you live in a predominantly white neighborhood and two blacks are in a car behind you," Lee had once famously declared, "there's a pretty good chance they're up to no good.") The Lee funeral—which was being covered by the local media with the kind of wall-to-wall intensity you'd see anywhere in the world following the death of an especially highly regarded head of state—provided the perfect ambience for my conversation with Tom, who was struggling with life as a cop in America's murder capital.

"A lot of these thugs came back after Katrina because they know how easy it is to commit crime in New Orleans," Tom says. "They know that if they're caught, there are rarely repercussions." He sighs. "The minute people start thinking this situation is normal, we've lost control," he says. "But given the number of shootings, robberies, and murders, it's hard to say we are in control of New Orleans right now."

The extent of the chaos was demonstrated in October by the murder of Thelonious Dukes, a nineteen-year NOPD veteran. Late one night, Dukes was working on his motorcycle in the garage of his home in New Orleans East, a middle-class neighborhood on the outskirts of the city, when two gunmen ordered him into his home and awoke his wife. They pushed the couple to their knees and demanded cash and jewelry. Dukes complied, but when the men began to threaten his wife, he lunged for his service revolver, squeezing off two shots before the intruders returned fire. His wife was hit in the foot and survived; Dukes took two bullets to the torso and leg and died soon after.

If the notion of a cop murdered in his own home wasn't scary enough, the kicker came two weeks later. One of the suspects in the case, twenty-year-old Elton Phillips, was found to have taken refuge in an unlikely hideout: the home of Orleans Parish district attorney Eddie Jordan. Eventually it was revealed that Phillips, the main suspect in the cop killing, was a friend of Jordan's live-in girlfriend. To this day, Jordan insists he was unaware that his houseguest was wanted by the cops. Though Jordan, the first African-American DA in New Orleans history (whose penchant for flashy haberdashery earned him the nickname "the Hat"), soon resigned, the damage the city sustained during his tenure endures.

Jordan's disastrous years in office were marked by thousands of releases under Article 701 of the Louisiana code of criminal procedure, which states that suspects cannot be held for longer than sixty days on felony arrest without an indictment. Murder suspects freed under Article 701 dubbed the charges against them "misdemeanor murder." While Article 701 was designed to ensure that suspects could not be held indefinitely, it ended up simply becoming a get-out-of-jail-free pass thanks to Jordan's dysfunctional office, which could not bring indictments in the allotted time. Jordan's office was also hit with a race discrimination lawsuit brought by dozens of white former employees who claimed they were wrongfully terminated due to race. The lawsuit resulted in a staggering $3.7 million judgment against the DA's office.

When Mayor Nagin said that the city did not have the funds to pay for the judgment—"I don't see how the city is going to come to the DA's rescue"—the DA's office faced a seizure of its assets by the plaintiffs. The state later stepped in and paid the bill, staving off closure of the DA's office. Yet as the post-Katrina murder epidemic claimed even Tom's fellow cops, he told me that none of his hard experiences compared to the horror of finding Addie's dismembered corpse in the kitchen of the North Rampart apartment. So when Tom and I met on that early October day in 2007, even though our conversation was dominated by the skyrocketing murder rate in New Orleans, the imminent resignation of Jordan, and the funeral of Harry Lee, he kept returning to that Tuesday night about a year earlier when he discovered Zack splayed out on the

Omni Royal's parking garage, and then, later, Addie in the kitchen of 826 North Rampart. "If you're not gonna throw up or anything," Tom suddenly blurts out, "I'd like to show the crime scene photos to you."

I hesitated—I knew that if I looked at the photos I'd never be able to erase them from my memory—but then agreed to take a look. As I had interviewed Zack's friends and former military buddies, my wife had occasionally angrily accused me of being too sympathetic to Zack, and I felt a responsibility to look at the photos, to see if viewing Addie's body would alter my perspective.

As soon as I agreed, Tom disappeared into his bedroom to fetch his laptop computer, where the photos were stored. When he returned, we sat down together on a long, black leather sofa in the living room.

Then it hit me: I was about to get perhaps the most intimate and corporeal glimpse imaginable of a case I had investigated for more than a year. They were difficult to look at; they are difficult to describe; and they may be difficult to read about. In the first photos, the thick, rotting flesh of Addie's charred legs were floating in some kind of yellow, viscous material in a tinfoil turkey pan. This was followed by a shot of a black cooking pot filled with Addie's long hair and decaying head. The only discernible physical feature among the deteriorating flesh and wet thicket of hair was her top row of teeth. Then Tom showed me a photo of Addie's legless, armless torso, which Zack had wrapped in a black garbage bag. For the police photo, Addie's torso had been removed from the garbage bag and placed into a plastic laundry basket, where it was "posed" for the cameras. The photo was so disturbing that it seemed unreal.

Tom then opened a folder on the desktop of his computer containing photos of Zack splayed out on the roof of the Omni Royal. Surprisingly, Zack hardly looked dead: there was little damage to his body and his eyes were halfway open, so he appeared to be sleeping. As I stared at the image of Zack's corpse, I noticed black lettering on his lower stomach just above his pubic hair, which was exposed because the force of the fall had loosened his pants.

"Zoom in," I told Tom. A close-up revealed a tattoo that read "FUCK IT ALL AND FUCKING NO REGRETS," a quote from Metallica's song "St. Anger" that had also appeared in Zack's suicide note. "This guy," Tom said, gesturing toward the photo, "was obviously in a lot of pain."

Tom next showed me a series of photos of the messages that Zack had spray-painted on the walls of the North Rampart apartment. "PLEASE HELP ME STOP THE PAIN" was the largest and most imposing of the messages. The words appeared in big, blocky letters that dwarfed all of the other messages, including "PLEASE CALL MY WIFE" and "I LOVE HER." Looking at the photo of "PLEASE HELP ME STOP THE PAIN," I understood what Tom meant when he said that this message in particular haunted him.

The images of Zack's and Addie's corpses got Tom thinking out loud about Katrina and its holdouts. During Katrina, Tom was a holdout of sorts: as his house in Slidell, Louisiana, took on three and a half feet of water, he holed up in the French Quarter's Omni Royal hotel. The hotel served as Tom's base of operations—from there, he went out on daily patrols in the Lower French Quarter and in the Marigny, all without communication by either overwhelmed or malfunctioning cell phones or police radios. It was brutal, round-the-clock work, and for days Tom subsisted solely on MREs (meals ready to eat); his conduct stood in contrast to that of hundreds of his fellow officers, who abandoned their posts and fled the city, some in expensive vehicles looted from New Orleans car dealerships.

After Katrina, Tom's marriage fell apart and he sold his flooded home in Slidell, downsizing to the one-bedroom condo in Gretna. Basic living expenses in New Orleans—rent, energy bills, home insurance—became significantly more expensive post-Katrina (the average rent, for example, has increased by nearly 50 percent since the storm), so Tom's NOPD paycheck doesn't go nearly as far as it once did (salaries for the NOPD range from about $34,000 for a new recruit to $59,000 for a captain). So, during his downtime, Tom finds himself thinking about taking a job on the police force in a safer city, like Phoenix. "Who," he asks rhetorically, "wants to be a police officer in the murder capital of the United States?"

As Tom got up from the couch to grab another sports drink from the kitchen, a newscaster interrupted the broadcast of Harry Lee's funeral to announce that the National Weather Service was predicting flash floods for the New Orleans area. We both rushed to the living room window to check out the weather, and indeed heavy sheets of rain were already falling, guaranteeing some flooding of Gretna. By late afternoon, approximately eight inches of rain would fall on the New Orleans area, the heaviest accumulation of rainfall since Hurricane Katrina two years earlier. "We're ready for any kind of storm," Tom says. He was talking brave about the NOPD—not the federal levee system. "But when state police and the National Guard leave"—both were at that time scheduled to stop patrolling the streets of New Orleans in June 2008—"it's gonna be rough. Unfortunately, we'll see a difference quickly." (Tom's fears about the National Guard have not been realized yet—in June 2008, newly elected Louisiana governor Bobby Jindal ordered that the approximately three hundred Louisiana National Guard troops remain in New Orleans. It would only be a temporary extension of the Guard's stay, however: they pulled out of the city in March 2009.)

Yet the NOPD's resources are so badly misallocated (in 2007 and 2008, a mere 10 percent of all NOPD arrests were for violent offenses) that the Second Wave Epidemic is likely to worsen. "We try not to look at the numbers," he says. "We gotta take it day by day; otherwise it's too overwhelming." He rubs his eyes. "How many murders are we gonna end up having this year?" Well over two hundred, I reply. He lets out a deep sigh. "This city," he says, "is dying because of murder."

———

Even sometime criminals like Squirrel were becoming fearful of New Orleans's streets. Soon after my afternoon with Tom Morovich in Gretna, I took Squirrel out for lunch at N'awlins Flava Cafe on North Rampart, just a few blocks away from Zack and Addie's former apartment. Over a plate of rice and beans, he lamented that "from Zack and Addie to the Malta thing, all the death here just blows my mind." Squirrel was particularly incensed by the losses he'd experienced since Katrina because he had found a sense of purpose for himself as a holdout. "I was technically a hero," Squirrel explained. "I broke my leg jumping from a two-story apartment building to save my neighbor's daughter. Now [the cops say] I'm a guy who beats someone to death."

Squirrel then told me a long, rambling story of his Katrina heroism: one afternoon, he encountered a woman outside Robert's on Elysian Fields Avenue—the supermarket where Addie had nearly been raped—who was lying on the street, bleeding profusely from a wound she had received after being beaten by a looter and then falling into the floodwater, where broken glass in the water had shredded her left calf. Squirrel and two other men forced the driver of a passing van to take her to a place where she could receive medical attention. Squirrel even hopped into the van to make sure that the woman would be helped, and later heard that she had been saved as a result of his quick thinking.

As I listened silently to Squirrel's story, I thought that it sounded suspiciously familiar—I wondered at first if he had read such a story in the *Times-Picayune* and made it his own. But as I called for the bill at N'awlins Flava, I remembered why Squirrel's story seemed so familiar. Cynthia Salerno, the New Orleans real estate agent who had shown houses to my wife and me way back in 2002, had told me after Katrina that she had been brutally attacked by a looter outside Robert's and then rescued by an unknown man who had trundled her into a van. When the van's driver deposited her on the street just outside the French Quarter, she had then been assisted by two reporters who had forced NOPD officers to take her for medical help.

In December 2005, Cynthia had e-mailed me to ask for assistance in tracking down the journalists who pressured the cops to help her; I told her to post her story at journalist Jim Romensko's popular media blog. This quickly led to confirmation that NBC News reporter Carl Quintanilla (now the cohost of the network's popular business program *Squawk Box*) and a freelance producer named Doug Stoddart had been the reporters who assisted her. Cynthia was thrilled to locate Carl and Doug but frustrated that she had been unable to locate her first anonymous savior.

So after saying a quick good-bye to Squirrel, I headed back to my apartment to find Cynthia's business card, which was still stashed somewhere in my moving boxes. When I found it, I called Cynthia at her new home in North Carolina and gave her a full physical description of Squirrel. The phone went silent; then she said, "That's him. Oh my God. That's him."

———

By Christmas, I was feeling depressed by the skyrocketing murder rate, an ugly debate over the future of the city's public housing, and, finally, the New Orleans City Council's December vote to approve the demolition of 4,500 apartments at the massive public housing projects B. W. Cooper, C. J. Peete, St. Bernard, and Lafitte. Though these buildings had been shuttered since Katrina, the decision to destroy thousands of affordable housing units during an epic housing crisis seemed insane, particularly as the sturdy brick buildings built in the 1940s had withstood the storm. The city's elite simply wanted to purge its poor (and black) citizens from the city. It seemed to me that Naomi Klein was right when she observed in her book *The Shock Doctrine* that disasters now "provide windows into a cruel and ruthlessly divided future in which money and race buy survival." In December, police had tasered protesters outside city hall as the city council approved the public housing demolitions.

Over the Christmas holiday I was so overwhelmed by the pain and ugliness of my new, adopted city that I bought a beautiful tree from the Bywater nursery Harold's and then shuttered myself in my living room with boxed sets of *The Wire* that I'd purchased as holiday gifts for my wife and me. Season 3—in which Mayor Clarence Royce presides over the demolition of the Franklin Terrace housing projects and declares a new era in Baltimore only to have crime continue—was particularly resonant.

But as much as I could feel beaten down by New Orleans, I also loved the craziness and mind-boggling complexity of the city. One afternoon late that fall, my wife and I went for Bloody Marys at Molly's at the Market and sat next to a bleary-eyed woman who was nursing a bad hangover with several cups of black coffee. Over drinks, she told us that she was sobering up for a night shift at a French Quarter strip club and then coolly mentioned that she also happened to practice witch-craft. (Indeed, she was carrying a "grimoire"—a textbook of magic—in her backpack.) New Orleans has perhaps the most glorious subcultures, which somehow manage to be simultaneously profoundly strange and historically resonant, in the United States—for example, the "Mardi Gras Indians," black, working-class New Orleanians who dress in spectacu-larly bright, almost psychedelic American Indian–style beaded costumes because of a long-held love of Native American style and empathy for their plight. Post-Katrina New Orleans is, as Levon Helm, the drummer for the Band, once said of 1970s-era New York City in Martin Scorsese's great documentary *The Last Waltz*, "an adult portion . . . an adult dose. It took a couple of trips to get into it. You just go in the first time and you get your ass kicked and you take off. As soon as it heals up, you come back and you try it again. Eventually, you fall right in love with it."

———

The New Year in New Orleans arrived with great promise—Carnival sea-son was just ahead, with an early Fat Tuesday on February 5. I was eagerly anticipating the parades by satirical "krewes," like Le Krewe d'Etat and Krewe du Vieux. Krewe Du Vieux's parade in January did not disap-point. The krewe marched through the Marigny and the French Quarter with floats themed the "Magical Misery Tour" that offered sharp cri-tiques of New Orleans's collapsed criminal justice system. One float—named "New Orleans Under the Gun"—had a massive pistol towering over a model-train-size city, which was dotted with signs reading "701" and "Kill-Ville." Later, a series of marchers wearing Groucho Marx glasses were labeled the "New Orleans Witness Protection Program";

another float, "Sgt. Eddie's Only Honkies Banned," lampooned DA Eddie Jordan's race discrimination settlement. When a subkrewe of Krewe du Vieux called Krewe of Pan rolled by with a tribute to Lafcadio Hearn, whose paean to the decimated beauty of post–Reconstruction-era New Orleans—"It is better to live here in sackcloth and ashes than to own the whole state of Ohio"—has become a motto for the post-Katrina city, I knew that I had come home.

Soon afterward, my wife and I marched with the Krewe of Eris, a walking, open membership club who staged an insect-themed parade (dubbed "the Swarm") that wound through the Bywater, the Marigny, and the French Quarter. The scrappy Eris revelers—who shunned the expensive throws and floats of most Mardi Gras krewes—wore perhaps the most inspired costumes of the Carnival season: there was a man dressed as an insect exterminator who sought to rid the planet of humans; another krewe member built a massive, nearly twenty-foot-tall papier-mâché sculpture of a roadkill dog; most beautiful, a group of "termite queens" walked through the foggy Bywater streets bearing massive lanterns. As I marched with Eris that night, I was sandwiched between a woman with a pink Mohawk pushing her baby in a stroller and two brass bands, one playing klezmer and the other jazz.

Well after midnight, we attended an Eris after-party at a home on Desire Street in the Bywater. The home's owner had hired a taco truck—taco trucks are now plentiful in the area because of an influx of Latino construction workers—to dispense burritos and tacos to drunk and hungry partyers in the sprawling backyard. At around four in the morning, a woman dressed in Annie Oakley regalia, complete with a real BB gun, began shooting beer cans and plastic cups perched on a wooden table near the taco truck. As "Annie" performed target practice in the midst of the packed party, one of her BBs ricocheted off a table and hit a party-goer in the eye socket, causing it to swell and turn a dark, ugly purple. With dawn approaching, the mood running out, and the possibility of the NOPD crashing the party because of a trigger-happy Annie, I convinced my wife that we should turn in for the night.

The peculiar, violent ending to the night was somehow appropriate: Eris, after all, is the goddess of discord and strife. And this Mardi Gras, sadly, was particularly violent and chaotic, even by New Orleans standards. Soon after the Krewe of Endymion—a neighborhood club that has participated in Mardi Gras since 1966—rolled out its massive floats for the first time since Katrina, five people were shot along its parade route when an argument erupted between two teens. This was just one among five separate incidents along the parade route that put nine people in the hospital with gunshot wounds—including one unsuspecting hotel guest struck in the head by a stray bullet in the lobby of a Holiday Inn near city hall. The mayhem shocked even NOPD superintendent Warren Riley, who denounced the "young, brazen thugs" ruining Carnival season.

Despite the violence, Carnival season—particularly the wild, inspired parades held by krewes like Krewe du Vieux and Krewe of Eris—sparked for me a new understanding and appreciation of post-Katrina New Orleans. The members of Krewe du Vieux seemed to grasp Samuel Beckett's notion that "nothing is funnier than unhappiness."

The handmade costumes and scrappy bands of Krewe of Eris proved that New Orleanians were years ahead of their fellow Americans in embracing a future in which dwindling resources would force music and art to be made more locally. Indeed, post-Katrina New Orleans already seemed like the "world made by hand" of social critic James Howard Kunstler's imagination. Furthermore, though the city's political and media establishment can seem comatose, signs of an energetic resistance to the status quo can be found everywhere in New Orleans: the dark humor of the krewes; the second liners, such as Glen David Andrews and the Rebirth Brass Band, who dance and drum in the Tremé, often in direct defiance of the NOPD; citizen activists like Karen Gadbois who have relentlessly battled with the city over its housing demolitions. It's this defiance that continues to make New Orleans the most vital place in America even as it stares down the barrel of a gun.

THIRTEEN

HOWARD H. WEISSINGER

AUBURN, COLUMBUS

Coming home from a combat zone is an alienating experience. America's deepening civil-military divide crystallized for me two weeks after I had returned from Iraq, while sitting at a Starbucks in the San Fernando Valley. I looked around the cafe and saw a dozen people ordering coffee, talking, reading and studying, while the baristas were busily serving drinks. All of a sudden, it hit me. Even though we are a nation at war, the war does not really seem to exist here in America.

—PHILLIP CARTER, an attorney who served with the army's 101st
Airborne Division in Iraq, *Los Angeles Times*, November 11, 2006

Our little group of people who still care about the Iraq war appears to be dwindling. . . . We few, we (un) happy few. We band of brothers.

—THOMAS RICKS, *Washington Post* military correspondent,
in a February 26, 2008, online chat

Just after ten o'clock on Saturday night, January 13, 2008, I powered up my laptop and pulled up the *New York Times*'s homepage, a weekly ritual for me, as I like to read the Sunday *Times* as soon as it hits the web. On the newspaper's site was a very familiar face: Zack's. I was so stunned by the photo of Zack that I read only the headline—"Across America, Deadly Echoes of Foreign Battles"—before I fired off a text message to Capricho. "Zack's on the front page of the New York Times," I wrote. "Why?" Capricho quickly replied. "Something about Iraq vets and homicides." Though we were only texting, I could tell that Capricho was shocked that Zack had landed on the front page of the *Times*. "Is he the poster boy or something?" he wrote back. Before replying again, I slowed down to read the entire piece, described by the paper as the first in a series of articles "about veterans of the wars in Iraq and Afghanistan who have committed killings, or been charged with them, after coming home." *Times* reporters Deborah Sontag and Lizette Alvarez had found 121 cases in which Iraq and Afghanistan vets had committed a homicide after returning home to the United States from war. Because neither the Pentagon nor the Justice Department tracks murders specifically by Iraq and Afghanistan vets, Sontag and Alvarez had found the cases through "a search of local news reports," and by having "examined police, court and military records and interviewed the defendants, their lawyers and families, the victims' families and military and law enforcement officials."

Many of the homicide cases highlighted by the *Times* were arguably as eerie as Zack's slaying of Addie: the piece opened with the story of a twenty-year-old Iraq vet named Matthew Sepi who was haunted by the killing of an Iraqi civilian by his unit. One hot summer night in 2005, as Sepi prepared to head out to a 7-Eleven in the Las Vegas area, he was "seized by a gut feeling of lurking danger," so he tucked an AK-47 into his trench coat. Outside the convenience store, Sepi shot two men who happened to be gang members. (One of Sepi's victims died of his wounds, the other survived.) Sepi apparently had believed that he was "breaking contact" with the enemy when he shot the two men. After the shooting, Sepi went home, loaded 180 rounds of ammunition into his car, and drove until he was pulled over by police.

The reaction to the *Times* piece—which featured a sprawling photo collage of Zack and twenty-three other vets—was swift and furious from some quarters. Right-wing blogs like Power Line accused the *Times* of smearing war veterans. "It's bad enough that the *New York Times* smears our military personnel when they are serving overseas," John Hinderaker wrote on Power Line. "Can't they at least leave them alone once they return home?" Military bloggers such as Lieutenant Colonel Bob Bateman, meanwhile, slammed the methodology that the *Times* reporters had employed in the series, which they said relied too heavily on anecdotes and did not prove the reporters' contention of a "quiet phenomenon, tracing a cross-country trail of death and heartbreak." Bateman argued that 121 murders hardly constituted a homicide epidemic among vets given the total number of Iraq and Afghanistan vets. Using the *Times*'s tally of murder cases and the number of Iraq and Afghanistan vets, Bateman calculated the homicide rate for vets of the two wars to be about 17.28 per 100,000. This is a murder rate that Bateman and bloggers like "Armed Liberal" noted is lower than the overall American homicide perpetrators rate for eighteen- to twenty-four-year-olds, which is about 26 per 100,000.

Times ombudsman Clark Hoyt later criticized the series, specifically the reporters' contention that the number of homicides involving active-duty military personnel and new veterans was 89 percent higher in the six years after the wars in Iraq and Afghanistan began than in the six years before. "It seems analytically shaky to compare admittedly incomplete news reports from two periods and express the difference as a precise 89 percent," Hoyt wrote, "especially, as a Pentagon spokesman said in the *Times*, given that the news media may not have been as sensitive to the military status of accused killers in the period before the wars." Hoyt concluded that "the questionable statistics muddy the message."

When I relayed the statistics in the *Times* piece to Peter Scharf, he said that it was impossible to provide an accurate homicide rate for Iraq and Afghanistan veterans because there were far too many unknowns involved. "Caution is appropriate here," Scharf told me, "because we aren't able to answer critical questions such as the percentage of Iraq and Afghanistan vets who were actually involved in combat." I also contacted Paul Sullivan of Veterans for Common Sense (VCS) about the *Times* piece, and he echoed Scharf's sentiments about the difficulties of tallying a murder rate for these two wars, though he noted that there was perhaps a purposefulness to why the Pentagon and the Justice Department weren't tracking such killings. "VCS tried to do this [provide accurate statistics on the number of Iraq and Afghanistan vets involved in homicide cases] nearly two years ago," Sullivan told me, "and the Justice Department has no records. This is the same old 'don't look, don't find' policy."

Despite any methodological flaws in the *Times*'s conclusions, the stories included were carefully researched and highly credible, and I recognized clearly behaviors and challenges similar to Zack's, and even shared by some of his fellow 527th MP Co. soldiers. The *Times* piece also hit Lana with an unmistakable and uneasy sense of familiarity, and not simply because Zack's photo was on the front page of the paper. (Zack's case was not detailed in the body of the story itself; instead, it was briefly covered in an accompanying interactive feature dubbed "The Cases.") The day the *Times* piece hit newsstands, Lana was in a New Orleans library with Jaxon and Lily. Lana would often travel to the library to use the Internet, as she had cut off Internet access at home in the wake of Zack's death (she didn't want the kids Googling Zack's name). On that Sunday in mid-January, however, Lana was reading the dead-tree version of the *Times*, which she had spotted lying on a table in the library. As Lana read the article, she thought not about the rates of homicides, or statistical analysis, but how much she recognized in the other cases described.

The *Times* piece spurred me to reconnect with Zack's fellow soldiers from the 527th. How were they managing the transition to civilian life? Were any of them struggling with PTSD? I was particularly interested in checking on two of Zack's closest friends from the company, Jeremy Ridgley and Todd Rauch. So in mid-February I began a series of phone and e-mail interviews with 527th soldiers and hit the road to meet with Jeremy and Todd, both of whom were discharged from the military and back in civilian life, with Todd enrolled in an undergraduate psychology program at Auburn University in Alabama and Jeremy working construction in his hometown of Columbus, Indiana.

———

After a seven-hour drive from New Orleans, I arrived in Auburn shortly after dark. As I pulled into a parking space in front of the three-bedroom apartment Todd was renting in a complex of condos called Creekside, built to resemble rustic log cabins, complete with wood porches and wood rocking chairs, Todd came rushing out his front door to greet me. If I hadn't known any better, Todd would have seemed like an ordinary, highly enthusiastic undergraduate: he wore black sweatpants and an orange and blue shirt, a jacket, and a baseball cap, all with the interlocking "AU" logo. With his ruddy, rounded cheeks and buzz cut, he also looked very much his age of twenty-two. Yet because I'd come to know Todd's story so well, his youthful appearance was discomfiting. At twenty-two years old, he had already lived a fuller and riskier life than many people ten or twenty years older than him (including me, nearly fourteen years Todd's senior): patrolling the mean streets of Abu Ghraib in the first months of the Iraq war, getting seriously injured in an attack by Iraqi insurgents, coming home to be awarded the Purple Heart by President Bush. After giving me a friendly clap on the back, Todd was more interested in having a few beers—and hearing about my investigation into Zack's case—than bragging about his own accomplishments.

But when we sat down in his living room and cracked open a six-pack of Abita Purple Haze (a Louisiana-brewed beer I brought Todd as a sort of memento of Zack's New Orleans), I wanted to hear about what Todd had been up to since September 11, 2003, when he met the president at Walter Reed. It turned out that President Bush was just the first of many high-profile visitors for Todd at Walter Reed: he met former deputy secretary of defense Paul Wolfowitz, comedian Adam Sandler, and, best of all for the *Forrest Gump* obsessive, "Lieutenant Dan" himself, Gary Sinise.

Yet Todd admitted that he found himself becoming testy and moody as he underwent nearly a dozen surgeries on his severely injured right hand and shoulder, until he was discharged from Walter Reed in 2005.

When Paul Wolfowitz visited Walter Reed in December 2003, he met Todd and his mom, Robin—who was also visiting that day—and autographed a copy of *Time* magazine for Todd that featured "the American Soldier" as its "Person of the Year." The Wolfowitz visit was a welcome reprieve for Todd from his roommate at the time, an injured Iraqi soldier who Todd says "brought back memories about how needy and impolite they [the Iraqis] are." Later that afternoon, after Wolfowitz had left, Todd went downstairs to get a Coke and the Iraqi soldier asked Robin if he could take the *Time* magazine into the bathroom with him. She agreed. When Todd returned to the room he was apoplectic over his mom's decision to allow the Iraqi to take his souvenir of the Wolfowitz visit into the bathroom. "You did not just give away my damn *Time* magazine," Todd shouted. "That motherfucker can get his own damn magazine and read it his motherfucking self." Chastened, Robin went down to the gift shop and purchased a separate copy of *Time* for the Iraqi soldier.

One afternoon a few weeks later, in an effort to encourage connections between Iraqis and Americans, the Walter Reed staff brought in Iraqis who had been tortured under the Hussein regime to meet American amputees at the hospital. But some of the American soldiers were struggling with PTSD and experienced intense flashbacks at the sight of so many injured Iraqis, some of whom had had their hands and tongues cut off under Saddam.

"The staff was trying to get people out of the clinic as fast as they could," Todd remembers. "The amputees were being rerouted through the back door. It was flashback central."

I then asked Todd if he had suffered from PTSD—or any other mental health–related issues—since returning from Iraq. "I've never had any problems psychologically," Todd replied, "but when I was at Walter Reed I had dreams. Listen, when you first come back from the war, the war is all you know. You don't have memories of going to the park with your family. You're gonna have dreams. I did." In one of the dreams that Todd had at Walter Reed, he is back in Iraq for a second tour. Strangely, the ground is densely covered with dry leaves, like one might see during a fall day in New England. Frightened by what might lie under the leaves, Todd walks four small steps ahead. But then he stops because he fears stepping on an IED. "I've been blown up once," Todd tells his team leader, "I can't go out again. I just fucking can't go out. I'm sorry. You have no idea what I've been through. I *cannot* do this again." Todd's team leader is furious. "You're not gonna go out?" he barks at Todd. "We're gonna go out without you." Todd is then left standing alone and helpless on the dry leaves. The dream ends.

After nearly two years at Walter Reed, Todd was finally discharged from the hospital on April 17, 2005. That day, he also received a medical discharge from the army, and because his injuries were so severe, he was given a 90 percent disability rating from the VA, which entitled him to approximately $1,500 per month. The incidents with the Iraqis aside, Todd had adjusted well to life at Walter Reed—he loved the constant visits from celebrities and high-level government officials, he made light of the often dirty conditions at the hospital (he and a roommate joked that whenever the bathroom door was closed, the huge cockroach that stalked their room was inside "with a newspaper taking his daily shit"), and he'd grown close with one roommate who had lost use of his left leg. "We were the dynamic duo," Todd remembers. "I'd help him put on his shoes and he'd help me pick up my coffee in the morning. It was very therapeutic." Daunting decisions lay ahead for Todd: he knew he had to live at home in Mattoon, Illinois, as he contemplated whether he would choose college or chance the local job market. But he wondered how long he would last in his parents' home, because his military service had encouraged him to become so strong-willed and independent. And, Todd explained, "I didn't want to live with my parents. I didn't want to be another story of another veteran not making it."

So even though Todd stayed with his parents for only one night before moving into an apartment of his own in Mattoon, living back in his hometown turned out to be just as fraught with career and personal problems as Todd had imagined. During a visit to a VA hospital in Danville, Illinois, a doctor urged Todd to talk with a PTSD specialist even though he insisted that he had suffered, temporarily, only from bad dreams. "He was supposed to be the number one PTSD psychologist in the world," Todd remembers, "but as soon as I walked in the room I felt uncomfortable. He told a joke and I didn't laugh. I felt like I was merely an experiment to this guy, like I was in a petri dish. So I said, 'I'm done,' and walked out of the room."

After enrolling at a local community college, Todd took a part-time job as a low-level sales clerk at an Abercrombie & Fitch. Todd remembers: "I felt dirty. It was rough. I didn't get the respect I needed. I had a twenty-three-year-old manager who would bring in secret shoppers to grade us. One day, a secret shopper gave me a zero because he claimed that I was one of three employees who didn't say hello. My manager told me, 'Whenever I'm here you're gonna be on dressing room duty,' and then he just walked away. Dressing room duty is the absolute worst job. So I went over to his office and waited for him outside like a cat waiting outside a mouse hole. When he came out I said, 'Don't ever walk away from an employee. I don't need this job. I came from the VA and I just needed something to do. This is hard enough for me as it is.'" Todd's manager recanted on the demotion, but Todd knew then that he had to find a more meaningful career, particularly after enduring the stresses of Iraq. "When I thought about my life I remembered that line in *The Truman Show*," Todd explains. "'How will it end?'"

By the spring of 2006, fortunately, Todd had fallen in love with a fellow student at the community college and he began preparing his application to Auburn University, where he would enter as a freshman in the fall of 2007. It was going to be the most exciting transition for Todd since he returned from the war—Alabama was far from home and Todd had always liked the warm people and the warm weather of the South. But that fall the *Truman Show* question that had dogged him since he returned from Iraq—"How will it end?"—was answered for Zack, one of Todd's closest friends from the 527th.

"What happened to Zack broke my heart," Todd remembers, "and I just couldn't make any sense of it. He was such a good guy; he was one of those guys who I respected. He was always doing the right thing. And people liked being around him. I don't know one person who didn't like him." The shock of Zack's end was intensified, and renewed, by Todd's awareness that other soldiers from the 527th MP Co. had died—by suicide, in car accidents, during inexplicable incidents in which they didn't wake up from their sleep—since returning from Iraq. "A lot of people from the 527th have died," Todd explains. "It's absolutely crazy. I think eight in all have died since we came home. You get a call: 'Did you hear so-and-so died?' You made it through a war and then . . ."

As I sat in Todd's living room—dominated by a big-screen TV and stacks of DVDs scattered across the floor, including the boxed set for HBO's World War II miniseries *Band of Brothers*—on that late February day, I thought about a conversation I'd had a few months earlier with Charles Adam Kotch, a specialist with the 527th's Second Platoon. Charles lamented to me that it seemed as though "everybody I deployed with either died suddenly or murdered someone." Charles was particularly upset by the death of Eugene DeMinico, the 527th soldier who had been involved in the fierce firefight with Jeremy and Todd in the Abu Ghraib market in July 2003. In late November of 2005, Eugene died in a car accident near his hometown of Pittston, Pennsylvania. Since returning from Iraq, Eugene had worked as a cop and as a security guard at the Wilkes-Barre/Scranton International Airport. He was just twenty-three when he died.

That night with Todd, I also couldn't stop thinking about his Abercrombie & Fitch story. At Walter Reed, the nation's leaders had congratulated Todd for his heroism. Just a few short months later, he was being scolded by an obnoxious twenty-something retail manager who had laid a trap to determine that he was insufficiently friendly to customers.

Then my thoughts drifted to Zack—Sergeant Bowen—returning to New Orleans from Iraq in 2005 only to peddle around the French Quarter on his bike delivering groceries. I asked Todd if it was possible to make such a staggering transition from military to civilian life and hold on to your sanity in the process. He said that he didn't think it was possible for most vets. "That's why I don't work now," Todd told me. "It just doesn't feel right."

Our conversation about Zack and the post-Iraq lives of the 527th then turned to another one of Zack's buddies, Jeremy Ridgley. Over the last beer in the Abita six-pack, Todd solemnly revealed that he had bad news about Jeremy. There had been a violent incident a few months earlier involving Jeremy that had started, apparently, with a telephone conversation I'd had with Jeremy about the war and Zack. Todd explained that after Jeremy got off the phone with me, he went to the bar in Columbus, Indiana, where he worked part-time as a bouncer. There, he had a flashback to Iraq—he actually believed he was back in the war—and attacked one of the bar's patrons. When several bar employees tried to restrain Jeremy, he wriggled free of their grip. The bar's manager, frightened that Jeremy was beyond their control, cleared the place of customers and called the cops. Only when riding in the back of a cop car on the way to the police station early that morning did Jeremy snap back to the present. Yet even then he could not recall what he had just done.

Fortunately, Jeremy spent only the rest of that night in jail, and when he was released the next morning, his boss at the bar assured him that he could keep his job. She knew several Iraq and Afghanistan vets in Columbus, understood what he was going through, and wanted to give him another chance. But Todd was deeply worried about the incident, particularly in the wake of what had transpired with Zack the previous year. So Todd asked me if I would try to convince Jeremy to leave Columbus and come and live with him in Auburn. My trip to Columbus, Todd told me, offered the perfect opportunity to get Jeremy thinking about the move. I didn't know what to say. My first reaction, I am sorry to admit, was to fear for my safety during my visit with Jeremy. When Todd told me about Jeremy's violent flashback, I thought back to the phone conversation that preceded the incident. During the call, Jeremy had described his job as a bouncer to me thus: "That job does me wonders as far as allowing me to have an aggressive personality legally." Jeremy had also admitted that he had "got into six or eight physical fights, a few of them causing significant damage to the other person." Despite my concerns, I agreed to talk to Jeremy about a potential move to Auburn. Both Jeremy and Todd had been enormously generous with their time, and even though Jeremy's hyperaggressiveness could be intimidating, I appreciated the straightforward way in which he spoke with me. In one of our first conversations I'd casually asked Jeremy what his life had been like since he returned from Iraq; without hesitating he said: "My life has gone to shit because I'm intolerable." I also found his devotion to Zack touching: he once tracked down and berated a journalist who'd written a tabloid-style story about Zack. "I felt like he'd written that Zack was born a psycho," Jeremy remembers, "so I called him and said, 'You don't know a fucking thing about the guy.'"

Thrilled that I'd agreed to accept the Jeremy mission, Todd then announced that he had another, more pleasant surprise in store for me. In honor of my visit from New Orleans, Todd was going to give me a nighttime tour of Auburn's Garden District. I had no idea that Auburn had a Garden District of its own, so I eagerly piled into Todd's truck and we headed toward an area near I-85. But as we pulled into the Garden District I realized it was a small, preplanned apartment community— dubbed the "Garden District" by its builders—meant to resemble the lush, uptown New Orleans neighborhood dominated by sprawling mansions, including the former homes of Anne Rice and Nine Inch Nails frontman Trent Reznor. "Isn't this great?" Todd asked as we drove past one building with New Orleans–style iron lattice balconies. It was like a Disneyland version of the real Garden District, but I was fascinated to hear Todd talk about the deep affection in Auburn for all things New

Orleans. And I savored the profound strangeness of riding through a faux Garden District with a member of the 527th; surely somewhere Zack had to be laughing at us.

It was late—well past midnight—so I took Todd up on his offer to crash in one of the bedrooms in his condo back at Creekside. After we parked the car and made our way upstairs, I stopped Todd in the hallway outside the bedrooms so he could tell me about all the medals displayed there. Against the backdrop of a huge American flag, Todd had hung his Purple Heart medal "for wounds in action received August 21, 2003," as well as an army commendation medal and several presidential coins. On the opposite wall was a framed photo of Todd and President Bush at Walter Reed on September 11, 2003. In the shot, Todd is dressed in a hospital gown and sitting upright in his bed as a grinning President Bush stands beside him. The most curious part of the whole display, though, was an old piece of notebook paper that Todd had hung under the flag. When I moved closer to get a better look, I saw what looked like a child's handwriting. It was a letter to a "US Army Soldier."

12/5/01

Dear US Army Soldier

Thank you for risking your life for me. I wish you good luck and want you to find bin laddeb [*sic*] I wish I could end this but I cant [*sic*] and they bombed assistant [*sic*] people that was just working. I want you to bomb the people that did that to us. Do not hurt the children. They did not do nothing wrong. I will always remember you as my hero. I love you bye.

Todd explained that the letter was written by a grade-school kid in Richmond, Virginia, as part of a letter-writing campaign to soldiers coordinated by a Richmond elementary school in the wake of 9-11. Though the letter was not addressed to Todd specifically, he said that he was moved by its sentiments and that he's held on to it because it continues to remind him of the heady days after 9-11 when he was eager to take the fight to the enemy. Todd is no less enthusiastic about the wars in Iraq and Afghanistan now: he is angered by critics and criticisms of the war, from the distant and famous, like Michael Moore (whom he accuses of exploiting injured soldiers at Walter Reed in *Fahrenheit 9/11*), to a group of antiwar protesters who Todd once confronted on the streets of Washington, D.C., during a visit. "I saw a guy sitting with an antiwar sign in D.C.," Todd remembers, "and I said, 'Do you mind if I ask you a question? Why are you protesting the war?' So the guy says, 'I don't protest the war. I protest the government.' That's just *bullshit*; when we hear about Americans protesting the war it brings about a sicker feeling in our stomachs than losing a soldier." Nonetheless, Todd admits that he is a much different person than he was in the immediate wake of 9-11. "I don't know one person," he says, "who came back from Iraq the same."

When I woke up at around nine the next morning Todd was already downstairs in the kitchen making coffee. Over coffee, Todd and I talked again about Zack rumors, specifically one floating around New Orleans that Zack had been involved in a violent incident in Baghdad that included Iraqi children. Todd was unaware of any such incident—though he acknowledged that he was in a separate platoon and was one of the first soldiers from the 527th to be sent home from the war—but he did say that the constant door-to-door raids in Baghdad carried with it a substantial risk of harming civilians.

"One day, we went into a building for a raid," Todd remembers. "We went inside and knocked on an apartment door and our interpreter started yelling in Arabic. I yelled to one of the Iraqi police officers working with us, 'What the fuck did he say?' And the police officer told me that the interpreter had said, 'We're here with the U.S. Army.' I couldn't believe it. Why the fuck would he say that? They're gonna be fucking loading their weapons inside the apartment and getting ready for an attack. So we open the door and—no shit—there are twelve little kids lying on the floor. I personally carried out every single kid. I probably looked like a New York City firefighter. But within minutes of getting the kids out the bullets started flying." Todd adds that because Zack was usually working operations back at Saddam's vice presidential palace, it would have been unlikely for him to experience such a close confrontation. "Back in headquarters," Todd explains, "you didn't see very much." I gulped down my last cup of coffee and headed upstairs to gather my belongings; I had to start the long road trip to Jeremy. On my way out the door, Todd gave me a hug and reminded me to talk to Jeremy about moving to Auburn. I told Todd that he had an open invitation to come down to New Orleans, and that my wife and I would be happy to show him the real Garden District.

———

The drive to Columbus, Indiana, from Auburn is very long—about 580 miles—but it's basically a straight shot up I-65, so it's not particularly challenging, and I had time to switch casually between my iPod and the radio for much of the ride. But as I passed through Kentucky and then crossed the Indiana state line, the temperature dropped about twenty degrees. The sky was dark and ominously cloudy, and two hundred miles south of Columbus I hit a nasty snowstorm, so thick I could barely see through my windshield. I then dialed Jeremy on my cell phone to let him know that I was going to be late—it was nearly nine o'clock. "Don't worry," Jeremy said laconically. "I'm going to be up all night." He hung up the phone.

Another hundred miles later the snowstorm became much more intense and, worse, the enormous trucks that dominate that stretch of I-65 whizzed frighteningly near my comparatively tiny Toyota Prius. So I slowed down to about sixty miles per hour—still probably too fast—and, out of range of most radio stations, sat driving slowly and silently in the darkness toward Jeremy.

Around midnight, I finally pulled off exit 68 on I-65 outside Columbus and spotted a Holiday Inn with a bright "Vacancy" sign outside. I checked into a cheap, outside-facing room, and freezing from my first blast of winter since moving to New Orleans the previous summer I turned the heat up in the room to eighty degrees. Then I called Jeremy.

"Listen, man," I explained, "we're gonna have to put off our plans for tonight." Jeremy seemed disappointed that I'd canceled, so I asked him what he was up to the next day after work. He then sheepishly admitted that he wasn't working at his day job in construction anymore. "I'm up real late these days," Jeremy told me. "I'll call you when I wake up and we'll make it a day."

The next morning, Jeremy called at about eleven thirty; fortunately I'd just woken up, too, having slept off the nearly six-hundred-mile road trip. I was starving—I remembered that I hadn't eaten dinner the night before—and it was nearly lunchtime, so I suggested to Jeremy that he come by the hotel and then we could head out for lunch. About twenty minutes later, Jeremy showed up at my hotel room wearing a camouflage T-shirt, jeans, and a baseball cap emblazoned with the Jameson logo. Every physical aspect of Jeremy was thick and muscled: he had a small, round face, a closely trimmed goatee, a shaved head, and big, fleshy biceps emerging from his short sleeves. He looked unusually uncomfortable standing in the doorway of my humid room, so I ushered him out to my car in the parking lot. As Jeremy crammed his massive frame into the front passenger seat of my Prius, I realized that he was not carrying a winter coat or even a sweater, though snow was still falling and the temperature appeared to have stalled at around twenty-five degrees. "I walk around all winter in short sleeves," Jeremy said as I started the engine, "because I get panicky when I'm hot. My apartment stays at sixty degrees." Jeremy explained as I pulled out of the Holiday Inn's parking lot that even moderate heat had been triggering panic attacks and flashbacks to Iraq.

As we drove toward town, Jeremy added that insects had also become a source of stress since he'd come home from Iraq. "Bugs," he says with a laugh, "oh man, I hate bugs now. Which is weird because I've always been a country boy." After parking just off Fourth Street in downtown Columbus, Jeremy and I walked in the bitter cold toward a restaurant and brewpub called Power House Brewing Company. On the way to the pub, we passed a construction site and Jeremy mumbled something under his breath about the company working the site refusing to hire him. When we arrived at Power House, a waitress who seemed to know Jeremy seated us at a booth by the front window and brought us a couple of local beers. "My life," Jeremy begins with a loud sigh as we settle into the booth. "Well, since coming back from Iraq my life is like I was at the top of the stairs and have been going down ever since." Like Zack, Jeremy and his wife separated when he was discharged from the military. "She said I wasn't the same person she married," Jeremy explained, even though the couple had only tied the knot in the fall of 2002. The collapse of Jeremy's marriage—followed by his wife taking custody of their daughter, who was born in early 2003—accelerated a downward spiral for Jeremy, involving unpaid credit card bills, sporadic drug use, and increasing disinterest in his construction-work day job. "I didn't take care of business," Jeremy says. "I don't know, man, life just got hard." Jeremy has also struggled with PTSD since his discharge from the military in 2004, and he said that the VA doctors have been of little help to him. "They asked me, 'Are you experiencing anxiety?' And I said, 'Yes,'" Jeremy explains. "'Are you nervous in public places?' And I said 'Yes' again. So they gave me Zoloft, Effexor, and Lexapro. But I'm not really so sure that I'm depressed. My problem is that I'm always on guard, always alert, always on point. And I react to things so fast because when you're in combat, time *is* lives. That never went away." Jeremy's experience with the VA has made him reluctant to seek talk therapy for PTSD. "I'm so hesitant to talk to anyone at the VA," he says, "because it is not operated by soldiers. They ain't been there."

Jeremy has recognized, however, that his almost reflexive instincts toward violence are endangering both himself and those around him. "I'm quick to fight and in the past my explanation always was, 'Well, I'm in combat,'" Jeremy explains. "But acting like that with civilians—well, that's a bad thing." Because our lunch—cheeseburgers—was on its way out from the kitchen, I was reluctant to bring up his flashback at the local bar. But when our waitress sat our plates down on the table, Jeremy provided—unsolicited—an intensely detailed account of the incident, so detailed and accurate because, as he explained, the bar's surveillance camera had been rolling, captured the entire event, and the owner later let Jeremy watch the tape in an effort to make sense of his own behavior. "The night I talked to you," Jeremy told me, "I went to the bar for dinner and had two drinks. I was sitting there at the bar eating and a guy walked past me to my right. I wiped my hands off, got up and walked over to the guy, and started acting aggressive. He was a Mexican who kind of looked Iraqi. I pushed him real hard and then people started grabbing me. I screamed, 'I'm not going back over *there*,' and I threw a stool. Then I started 'low crawling'"—a military term for a maneuver in which a soldier crawls close to the ground in order to avoid being seen or shot—"around the edge of the bar. The bartender cleared out of the bar everyone who did not know me, and because she had friends who had been to Iraq she knew I was flippin'. I crawled around the bar and they just grabbed me and put my back against the wall but I just pushed my back *through* the wall. Then they called the police and they came and arrested me and calmed me down. I spent the night in jail—I was charged with public intoxication even though my blood alcohol level was .08." When Jeremy was released from jail the next morning, a platonic female friend was waiting for him at his house to see if he was okay. "I dated her for two months afterward," Jeremy explains, "and it was a big turning point for me. She made me want to take care of myself and get back on my feet." Jeremy had since broken up with the woman and even made a shot at reconciling with his wife. "I'm trying to fix things up," Jeremy said, "put my head down and charge through it just like I did in the army."

Because Jeremy was comfortable with talking about his flashback, I decided to spring Todd's idea of moving to Auburn on him. Without hesitating, Jeremy declined the offer—he said that he felt like he was finally turning his life around in Columbus and he wasn't sure what he would do in Auburn anyway. But as we finished up our cheeseburgers, Jeremy made a strange declaration: "I don't feel like I should have walked away from Iraq." I asked him what he meant. "Well, once I had an RPG pass about one foot over my head," he explained. "It was so close that I could smell the gases coming off it. If it was just a little bit lower it could have taken my head clear off." He wiped his mouth with his napkin. "How did I get away from that?" When Jeremy thinks about his good fortune in surviving the streets of Baghdad, he's reminded that the traits that allowed him to thrive there—a heightened and permanent sense of alertness, a precise and quickened skill at killing with his .50-caliber machine gun—are also making the transition to civilian life back home so difficult. Jeremy thinks a lot about the 527th soldiers who did not make it: most often Rachel Bosveld and Zack.

For Jeremy, the good memories of Zack—Christmas 2003, when he and Zack had just returned from Iraq to Giessen and took their kids to see Santa Claus, all the while joking about the recent capture of Saddam Hussein—are sometimes overshadowed by the bad, namely, a friend calling with the news about Zack and Addie at the end of 2006. And though Zack didn't die in combat, Jeremy has survivor's guilt, the terrible feeling that it could—and maybe should—have been him.

"To be honest with you, I can see someone like me doing something like this," Jeremy says of Zack's murder of Addie. "But Zack—no way."

Pondering Zack's fate also brings up thorny mental health issues for Jeremy: the panic attacks, his hair-trigger temper, and even the flash-backs triggered by innocuous items such as plastic bags. "When I drive I think that every piece of plastic, every piece of paper, every hole in the road could be a roadside bomb," Jeremy explains. "In Iraq you live in constant fear of those things and that's what helps you survive. But back here—well, it's not healthy for the human mind."

That night, after saying good-bye to Jeremy, I brought in take-out food from a nearby restaurant and ate dinner alone in my cramped room at the Holiday Inn to watch the Ohio Democratic debate. Though Hillary Clinton and Barack Obama fielded numerous questions about Iraq policy from moderator Tim Russert, most of the questions focused on the initial vote to authorize the war.

As journalist and blogger Philip Weiss later observed: "American elites have no personal stake in this disaster, apart from the parlor game in which I am myself a player: Who was right in the debates of '02–'03?"

As I watched the Ohio debate, I was hit again with a feeling that had been with me off and on ever since I started writing about Zack. Even throughout the height of the national election season, the war did not exist for most Americans. There are many reasons for the civilian-military divide—from an all-volunteer military, to a series of base closures in the 1990s that have reduced the number of military communities, to the long wars in Afghanistan and Iraq, of which the public is understandably growing weary. But nearly all the vets I have talked to—including enthusiastic advocates of the Iraq war, like Todd—have told me that the disinterest and detachment on the public's part foments profound feelings of alienation among them. "When it comes down to it," Todd told me when I was in Auburn, "America isn't interested in us. Now, I'm not saying that America doesn't appreciate us—they're just not interested." Similarly, Jeremy explained that he'd noticed a huge drop-off in the public's interest in the war from when he was discharged in 2004 to when we sat down for lunch in 2008. "When I first got back it was 'Support our troops' and I was welcomed with open arms," Jeremy remembers. "Everywhere I went I was bought drinks and one time on an airplane I was even upgraded to first class. But the years go by and the war gets forgotten and so do the soldiers. Now, the public walks the streets every day like ain't nothing goin' on."

Watching the Democratic debate grind on that night, I was reminded of a comment that Paul Rieckhoff of Iraq and Afghanistan Veterans of America made to Bob Herbert of the *New York Times* back in May 2007: "The president can say we're a country at war all he wants. We're not. The military is at war. And the military families are at war. Everybody else is shopping. . . . One of the key things we [vets] all have in common is this frustration with the detachment that we see all around us, this idea that we're at war and everybody else is watching *American Idol*."

FOURTEEN

CHARLES SILVER

OURSELVES ALONE

That's probably how we're gonna get outta this mess, by ourselves. I'm not banking on anyone to do anything, because that's part of the White House strategizeing [*sic*]: wait us out until we're bankrupt from mortgages and rent and no jobs, and then buy us out and create vinyl-sided McMansions. I think that they're forgetting how hard-headed we are, and how we won't bow down. They ain't gettin' nuttin' from us. Especially Mardi Gras.

—ASHLEY MORRIS, New Orleans blogger, February 19, 2006

The next morning, because my wife had been alone in our apartment for days, I made the long drive back to New Orleans without an overnight stop. While I had been in Auburn, our street had been ranked at the top of NOCrimeline's list of "The Mean Streets . . . in the French Quarter and Marigny Triangle."

The collapse of the criminal justice system continued apace. In mid-April, a New Orleans jury acquitted David Bonds, the accused killer of Hot 8 drummer Dinerral Shavers, on all charges in the case. Shortly afterward, Guy McEwen—who had been riding in the car with Dinerral and his son when Dinerral was murdered in 2006, and who served as a witness during the Bonds trial—was cut down in a hail of bullets on an Uptown street. Then, early on the morning of May 4—about two weeks after he was cleared in Dinerral's murder—Bonds allegedly got into an argument with a twenty-five-year-old man at the corner of Canal Street and St. Charles Avenue and shot the man in the torso. On May 16, Bonds was picked up by cops in Thibodaux, Louisiana, about sixty-five miles from New Orleans.

Yet another unhappy epilogue to the tragic Dinerral Shavers tale was the death of fiery New Orleans blogger Ashley Morris in April. Though I disliked how Ashley had portrayed Zack as an outsider back in 2006, I felt that he was nonetheless one of post-Katrina New Orleans's most lucid voices. In one post, he suggested that New Orleanians appropriate the name of Ireland's oldest political party, Sinn Féin ("Ourselves Alone"), as their own because Katrina and its aftermath had proven that the rest of the country simply didn't care about the city's fate. I'd also come to admire Ashley because he proudly participated in the January 2007 anticrime march on city hall after the murders of Dinerral and Helen Hill, had taken part in the great tribute to Lafcadio Hearn during Krewe du Vieux, and he'd written passionately on his blog about Dinerral's struggle to gain acceptance into Musicians' Village just before he was murdered. In the fall of 2007, Ashley's blog linked to a *Times-Picayune* story about Dinerral's family (he is survived by a young son, D.J.) and lamented the dysfunctional criminal justice system in New Orleans: "If Ray Nagin has a heart . . . if Eddie Jordan has a soul . . . they'll fix this mess. For DJ, if nobody else." Yet soon after Ashley died from heart failure in a Florida hotel room in early April 2008, Dinerral's accused killer walked free, only to again contribute to the rising tide of violence.

Still, Ashley's work on his blog—and on a website dedicated to *The Wire* dubbed "Got That New Package"—would not be forgotten. In Ashley's honor, *The Wire* creator David Simon delivered the commencement address at DePaul University in June 2008. (Ashley was an assistant professor at DePaul College of Computing and Digital Media and was such a devoted New Orleanian that he commuted to Chicago weekly to teach.) "Ashley was angry on behalf of others," Simon told the *Chicago Tribune*, "which in my mind makes all the difference. . . . I am convinced that Ashley loved his city and he loved the people of his city, and he was short and to the point with people who tried to [evade] the real questions using ad hominem and decorum and false civility."

———

As New Orleanians confronted a skyrocketing murder rate, Iraq and Afghanistan veterans struggled with psychological wounds and a staggering increase in the rate of suicides among their ranks. In May 2008, the Rand Corporation published a study called "Invisible Wounds of War: Psychological and Cognitive Injuries, Their Consequences, and Services to Assist Recovery" in which its researchers found that nearly 20 percent of Iraq and Afghanistan veterans—about three hundred thousand in all—report symptoms of PTSD or major depression, yet only slightly more than half have sought treatment. Furthermore, the Rand Corporation researchers found that even among those who seek help for such mental health issues, only about half receive treatment that could be considered "minimally adequate." Tellingly, when the project's coleader Lisa Jaycox described the "cascading consequences" that can occur when PTSD goes untreated—drug use, marital problems, unemployment, homelessness, and even suicide—she neatly characterized nearly every problem that befell Zack when he returned to New Orleans from Iraq. The same month that the Rand Corporation researchers found a significant percentage of Iraq and Afghanistan veterans suffering from PTSD, a National Institute of Mental Health (NIMH) official said that postwar suicides among Iraq and Afghanistan vets may *exceed* the number of combat deaths because of inadequate mental health care. "It's quite possible that the suicides and psychiatric mortality of this war could trump the combat deaths," NIMH director Thomas Insel told reporters at the American Psychiatric Association's annual meeting in

Washington, D.C., on May 4, 2008. "It's a gathering storm for the civil-ian and public health care sectors."

The Pentagon changed its policy of requiring applicants for some military positions to disclose whether they'd undergone psychiatric care. It is hoped that the Pentagon's move will make troops less reluctant to seek help for mental health problems like PTSD, though many vets are unwilling to admit to such problems simply because mental health treat-ment carries a heavy stigma in the military.

Yet as the mental health epidemic grows, screening for PTSD remains woefully inadequate. After their tour, troops are supposed to fill out a Post Deployment Health Assessment (PDHA); six months after that, they are required to fill out a second form, the Post Deployment Health Re-Assessment (PDHRA). Oftentimes, these forms are reviewed by health care professionals who do not have experience in the mental health field, and, much more problematic, troops must self-report their own mental health problems on the PDHA and PDHRA. In January 2007, Army Surgeon General Kevin Kiley admitted that "if an individual checks nothing [on his/her PDHA], 'I have no mental health issues,' they're not necessarily being sent to mental health counseling."

An earlier 2006 study by the Walter Reed Army Institute of Research confirms Kiley's claims: only 19 percent of troops returning from Iraq self-reported mental health problems, yet 35 percent of those troops sought mental health care in the year after their deployment. Relying on troops to self-report mental health problems on the PDHA or PDHRA is ineffective in identifying mental health problems like PTSD among returning troops. "They give you these little tests and questionnaires when you come back," Staff Sergeant Larry Berreman explains. "You're not gonna answer truthfully on questionnaires. You're not gonna tell people that you can't sleep, that your nerves are shot, especially when, like most guys, you can't put a reason on it. When you can't figure out why you're different you don't report that."

In December 2005, a twenty-two-year-old former MP named Joshua Omvig, who had served in Iraq for about eleven months, returned to his home in Grundy Center, Iowa, and committed suicide soon afterward because he believed his PTSD would prevent him from gaining employment as a police officer. Omvig's suicide inspired Congress to enact the Joshua Omvig Veterans Suicide Act, which directed "the Secretary of Veterans Affairs to develop and implement a comprehensive program designed to reduce the incidence of suicide among veterans." The bill—which also required that there be a suicide prevention counselor at each VA medical facility—passed the Senate in the fall of 2007, and soon afterward President Bush signed it into law. Still, even well-meaning legislation has a long way to go in changing habits, practices, and systems.

Though war-related trauma has afflicted warriors for as long as there has been conflict—it was identified by a grab bag of symptoms and terms after the Civil War, such as "irritable heart" and "acute mania"; and during and after World War I, it was known as "shell shock"; and "gross stress reaction" during and after World War II—PTSD was only formally recognized as a medical condition fairly recently. Due largely to a surge of mental health problems and increasing public and professional awareness in the wake of the Vietnam War—one study found that 30 percent of all male Vietnam veterans and 26 percent of the female veterans of the war suffered from PTSD at some time during their lives—PTSD was listed as a subcategory of anxiety disorders in the *Diagnostic and Statistical Manual of Mental Disorders* (*DSM-III*) in 1980.

PTSD—defined broadly as an anxiety disorder that can develop after exposure to a traumatic event, such as combat or a severe physical injury—has symptoms that are well known. They can include emotional numbness, hyperarousal to stimuli, "reexperiencing," where an innocuous event can bring back memories so vivid that the sufferer feels he or she is literally reliving an experience; for example, hearing a car backfire may lead the sufferer to believe he or she is under gunfire. Yet, despite the familiarity of the disorder, the wars in Iraq and Afghanistan present special and severe mental health challenges. Because soldiers face constant attacks by insurgents using IEDs, RPGs, and roadside bombs, the Iraq conflict has been described as a "360-degree war," with no real front

or rear, and no safe zone. Asymmetrical conflict exacerbates the stresses
of war, and for those who thrive in such an environment the transition
from military to civilian life becomes all the more perilous. "This kind
of war makes it ten times harder to 'turn off' when you get out of combat," Jeremy Ridgley explains.

Even for Larry Berreman—who has adjusted well to civilian life as a
911 dispatcher in Fort Carson, Colorado—anxiety-inducing reminders
of combat come surprisingly often, and from surprisingly banal sources.
In Baghdad, Larry was involved in two incidents where the truck he was
riding in was blown up by a roadside bomb (he escaped both attacks
without injury). "Now I'll be driving and see a McDonald's bag on the
side of the road," Larry explains, "and I'll end up shooting across four
lanes of traffic going the wrong way to avoid that McDonald's bag."

As a 911 dispatcher in a military community, Larry witnesses firsthand the costs of the war back home. "There are a lot of vets dealing with
traumatic brain injuries," Larry explains, "so whereas we used to get
about one or two calls in a week about a seizure, now we're getting three
to five calls per day. And suicide rates are through the freaking roof
because of what's happening there and what happens when they come
back *here*. Because of all the money we're spending over there to keep the
damn thing going, we're not taking care of our soldiers over here."
Indeed, suicides—and even homicides—are frighteningly commonplace
among Fort Carson Iraq veterans. At least *five* homicides in the Colorado Springs area have been tied to Fort Carson Iraq vets, prompting
Colorado Democratic senator Ken Salazar to request that the army
investigate mental health treatment for Iraq vets in Fort Carson. Such an
investigation—called for by Salazar in October 2008—is long overdue:
Larry says that Iraq vets at Fort Carson believe that the army is shirking
its responsibilities to vets because of the staggering costs involved in caring for them. "I have a group of friends that I run with here," he explains.
"One was a sergeant major. He is the most amazing soldier you would
ever meet. But he is not the same guy since he came back from Iraq.
He'd gotten an eighty percent disability from PTSD. About three weeks

ago he received a letter from the VA telling him that his benefits were going to expire and his rating was going to drop to twenty percent. This is why I refused from day one to make a claim for PTSD. I don't give a shit if I end up under a bridge with my hair down to my ass. They treat you like it [PTSD] doesn't exist and you're lying." Similarly, Charles Adam Kotch of the 527th MP Co. says that the VA psychiatrists "try and convince you that you're suffering from depression, not PTSD. The VA doctors are instructed to prevent care; the VA does not want to pay disability."

Unfortunately, Larry and Charles's suspicions that the VA purposefully avoids diagnosing Iraq vets with PTSD are confirmed by some of the federal agency's own actions. In mid-May 2008, the congressional watchdog group Citizens for Responsibility and Ethics in Washington and VoteVets.org (an Iraq and Afghanistan war veterans lobbying group) distributed an e-mail written by a VA employee that suggested doctors avoid diagnosing vets with PTSD and instead consider a diagnosis that might result in a lower disability payment. "Given that we are having more and more compensation-seeking veterans," the VA official wrote in a March 20, 2008, e-mail with the subject line "Suggestion," "I'd like to suggest that we refrain from giving a diagnosis of PTSD straight out. Consider a diagnosis of Adjustment Disorder. . . . Additionally, we really don't have time to do the extensive testing that should be done to determine PTSD."

The economic environment for Iraq vets is also unforgiving: as of the spring of 2008, foreclosures in military communities were increasing at a pace nearly four times the already alarming national average, and educational benefits offered to veterans are far lower than the original GI Bill established in the wake of World War II. Under the Montgomery GI Bill, after paying a nonrefundable contribution of $1,200 from their first military paychecks, troops can receive up to $39,600 toward their education, which covers only about 60 percent of the average cost of four years at a public college or university or less than two years at a typical private college.

A new GI Bill cosponsored by Virginia Democratic senator Jim Webb and Nebraska Republican senator Chuck Hagel dubbed the "Post-9/11 Veterans Educational Assistance Act" proposed a dramatic expansion of educational benefits to Iraq and Afghanistan veterans: veterans would have up to fifteen years, compared to ten years under the Montgomery GI Bill, after they leave active duty to use their educational assistance entitlement; it would also allow veterans pursuing an approved program of study to receive payments covering the charges of their program up to the cost of the most expensive state school. Webb's GI Bill passed the House and the Senate in the early spring of 2008 even though it faced opposition from key legislators, such as Arizona senator and then presidential candidate John McCain (who was not present for the vote but argued that it would discourage reenlistment because it would pay full tuition and other expenses at a four-year public university for vets who served in the military for at least three years since 9-11). It also faced a veto threat by President Bush. But supporters of Webb's GI Bill argued that FDR's original GI Bill in 1944 gave a huge boost to the economy and demonstrated the country's commitment to vets. (FDR said that the GI Bill "gives emphatic notice to the men and women in our armed forces that the American people do not intend to let them down.") The bill's proponents also pointed out that attending college or university greatly eases the transition to civilian life for vets. Making that transition less difficult for vets is critical, as PTSD rates among Iraq and Afghanistan vets are skyrocketing. Fortunately, President Bush backed down from his veto threat and the Post-9/11 Veterans Educational Assistance Act was signed into law on June 30, 2008.

The passage of an adequate, wise, and generous new GI Bill could not come soon enough. Just as one example, Todd Rauch is a rare 527th MP Co. soldier who is truly thriving back home; and it is likely no coincidence that his relatively high disability payments have enabled him to attend Auburn University full-time without having to take on a day job. "School is a safe place to be for vets," Paul Rieckhoff of Iraq and Afghanistan Veterans of America explains. "You feel like you're doing something productive." It's worth noting, however, that Todd's "benefits" came at an enormous cost—namely, lifelong injuries to his right hand and shoulder—and he says that he still battles with the VA over his disability rating. He believes that he should be assigned a full, 100 percent disability instead of a 90 percent rating.

————

As the Post-9/11 Veterans Educational Assistance Act passed the Senate in a 75–22 vote just before Memorial Day weekend, I received an unexpected call from Leo Watermeier. The roof was leaking in Zack and Addie's former apartment at 826 North Rampart; he would be spending the holiday weekend fixing the leak; and he asked me if I'd like to see the inside of the apartment. It would be the first time I'd see it in person.

I hadn't been by the building since Lundi Gras—the festive day preceding Fat Tuesday—when I had marched in an exuberant second-line parade on North Rampart organized by the New Orleans Social Aid and Pleasure Club Task Force. The Social Aid and Pleasure Club members had donned bright yellow fedora hats and robin's egg blue suits, and waved matching plumes of yellow and blue feathers while dancing to the tune of brass bands playing everything from New Orleans standards like "Down by the Riverside" to a jazzed-up version of funk maestro George Clinton's "Atomic Dog." One Social Aid and Pleasure Club member confined to a wheelchair rocked himself back and forth in perfect sync with the beat. As we passed 826 North Rampart, Priestess Miriam Chamani appeared and began dancing in the doorway of the Voodoo Spiritual Temple. A few feet farther down North Rampart, we rolled by a bar called Starlight by the Park—where Zack had once tended bar and played the Suicide King drinking game—and a transvestite rushed out and joined us in the second line. Just then, I remembered a second line that had taken place in the Seventh Ward at the end of 2007 for a twenty-one-year-old New Orleanian named Chanell "Chanel" Sanchell, who had been murdered just before Christmas. It was a particularly emotional second line, as the paraders had danced and played music in the very spot where Chanell had been killed. "It was the New Orleans way," Chanell's cousin Joshua told me soon after the second line, "to shake the devil off!"

On that Lundi Gras day—as the bands wailed and the people danced in front of the site where Addie's life had ended, and where Zack had resolved to end his own—I hoped that we were somehow freeing their spirits of pain, and somehow easing the anguish of those whom they had left behind.

With that great memory of the second line, and the appropriate, lively and holy feeling surrounding it, I was reluctant to accept Leo's invitation to visit 826 North Rampart over Memorial Day weekend. But I forced myself to do it—I felt it was my responsibility as a reporter. So just before sunset on Sunday, May 25, 2008, I made the short trip from my apartment on Burgundy Street to 826 North Rampart. It was an uncomfortably hot and sticky—eighty-five degrees plus—New Orleans day, with a low sky filled with ominous clouds, and punctuated by loud thunderclaps. When I met Leo outside the heavy iron gates leading to the courtyard behind 826 North Rampart, we must have both looked frazzled and droopy. After greeting me with a strong handshake, Leo unlocked the gate and then led me through the courtyard, where Addie's bike with its MAKE LEVEES NOT WAR bumper sticker still sat next to a cluster of potted plants. As we approached 826 North Rampart, I saw a green colored door leading into the building that read "PRIVATE." I thought back to the fall day in 2006 when I had first met Leo and we talked in the courtyard just a few feet away from the green door, which was covered then in thick yellow police tape. Back then, the cops would not allow even Leo into the apartment. So as Leo now slid the key in the lock and opened the door, it felt like we were trespassers.

As we climbed the short, wooden staircase that led to the apartment, the heat rose with us and I felt a little dizzy and disoriented. But when Leo opened the front door and we stepped into the living room, the apartment was surprisingly airy and spacious, even though its seven-foot ceilings were very low by New Orleans standards. The floors in the living room were a dark-hued wood; a wide, arched entryway to the right led to a bright, white kitchen with a small refrigerator and a farmhouse-style sink. Connected to the kitchen on the left was a bathroom with a rectangular, art deco–style bathtub and shower and white subway tiles on the floor. Leo explained that the bathroom and kitchen had been remodeled in an art deco style by the building's owner during the 1930s. Both the bathroom and kitchen had small windows that looked out onto the tall, imposing oak tree in the courtyard as well as the back building.

As I peered out of the kitchen window to the courtyard, it seemed like a surprisingly idyllic little place, hardly the "house of horrors" of the media's imagination. But then Leo joined me by the window and mentioned that he, like jazzman and former renter John Boutté, had noticed that Zack had left the bathroom light on during the long days when—unbeknownst to his neighbors—he was slowly, methodically dismembering Addie in the kitchen and bathroom. And when I went into the bathroom to more closely inspect it, I noticed that there was a thick, black substance between the shower tiles, which Leo explained were the remnants of Zack's spray-painted messages. We exited the bathroom, passing through the kitchen and living room again, and then pushed open the door that led to a tiny bedroom with very little headroom, due to the downward-sloping front roof. There was also a loud, rumbling air-conditioning unit in the bedroom's front window, blocking out the view of Louis Armstrong Park and darkening the room. The bedroom had a cramped, claustrophobic feel—and I wanted to get out fast. Sensing my discomfort, Leo said, "John Boutté always thought there were ghosts in here."

Perhaps due to the heat in the apartment—the air-conditioning in the front room was turned off because Leo was in and out of the unit, fixing its leaky roof—it had begun to feel like something was trapped in there, so I had Leo lead me down the stairs and into the courtyard. The sense of freedom and exploration that I'd felt moments earlier, visiting a place that for me had been glimpsed only in crime scene photos, was replaced by a queasy, sick feeling about what had transpired between Zack and Addie inside.

At about midnight that Sunday night, as I prepared for bed, I noticed that I had missed a call from Jeremy Ridgley on my cell phone. When I punched in the code for my voice mail, there was a long message from Jeremy, who I hadn't spoken with since I left Columbus in late February:

> This is Jeremy Ridgley, the friend of Zackery Bowen. I was interested in talking to you tonight because me and a bunch of the guys are in D.C. for the Memorial Day weekend. We make it a yearly event actually. We come down here, man, and pay our respects to those who have fallen in combat. We're down here respectin' Rachel and Zack tonight, even though he didn't fall in combat. We were talking about you. We really appreciate what you're doing even though we're taking kind of a gamble by talking with you. We hope the book talks about the good things and not the hardships and bad things too much. Well, do me a favor and give me a call.

I tried calling Jeremy on his cell phone several times the next day—Memorial Day—but it went straight to voice mail. So I called Todd because I'd figured he'd been with Jeremy in D.C. and might know how he was doing. Todd was unusually tight-lipped when I called—he said that he had indeed been with Jeremy in the nation's capital over the holiday weekend and he recalled that when Jeremy was feeling stressed he would stop answering his phone entirely. Todd's explanation made sense to me: when I had lunch with Jeremy at the Power House Brewing Company in Columbus, his phone rang constantly, and even after we finished talking he refused to pick it up. But I still wanted to know what had happened in D.C. that made Jeremy so stressed that he couldn't pick up the phone. Todd said that he didn't want to get into too much detail about the D.C. trip because it had been a very private gathering for the soldiers of the 527th. He did say, however, that excluding a solemn visit to the Arlington Cemetery, the long weekend hadn't gone all that well, and that there had been a lot of drinking and fighting among the soldiers—Jeremy, Todd, and Specialist Adam Bagby, who had been very close with Rachel Bosveld—who had made the trip. Late Sunday night—the same evening that Jeremy had left the message on my cell phone—there were tearful reminiscences about Rachel and Zack. "It was," Todd says, sounding a little bit embarrassed, "an Oprah weekend."

When I got off the phone with Todd, I checked the newspapers to see if Memorial Day was bringing increased attention to Iraq's and Afghanistan's vets. There were articles and op-eds about the war, but the tone of the dialogue from politicians and journalists alike reflected merely weariness with wars that had already exceeded the length of World War II, and were the nation's longest-fought conflicts with an all-volunteer military since the Revolutionary War.

For the soldiers of the 527th and their families, of course, the war is not experienced with the detachment of a pundit or a politician. And for Zack's family—Lori, Jed, and Lana—I sensed a need to examine the war as closely as possible, the desire to find some clues as to what had led to Zack's terrible end. Zack's hints that he had committed atrocities in Iraq made them hopeful that there was a simple explanation for the monstrous, previously inexplicable act he had committed back home. But the deeper I delved into Zack's case, the less likely it seemed that he had slaughtered innocents in Iraq. All of the rumors that had swirled about Zack in New Orleans—including whispers of a record of disciplinary problems that began as soon as he enlisted in the army in 2000, a massacre of an entire family in Kosovo, and a dishonorable discharge from the military—*all* turned out to be false. After reviewing Zack's entire employment history and his criminal record (which amounted to an arrest for possession of drug paraphernalia in 1998 and a drug possession arrest in 2006); interviewing 527th soldiers including Jeremy, Todd, and Larry; and reviewing Zack's complete, *unredacted* military record, I found consistent, thorough, and convincing evidence that Zack was a hardworking civilian turned capable soldier with no record of disciplinary problems—excluding a few failed PTs at the very end—who had been fast-tracked from private to sergeant in just a little more than two years. Furthermore, in Iraq, Zack spent much of his time in operations in Saddam Hussein's vice presidential palace in Baghdad, far from a lot of the intense combat that Jeremy and Todd had engaged in while on patrol in the Abu Ghraib district. That does not mean that Zack—who had disparagingly joked about himself as a "back-office bitch"—was spared the stresses of the war. Quite the opposite: Zack had been a gunner in Kosovo and had uncovered mass graves there as well; the 527th served during some of the roughest and most confusing months of the war, and several members of the company were seriously injured or killed in just a few short weeks in the late summer and early fall of 2003.

Even before he left Iraq, Zack was suffering from severe depression, the result primarily of being kept from Lana as she underwent chemotherapy treatments, and of the ineradicable pressures he felt by serving in a war that he opposed, and that was claiming his closest friends. When Zack returned to Giessen in late 2003, he exhibited symptoms of PTSD such as sleeplessness and severe headaches. Adding a lasting insult to injury, though Zack had hoped that he would get an honorable discharge after failing his PTs, he was unfairly given a general (under honorable conditions) discharge. That Zack's PTSD went untreated unleashed what Rand Corporation researchers have in similar circumstances called "cascading consequences": the dissolution of his marriage to Lana, drug and alcohol abuse, the terrifying prospect of homelessness, and, finally, the murder of Addie and his own suicide.

Though the tragic arc of Zack's story had finally become clear to me, I wanted to make sure that I wasn't misreading his psychological profile. So I called Chad Peterson—a psychiatrist who has treated hundreds of combat veterans at the San Francisco VA Medical Center and through the Coming Home Project, a nonprofit organization devoted to providing care, support, and stress management tools for Iraq and Afghanistan veterans and their families—to get his perspective on Zack's case. We spoke for several hours by phone one afternoon in early June 2008, with much of our time devoted to me filling Chad in on the many complex details of Zack's story. Chad said that he understood why I had delved so deeply into Zack's military record to look for any evidence that Zack had committed atrocities in Iraq, but that I needed "to let go of the fantasy that this can be wrapped up into a neat little package."

Chad told me that there were likely multiple causes driving Zack's downward spiral in New Orleans: the loss of friends in Iraq; the collapse of his marriage; suffering from what psychiatrists call a "narcissistic wound" of transitioning from the military to a low-level civilian job; enduring and thriving amid the horrors of Katrina and then the comedown of the nonexistent recovery afterward; and, finally, Addie taking the North Rampart apartment from him. Chad told me that PTSD-stricken vets often look to their mates to create a safe space for them because they are uncomfortable talking about the war with *anyone* else, including family and friends (this was true in Zack's case, as he said little about the war to Lori, Lana, or Jed). Addie's act of violating that safe space, then, became the ultimate betrayal for Zack. Their troubles had led to the last act in their tragedy.

Chad then offered insights into Zack's final partying spree. Chad said that he'd treated marines who'd told him that after killing the enemy they adopted an attitude dubbed "FIDO," an acronym for "Fuck It and Drive On."

"The marines have just suffered a horrific trauma," Chad explains, "but they still need to function at a very demanding level. So they 'split off' or compartmentalize the horror. They wall it off and move on." That Zack could party with Capricho and Squirrel as Addie's dismembered corpse was stored in the stove and refrigerator of the North Rampart apartment was an extreme manifestation of the FIDO mentality. And the Metallica quote that Zack had tattooed on his stomach and that also appeared in his suicide note—"Fuck it all and fucking no regrets"—expressed an ethos very similar to FIDO. Chad also described Zack's good-byes to Capricho, Jack Jones, and Squirrel as "Zack's last mission." Finally, Chad said that he viewed the suicide as Zack's way of saying, "Something happened to me, I don't know what it is, and I can't take it anymore," a more clearheaded though still anguished version of the sentiment seen in the messages that Zack had spray-painted on the apartment's walls: "PLEASE HELP ME STOP THE PAIN."

———

For those who had been closest to Zack and Addie, the pain will probably never cease, and any explanation will be inadequate. On a sticky, mid-July evening in New Orleans, I arranged to meet with Lana at the Swizzle Stick—a bar in the Central Business District that serves some of the best and strongest drinks in the city—to see how she had been coping lately. When we sat down at a small table in a quieter back room, I noticed that Lana looked much better than I had seen her in months. We had met regularly at the Swizzle Stick since I had moved to New Orleans, and the last time we met for drinks, Lana told me that she had been feeling depressed, panic-stricken, and angry, and she had lots of dark personal revelations to share. A January article in *Maxim* about Zack and Addie, accompanied by illustrations more appropriate for a horror movie poster, such as a massive skull looming over the French Quarter, had deeply upset Lana. "I think I'm okay," Lana had said, "and then shit like the *Maxim* article comes out." She then confessed that she had tried to overdose on prescription pills after the *Maxim* piece hit newsstands. She also talked about real-life horrors more frightening than a campy magazine illustration. She said that discomfiting memories of Zack haunted her. She thought often about Zack rolling across the Iraqi desert in his Humvee, shouting along to the words of alt-metal band Drowning Pool's song "Bodies"—*"Let the bodies hit the floor!!!"*—and she told me that she had just remembered a fight in Giessen with Zack over photos she had found on his computer of dead Iraqis. "Get rid of them," Lana scolded Zack. "I don't want these anywhere in the house and I certainly don't want Jaxon or Lily to see them." Most frightening, Lana said that she had been haunted by a fear that when Zack invited her out the night of their eighth wedding anniversary, October 10, 2006, after he'd killed Addie, he had meant to lure her back to the North Rampart apartment and take her life as well. Lana even said that when she was feeling depressed, she wished that she would have met Zack at the Hustler Club on that early October night, and then gone back to the North Rampart apartment to meet her death by her husband's hands. "I go through days when I wish I had gone to see him," she had told me. "I mean that."

But on this hot mid-July afternoon, the anguish seemed to have vanished from her face. She enthusiastically talked about finally reaching the point where she can at least cope with what happened with Zack; she realizes, obviously, that she will never be the same and that there will be tough months every year: May because of Zack's birthday, October because of their wedding anniversary and Zack's killing of Addie and then himself. But the intense fear and panic that had relentlessly dogged her since the horrible fall of 2006 seemed to have passed at last. Ironically, she had found some solace following accounts of the unleashed storm of mental health problems for Iraq and Afghanistan vets, because with them came greater attention to the issue and respect for the suffering.

There had been a recent torrent of suicides involving Iraq and Afghanistan vets: on June 28, 2008, Specialist Joseph Patrick Dwyer—made famous in 2003 when he was photographed carrying an injured Iraqi boy during a battle between the army's Seventh Cavalry Regiment and Iraqi forces near the village of Al Faysaliyah—died of an accidental overdose in his home in Pinehurst, North Carolina, after struggling with PTSD.

Like Zack, Joseph had said he was haunted by an incident involving a child: he told friends that he was standing next to a soldier during a firefight when an Iraqi boy rode up on a bicycle and stopped beside a weapon lying on the ground. A soldier next to Joseph whispered, "Don't pick it up, kid; don't pick it up," but the Iraqi boy grabbed the weapon and was blown off his bike.

For the first time, Lana says, she does not feel alone in her pain. "The government is sending hundreds of thousands of little girls and boys off to war and not taking care of them," Lana explains. "The gravity of what Zack did is unusual. But that it happened is not."

I had brought news and other items for Lana that day at the Swizzle

Stick, too: I brought a copy of Zack's full military record, which included their marriage certificate (a document Zack provided to the army when he enlisted back in 2000) and proof that Zack took out $250,000 in Servicemembers' Group Life Insurance (SGLI pays out in situations, such as death by war or suicide, where other plans do not).

As Zack's military record was spread out on the table in front of us, I showed Lana the paperwork recommendation of an honorable discharge for Zack from his company commander, Captain William A. Rodgers, as well as the recommendation of a general (under honorable conditions) discharge from Colonel Lou L. Marich. I then told Lana that Zack's military attorney strongly believed that the general (under honorable conditions) discharge was not appropriate for Zack given that he had merely failed a series of PTs. Tears immediately welled up in her eyes.

"Would I be sitting here with you today," Lana asked, "if Zack had received an honorable discharge?" Lana told me she was too upset to stay at the Swizzle Stick any longer, so I called for the bill—even though we hadn't even made it through our first round of drinks. As Lana got up from the table to leave, I told her that I'd been thinking about our last meeting, when she said that Zack wanted to kill her the night he called from the Hustler Club. I told Lana that she was wrong; I believed that Zack wanted to see her as part of his "last mission" to reconnect with the people—Jack Jones, Capricho, Lana—that he loved. "Thank you," Lana said, gripping my hand over the table. She turned around and left.

After I paid the bill, I hopped on my bike and began the ride from the Swizzle Stick to my apartment in the Lower Quarter. My route home, oddly, turned out to be a tour of Zack's last days in New Orleans: when I crossed Canal Street, I headed downriver on Chartres Street, which took me past the Omni Royal and then around Jackson Square and back onto Chartres once again, where I passed the balcony of Jack Jones's apartment. Just past Jack's apartment, I made a left on Barracks Street and crossed the Lower Quarter all the way to my street, Burgundy. There, I decided to stop in front of Zack and Addie's apartment on Governor

Nicholls between Burgundy and North Rampart, where I noticed a "For Rent" sign on the other side of the house, 814 Governor Nicholls. Then I made the short last leg of the trip home, and soon after I arrived there was a call on my cell phone from Leo Watermeier.

Leo explained that just a few weeks after he showed me Zack and Addie's apartment on Memorial Day, the tenant in the unit had moved out (not because he was spooked; he simply wanted to find a place closer to where he worked, in Mid-City). When Leo lost the tenant, he faced the daunting task of finding someone who would be comfortable living in Zack and Addie's apartment, amid a slowing rental market. "I didn't want to put the Zack and Addie story in the craigslist ad," Leo says with a laugh. So Leo decided to just explain the story as briefly and bloodlessly as possible to the few prospective tenants who came to see the place. Unsurprisingly in this hard-to-spook city, none of Leo's prospects was turned off by the apartment's history—instead, they balked at the rent ($750 per month). So Leo lowered the rent to $650 and quickly found a tenant, a dancer at a French Quarter strip club. I told Leo that I was glad things had worked out for him, and our conversation reminded him that he'd just run into the New Orleans attorney, and his wife, who'd rented my place on Burgundy Street just before we moved in last year. Leo said that they'd wondered how my wife and I were doing, and then Leo told me that I was welcome to stop by his place over at 812 North Rampart for a drink. When I hung up the phone, I savored the notion that in New Orleans someone was always asking about you or offering a drink.

I was home again.

EPILOGUE: STILL HERE

We are a city of walking wounded, where there's something wrong
with you if you don't have some form of PTSD.

—LOUIS MAISTROS, New Orleans blogger and author of
The Sound of Building Coffins, September 14, 2008

New Orleans has rehearsed the complete collapse of the American
Dream for the last three years, and yet every day you can find us at the
neighborhood bar sipping a cold one while discussing the Saints and
the venality of politicians, or at that restaurant around the corner getting a po-boy. Life goes on. Come the Fourth of July, you'll find us
Going Fourth on the River, a bit choked up as we watch the bright
red, white and blue bombs bursting in air. No, we don't believe in that
old American Dream anymore, at least not in the way you still do,
America. We have a clear-eyed take on what government has become,
what insurance companies (for us) or banks (for the rest of you) are
really about. . . . The way the economy plays out may be the last straw
for some of us–the ones with empty 401(k)s and maxed-out credit cards
and a house still not finished, but not for most. We've been tested and
in spite of all the lies you've heard about shiftless Orleanians waiting

for their government handout, it's all bullshit: New Orleans done it on their own. There is nobody in America alive today under the age of 80 who understands hard times better than New Orleans. You can and will get through this, even if it plays out in the worst way you can imagine, but you are going to have to help yourselves. If you want a lesson on how to survive the next few years, I suggest you hop on a plane or gas up the car and come on down to New Orleans—before someone cuts up those credit cards—and we'll show you how it's done, and throw in a good time to boot.

—MARK FOLSE, New Orleans blogger and author of

Carry Me Home: A Journey Back to New Orleans, October 21, 2008

On a hot day in June 2008, Capricho packed up his belongings in the downstairs apartment of our rented Creole town house, walked over to the Greyhound station on Loyola Avenue in downtown New Orleans, and then took a bus to Imperial Beach, California, a small, picturesque surfing town about fifteen miles south of San Diego.

Capricho's lease was up at the end of June, but he didn't leave because he couldn't find a new place. He took the nearly eighteen-hundred-mile bus trip because he was finished with New Orleans. His departure was no surprise: during the year he lived in our house, he had often lamented the murder rate, the loss of Zack and Addie, and a job at Matassa's with which he'd grown weary. Capricho chose Imperial Beach for its idyllic surroundings—its sprawling, magnificent pier and reddish purple sunsets served as the backdrop for HBO's short-lived surfer-dude series *John from Cincinnati*—and because his sister lived nearby in San Diego. When Capricho called me in July from Imperial Beach, he sounded ecstatic about his new life.

"Every day, I either surf or ride my bike for about eight miles," Capricho explains, "then I go to work at a beach bar and bartend. About a week and a half ago I woke up and thought, 'I feel alive again.'" Capricho also talked enthusiastically about starting a band with some new friends. They called themselves the Smokestacks, and Capricho even came up with an apropos title for the band's debut album: *Closure*. Capricho already seemed happy in his new Imperial Beach home, so it wasn't surprising that when I asked him about New Orleans his mood grew dark. "Getting out of New Orleans," he said, "saved my life. It got to the point where every murder took a piece out of me."

I understood Capricho's despair, though not entirely, because I thankfully have never experienced personally a staggering loss like he did with Zack and Addie. Still, I had moments in New Orleans—such as the Christmas of 2007 when the projects were bulldozed, protesters at city hall were tasered, and an armed robbery epidemic spread through my neighborhood—when I thought I would be overcome by the craziness and cruelty of the post-Katrina city. But during the spring of 2008, I felt that I had made peace with the madness here, thanks in large part to the inspiration provided by New Orleanians like Karen Gadbois who were so bravely fighting for their city. Karen even offered me a crucial piece of advice when I was at a low point at the beginning of the year. "New Orleans is the dark and the light," Karen told me. "Just like life. Most people spend all their time looking for light when the dark has some beautiful places, too."

Soon after Capricho's call in early July, however, darkness seemed to envelop the city.

Later that week, interim district attorney Keva Landrum-Johnson—who had taken over when Eddie Jordan resigned in the fall of 2007 after a disastrous tenure as DA—dropped charges in the November 2005 murder of New Orleans resident Joyce Rader, the very first homicide after the levees broke. Rader was killed when she came to the aid of Jon Newlin, a beloved employee in the great French Quarter bookstore the Librairie Book Shop, who was being brutally beaten in his Marigny home. When Rader arrived on the scene to help Newlin, she was stabbed to death. A two-year manhunt yielded the capture of a forty-one-year-old man named Cleveland Moore—yet Landrum-Johnson quietly and mysteriously dropped the charges against Moore in July 2008. (First- and second-degree murder charges were reinstated in February 2009.)

In August 2008, Jessica Hawk, a thirty-two-year-old botanist who worked at the beautiful Bywater nursery Harold's, was stabbed to death in her Bywater home. That the murder occurred on a busy stretch of the Bywater—she lived two doors down from beloved New Orleans folk artist Dr. Bob (best known for creating signs reading "BE NICE OR LEAVE") and just down the street from the New Orleans Center for the Creative Arts (NOCCA)—stunned her neighbors. It was also discomfiting that the NOPD had no suspects in the killing; the police simply released a sketch of an unnamed "person of interest." On the Bywater forum on the *Times-Picayune* website, one resident fumed about the killings that had taken so many from the neighborhood—Helen Hill, Robin Malta, and Jessica Hawk—and about the fear and anger she felt when passing its numerous murder scenes:

Who ISN'T overwhelmed by the violence that seems to have touched us all?

I didn't know her except in the briefest of passings, but I think about Helen Hill almost every single day. I drive down N. Rampart on my way home from work—and passing her house triggers my brain and I think of her and the life that she's missing out on . . . and the anger flares once again.

I know that we all still care about what happened to her. I know that we are all still hurt by the loss of Helen. I remember how I stood in my neighbor's living room and painted signs for the City Hall march after Helen was killed and how it felt like I was doing SOMETHING—and I remember the feeling of awe that I had when we rounded the corner near the start point of that march and I saw how MANY people cared. It gave me hope that change was in the air, that something beneficial and positive would come from her death, and the deaths of the others whose names were on that roll call of victims.

Yeah, right. Not a damned thing has changed. Has it? Am I missing something?

And now we have Jessica. And I'm angry again, except now my anger for Jessica is piled on top of the anger I feel about Helen, and about ALL of the violence here. What else can we do? Marching is not enough. Complaining is not enough.

More than that, I am HURT. I will never look at my crape myrtles again without thinking of her, and how she laughed at my impatience for them to hurry up and grow. She was beautiful, and sweet . . . and I wish now that I'd known her a bit better.

Also, I am scared, and worried, about my neighbors, my friends, my own husband and daughters. We are not safe here—and I'm sure you all agree that it's a terrible thing to have to live with the fear that we are not safe in the sanctity of our own homes.

I want ANSWERS. I want a police department that is held ACCOUNT-ABLE to the public for dispersing information that can help us help ourselves, and the victims of crime. We are the eyes and ears of this community, but without information we are paralyzed.

How much more do we have to take before something changes? How do we make it better?

But New Orleanians yearning for integrity or accountability from their city government were about to be disappointed yet again. Late in the morning on August 11, just hours after the body of Jessica Hawk was found in her home on the three thousand block of Chartres Street, a team of agents from the FBI and HUD (the Department of Housing and Urban Development) raided the Poydras Street offices of a city-financed nonprofit called the New Orleans Affordable Homeownership Corporation (NOAH).

In 2006 and 2007, Mayor Nagin urged low-income and elderly New Orleanians to sign up for NOAH's $3.5 million home remediation program, meant to perform critical poststorm services such as house painting and gutting. But a July 2008 investigation by local TV news reporter Lee Zurik and Karen Gadbois found that contractors working for NOAH—some of whom had made vast, six-figure sums—charged the city for work that they did not do and for addresses that did not exist. Soon after the revelations were brought to light, NOAH was shuttered and the feds began an investigation into its home remediation program, followed by the raid on the agency's offices.

By mid-August, there was a tangible sense of fury in New Orleans at the NOAH scandal, the glacial pace of the recovery (a study by the Greater New Orleans Data Center found that nearly one in three New Orleans residence addresses were vacant or unoccupied), and the relentless pace of the killings. So when a group called the Excellence in Recovery Host Committee sent out invitations announcing an August 22 ceremony at the Ritz-Carlton in New Orleans that would honor Nagin with an "Award of Distinction for Recovery, Courage, and Leadership," New Orleanians were apoplectic (it didn't help that one cochair of the Excellence in Recovery Host Committee was the mayor's personal photographer).

When I arrived at the Ritz-Carlton the night of the awards ceremony, dozens of furious protesters marched in front of the hotel holding signs reading "NOAH? Murder Rate? Recovery?" "A Mayor in His Own Mind" and the defiant "We're Still Here, Ya Bastards." Karen Gadbois, meanwhile, was circulating through the crowd outside the Ritz, handing out Oscar-style statuettes to the protesters, whom she called the real heroes of the recovery. "We're here to celebrate the lunacy of this award ceremony," Karen told the *Times-Picayune* that night.

When an SUV carrying Nagin pulled up to the Ritz at around eight o'clock, protesters jeered loudly. The ceremony—held in a ballroom at the Ritz—went on as planned, but the *Times Picayune*'s coverage of the event was brutal. The headline read: "Inside, Nagin's a Hero, Outside He's a Joke."

More ominous for Nagin, later that night New Orleans inspector general Robert Cerasoli showed up unannounced at an opening party at Buffa's for Rising Tide, an annual conference "on the future of New Orleans" held by local bloggers. Cerasoli, along with Louisiana's much-feared federal prosecutor Jim Letten, had just begun investigating NOAH's home remediation program, and the bloggers in attendance were floored that Cerasoli would show up at Buffa's. "The city's swells were still at the Ritz, enjoying a fine fete, and the man in charge of putting the shiznit that is this city in order was at a convention of . . . bloggers?" wrote the *Gambit*'s Kevin Allman. "It was like Eliot Ness skipping an FBI banquet to attend a Dungeons and Dragons convention . . . seems he thinks that the local blogging community might be onto some chicanery, some jiggery-pokery, some shenanigans, that the mainstream media may be missing. . . . I would not want to be on the wrong side of Robert Cerasoli. He seems to exemplify . . . shall we say . . . excellence in recovery."

Nagin seemed oblivious to the rising tide of discontent in New Orleans, but when he spoke to reporters outside the Ritz-Carlton, he correctly gauged the city's mood just before the third anniversary of Katrina.

"I think around the anniversary we get edgy," Nagin said coolly, "and I think we're edgy right now, and I think we'll get past it." At about noon the next day, long after Inspector General Cerasoli and Mayor Nagin had gone home for the night, I rode my bike over to the Zeitgeist Multi-disciplinary Arts Center in Uptown New Orleans to attend the Rising Tide conference (I was also asked to participate on a panel about local politics).

When I arrived, a panel on charter schools was wrapping up, so I stood toward the back of the cavernous Zeitgeist space to avoid disturbing anybody. About five minutes after I arrived, however, I heard a scuffle behind me, and when I turned around I saw two men being physically separated from each other.

Apparently, a fistfight had broken out between two bloggers—over server space, no less—and one bruised blogger was threatening to call the NOPD. Fortunately, mutual friends of the bloggers intervened and convinced them that they should come to an agreement over the server space instead of bringing the NOPD down to Zeitgeist. They agreed, but the strange, disconcerting fight made me retreat even farther back into the room, this time by a table of books set up by Tom Lowenburg of the great Uptown bookshop Octavia Books.

Just moments after I started talking with Tom, however, a frazzled-looking woman with long, dirty blond hair who looked to be in her late forties stumbled through the doors of Zeitgeist nursing an Abita. She had a furious look on her face—her brow seemed permanently furrowed—and she made a beeline toward Tom and me, shouting, *"Where were you when the shit went down?"*

We were initially speechless, but with the third anniversary of Katrina just days away, both of us immediately understood what she was asking. I stammered that I'd just moved to New Orleans in 2007 and Tom politely explained that he'd evacuated before Katrina made landfall.

The woman appeared to be annoyed by our answers and she then went on to tell us her Katrina story: she had refused to heed Nagin's call for a mandatory evacuation and instead shuttered herself inside her home in low-lying St. Bernard Parish. When the levees broke and the floodwaters rose, she climbed onto the roof of her house and stayed there for several days until she was rescued by a helicopter. From there, she was put on a bus that, after thirty-six hours on the road, deposited her somewhere in Oklahoma. She didn't tell us how she made it back to New Orleans or if her home in St. Bernard Parish had been rebuilt; she simply walked away. But the fury in her original question— *"Where were you when the shit went down?"*—rendered the rest of the story irrelevant. This was the distilled anger of holdouts like Zack and Addie, and she just wanted to unload some of that fury on us. Though I knew how some of the holdouts felt thanks to interviews with Jack Jones and others, I'd never been confronted in such a way with their anger, nor did I realize how hot the anger still burned three years later.

The rest of the afternoon at Rising Tide was a blur, even though I spoke for a few minutes about the murder rate during the local politics panel. I couldn't stop thinking about Zack and Addie all day—the fury of the woman from St. Bernard Parish was such a striking, unforgettable demonstration of the resentment of the holdouts. The brawl between bloggers, meanwhile, was a reminder of the violence that creeps into post-Katrina life even in the most innocuous places. Nagin was right that the city was feeling "edgy" on the third anniversary of Katrina. But that description only begins to cover the combination of despair, rage, and hopelessness—the anguishes that, when they acquire symptoms, we call PTSD—that lurks in so many here.

———

If the Rising Tide weekend was edgy, the next day—Monday, August 25—pushed the city over another edge. A new hurricane—Gustav—began forming about 260 miles southeast of Port-au-Prince, Haiti. The following day, Gustav strengthened into a Category 1 hurricane. When it came ashore in Haiti that afternoon, it caused flooding, landslides, and dozens of deaths. From Haiti, Gustav moved slowly across the Gulf of Mexico, with New Orleans directly in what the National Hurricane Center called the storm's five-day "track forecast cone."

By Wednesday, I'd started preparing for an evacuation, purchasing essentials such as bottled water, meticulously storing all of my important documents in Ziploc bags, and, finally, making hotel reservations in Memphis. I briefly contemplated hunkering down for the storm in Jack Jones's Chartres Street condo, but awareness of the grim reality of becoming a holdout didn't allow me to consider the idea for very long. New Orleans, after all, had been spared from hurricanes during the calm summers of 2006 and 2007; it seemed unlikely that the city would make it through another hurricane season unscathed. On Thursday night, a quiet—almost contemplative—and surprisingly genial mood settled over the city; it seemed like New Orleanians were resigned to what was coming and were intent on making the experience as painless as possible for their friends and neighbors.

Early the next morning, I attended a ceremony on the grounds of the former Charity Hospital Cemetery (Charity has been shuttered since Katrina), in which seven people who perished during Katrina were interred in mausoleums designated for the remains of those who were unidentified or whose families did not claim them after the storm. The ceremony was meant to mark the third anniversary of Katrina, but the mood was distracted, as Gustav was bearing down on the Gulf Coast. Nagin, who was dressed casually in a light blue short-sleeved dress shirt and a dark blue blazer, seemed defensive and irritated, even though he was standing in front of a cheery blue banner reading "ONE NEW ORLEANS." He seemed more concerned with his personal gathering storm of critics than with the larger Katrina remembrance. "When people talk about their love for this great city," Nagin told the small audience of city council members, reporters, and everyday New Orleanians, "and then you go to a blog, or you read something and it is divisive, it is hateful, it is mean-spirited, my question to you is: How can you love New Orleans if you don't love all of us?"

The atmosphere was made even tenser after Nagin ended his speech and Lieutenant General Russel L. Honoré, onetime commander of Joint Task Force Katrina, responsible for coordinating Gulf Coast relief and once praised by Nagin as a "John Wayne dude," strode to the lectern and blasted the glacial pace of the recovery. "God is watching us," Honoré said ominously. "We cannot wait another three years to see hospitals open."

When the Charity Hospital ceremony ended, I ran back home to check meteorologist Jeff Masters's popular Weather Underground blog. Masters predicted that Gustav would strengthen into a Category 3 or 4 hurricane, and a few hours later I felt the mood in New Orleans grow tense and panicky again. My favorite host on WWOZ—Bob French— launched into an impassioned on-air rant about the slow recovery in New Orleans and the defiance of its citizenry in the face of a new storm. "We ain't all right," Bob said in his husky drawl, "but we are New Orleans. We can take it." The pre-Gustav defiance *was* New Orleans, and I felt proud to live here. That night, my good feelings dissipated when Michael Moore went on Keith Olbermann's show to proclaim that Gustav's arrival on Katrina's anniversary amid the opening of the Republican National Convention in Minneapolis–St. Paul offered "proof that there is a God in heaven." I wanted to reach through the TV screen and flatten

Moore's face with my fist—and for the moment I briefly understood the rage New Orleanians felt when the city was bashed by idiot TV pundits like Glenn Beck who declared on the second anniversary of Katrina, "How much do I think should be spent rebuilding New Orleans? Zero. Nothing. Not a dime."

There was no time for sulking, however, as my wife and I were set to evacuate the next morning to Memphis. Soon after we woke up, the reality of evacuating—and the fear that New Orleans could take a direct hit from Gustav, on the third anniversary of Katrina, no less—became uncomfortably real. So instead of being practical on an empty stomach and packing up the car, we decided to enjoy a full and glorious meal and went over to one of our favorite restaurants, Elizabeth's, for brunch. As I feasted on Redneck Eggs—fried green tomatoes, poached eggs, grits— someone at a nearby table muttered to themselves darkly, *"Last supper."* I got the bill and then we headed back to the house to start packing. My wife and I were quiet on the drive from Elizabeth's until we passed a mural just off North Rampart Street by the great, mysterious British graffiti artist Banksy, who had just secretly visited New Orleans—in his typically guerrilla art style—and left several pieces spray-painted across the city as evidence of his visit. We pulled the car over to closely inspect the Banksy piece. It was tremendously affecting: a little girl in a black-and-white dress stood under an umbrella. Instead of the umbrella protecting the girl from the rain, a torrent of rain poured out, straight down *from* the umbrella onto the girl.

Back at home in the French Quarter, we quickly packed the car, readied our dogs for the nearly four-hundred-mile drive to Memphis, and then set off to find some food for the trip in case we got stuck in traffic. As we drove through the neighborhood that afternoon, it was much emptier than I'd imagined, excluding the gay partyers who were in town for the Southern Decadence festival. When we drove by a gay bar called Good Friends, there was a group of hairy, bearish-looking guys in their underwear with their arms around one another. One guy wore a string of small glitter balls around his neck. If New Orleans was going to get slammed by Gustav, I imagined that these guys would happily go down with the ship.

Unfortunately for us, however, most of the restaurants in the French Quarter were closed (a few were even boarded-up), so we went to Matassa's and grabbed whatever we could pull off the shelves—hummus, Wheat Thins, Zapp's chips. It was nearly five o'clock when we pulled off and there was no time for any more stops. But as we headed toward the entrance to I-10 West, one of our dogs vomited all over the backseat, so I had to pull over in Tremé, at the corner of Basin Street and North Robinson. As I stood on the street corner I had an ominous thought: *This is the last time I will stand in New Orleans.* Then I remembered that on Fat Tuesday I'd stopped at this very corner in heavy traffic. Back then, a fiftyish African-American man was in the car beside me. Since we were both idling in traffic, we struck up a conversation: he told me that he'd been living in Houston since Katrina and wasn't able to move back; he was only able to visit for Mardi Gras. "It's good to be home," he had said.

About three hours into the nine-hour trip to Memphis, we tuned in to Nagin's press conference on Gustav. "You need to be scared," Nagin warned, "and you need to get your butts out of New Orleans right now." The Category 4 Gustav, Nagin continued, was going to be a mighty "mother of all storms," much worse than Katrina in 2005 and, before that, Hurricane Betsy in 1965. As we drove on to Memphis that night, I wondered where my wife and I would live next if Nagin was right. Then I turned the dial on the radio and, surprisingly, found a station playing New Orleans trumpeter James Andrews's song "Got Me a New Love Thing," which is regularly spun on WWOZ. It's one of those archetypal New Orleans songs about how love—for a city, for another person—can carry you through hard times. "I lost my job but I don't care," Andrews sings. "I wrecked my car but I don't care / My house burned down but I don't care / I got me a new love thing."

Gustav, of course, was not the mother of all storms. Nor was it worse than Katrina. At about nine in the morning on Monday, September 1, Gustav made landfall in Louisiana as a Category 2 storm, and just hours later it dropped to a Category 1. Thankfully, our short evacuation to Memphis was uneventful. Thousands of New Orleanians were not as fortunate as we were, however: though nearly the entire city was evacuated (only about ten thousand residents remained in New Orleans), publicly assisted evacuees were sent on long, excruciating trips, often without being told their final destination. "As the passengers settled in, no one seemed to know where the bus was heading," wrote a *New York Times* reporter onboard a bus packed with city-assisted evacuees. "A helpful volunteer had informed riders that it would be Arkansas. A rumor went around that it was Tennessee. Finally, as the bus pulled out of the terminal, the driver was handed a map to Cuba, Alabama, a town of 322 people on the Mississippi state line."

New Orleanians who could afford to drive out of the city, meanwhile, were stuck in a snarl of traffic on I-59 North through Mississippi when the state's "Contraflow" plan (in which lanes on specific highways are converted so that all traffic is flowing in the same direction during an evacuation) stopped at Poplarville, Mississippi, instead of of the much larger and more useful—and anticipated—hub of Hattiesburg, Mississippi, about forty miles farther north. One furious and evacuation-weary blogger wrote of his trip up I-59 that "Contraflow is the Superdome of Gustav." As we made our way back to New Orleans from Memphis later that week, the Nagin administration's reentry process was a confusing, infuriating mess. At the outset, the city announced a tiered process whereby first-responders would be allowed to reenter the city limits first. They would be followed by so-called recovery support—defined too loosely by the city as "major employers or businesses that are essential to the return of residents and the city's economic viability." But the city scuttled the reentry plan when New Orleanians—their memories fresh of being kept from their homes for several weeks after Katrina because of Nagin's infamous Promulgation of Emergency Order, and furious that they could be classified as "third tier" after having persevered through the slow recovery—howled at the classifications.

Gustav glanced New Orleans and damage to the city's buildings and infrastructure was minimal. But nearby, low-lying parishes like Terrebonne Parish were slammed by Gustav; though it went mostly unreported outside Louisiana, the southernmost parts of Terrebonne Parish—which are populated by Indian tribes such as the United Houma Nation—were nearly wiped out by the storm.

In New Orleans, thousands were financially tapped out due to the costs of evacuating. On September 10, thousands lined up at the Ernest N. Morial Convention Center for emergency food stamps, the very place where nearly twenty thousand New Orleanians waited in vain for help in Katrina's aftermath. In Gustav's wake, the Nagin administration put its troubled post-Katrina demolition of single-family housing into fast-forward. Nagin signed an executive order suspending the operations of the Neighborhood Conservation District Committee (NCDC)—which reviews demolitions in historic neighborhoods—because of, he said, the "state of emergency" associated with Gustav. Nagin insisted that the suspension of the review process would expedite the demolition of homes in "imminent danger of collapse," but the mayor already had the authority to order "imminent danger" homes to be razed without consulting the NCDC. After preservationists and city council members alike cried foul, Nagin rescinded the executive order.

With Louisianans struggling in the wake of Gustav, I decided to check in with the ultimate storm survivor, Jack Jones. I'd heard that reporters were once again filing stories from Jack's Chartres Street condo, so I was particularly keen on meeting with him. When I pushed the buzzer outside Jack's building on September 10, he gruffly shouted through the intercom that he wanted to get out of the house and grab some coffee. "These storms," a weary-looking Jack said as he greeted me at the door, "are wearing me out. But I tell you, compared to some of these people out here I'm doin' all right. Everyone else looks like a bunch of whupped puppies."

We decamped to Cafe EnVie on Decatur Street and over black coffee Jack told me that a pair of reporters from the Associated Press who had just covered the Beijing Olympics had hunkered down with him for the storm at the Chartres Street condo. Jack's building lost power for only a few hours: on September 1, the day Gustav made landfall. That afternoon, Jack had sat in the dark with the Associated Press reporters and was nearly overcome with memories of Zack and Addie. "When the lights went out I immediately thought of Zack and Addie," Jack recalls. "I thought of them building a huge campfire out of an old mattress out there on Governor Nicholls Street when we lost power."

Remembering Zack and Addie seemed to depress Jack; he changed the subject and railed at the city government—"They were down in city hall just pattin' each other on the back"—and New Orleanians who he believes still do not grasp what it takes to make it as a holdout. "They think they're gonna make it on a generator," Jack says dismissively. "Well, let me tell you, if you're stuck here for several weeks you're gonna need *thousands* of gallons of gas to run that generator."

Jack told me that he was setting up an electrical system in his condo whereby essentials like a refrigerator and fan can run on a twelve-volt battery. He was also thinking about starting a "disaster business" in which he would rent an eighteen-wheeler, pack it full of essentials like ice and water, and haul it to disaster-stricken cities around the country. The plan might sound crazy, but Jack and his truck would be stepping in where FEMA has continued to fail: during Gustav, the agency's officials promised Louisiana governor Bobby Jindal that they'd have 160 trucks delivering essentials such as bags of ice and MREs to the state, but only 45 showed up. "There are a lot more of these disasters happening nowadays," Jack said, pointing to the Midwest flooding during the summer of 2008. "It could be a good business."

As Jack and I talked that afternoon, a huge new storm—Hurricane Ike—churned toward Galveston, Texas. When I returned home, I checked the Weather Underground blog and found a stark warning: "Although still of Category 2 strength, Ike remains larger and more powerful than Category 5 Katrina or Category 5 Rita. . . . Ike's storm surge potential rates a 5.1 on a scale of 1 to 6."

That night and through the next couple of days, Ike's outer bands lashed New Orleans with heavy rain and forty-mile-per-hour-plus winds. It was terrifying to experience the effects from a storm that was well over three hundred miles west of New Orleans. Sure enough, Ike cut a devastating swath through Texas after it made landfall in Galveston as a strong Category 2 storm on September 13. Communities along the Bolivar Peninsula, an area in Galveston County that separates the eastern part of Galveston Bay from the Gulf of Mexico, were nearly eliminated and millions lost power in the Houston area for weeks. Incredibly, Ike's destruction was not limited to Texas: storm-related power outages were reported as far away as Kentucky, Ohio, Pennsylvania, and Indiana.

In this era of strong and frequent storms, there is, as Priestess Miriam might say, nowhere to run. And the failures seen during Katrina are not confined to New Orleans. FEMA struggled to supply Texas residents with food, water, and ice, leading one Houston blogger to dub the storm "IkeTrina." As ominous is the fact that alarming scenes such as desperate New Orleanians at the Superdome and the Convention Center being treated as disposable citizens are losing the power to shock. After Ike passed, the *Houston Chronicle* ran a story about a local senior center called the Villas on Winkler that passed out flyers to residents before the storm reading, *"Are you prepared for a hurricane? . . . Villas on Winkler is not responsible for your evacuation!"* Personnel at the center left the seniors in the care of the *maintenance* crew. When the storm hit, the center's desperate residents held handwritten signs up to their windows reading, "Seniors! Disabled! Need food!"

At every level, we're a "you're on your own" society. It is one of the perversities of the "you're on your own" style of governance that it applies largely to those who most need and most deserve the government to work for them: people such as Iraq vets and Katrina survivors. That the apocalyptic fall of Gustav and Ike climaxed with a financial collapse in which the Treasury Department initially proposed a $700 billion bailout to purchase troubled, mortgage-related "toxic assets" demonstrated just how topsy-turvy the country's priorities have become (economist Nouriel Roubini rightly described the bailout as socialism for the rich and well connected). I became fascinated with Zack's story—and New Orleans itself—in part because I believe that Katrina was about much more than the end to any national pretense of an engaged or effective Bush presidency (the president's approval ratings never recovered after the levees broke in 2005) or even the fall of a great American city. I believe that the "wrecking crew" (to borrow Thomas Frank's great phrase) of incompetents running critical government agencies like FEMA; the passage of unpopular legislation in the wake of national shocks (such as the Patriot Act after 9-11, or President Bush's post-Katrina suspension of the Davis-Bacon Act, which sets a minimum pay scale for workers on federal contracts by requiring contractors to pay the prevailing or average pay in the region); and the "you're on your own" style of governance represented by Katrina's aftermath was not exclusive to New Orleans—it could be seen across the nation. In the three years since Katrina, tent cities resembling the sprawling encampment outside New Orleans's city hall have sprouted up everywhere from Reno, Nevada, to Seattle, Washington. Post-Katrina-style blight—with its emptied homes and overgrown lawns—has spread in cities where foreclosures have been rampant, such as Lehigh Acres, Florida, an exurb of Fort Myers. There have been levee failures in the Midwest and the collapse of a major bridge in Minneapolis. Finally, there's the epic financial crisis, pure New Orleans in both its creation—speculation worthy of John Law—and the disaster left in its wake: an emergency declared, followed by a rescue for the superrich. The *Wall Street Journal* even dubbed the financial crisis "a Category 5 test of our financial levees."

Just as aptly, Nobel Prize–winning economist Paul Krugman characterized the initial wrongheaded bailout plan by the Treasury Department as the "Femafication of government under President Bush." Indeed, the sharpest commentary on the bailout came from a political cartoonist who viewed the entire financial crisis through a New Orleans prism. In the *Rocky Mountain News*, political cartoonist Ed Stein depicted a map of America divided not by red and blue states but by wealth and privilege. In the Stein cartoon, *all* of America is the Lower Ninth Ward save for Wall Street, which is surrounded by a high and seemingly impenetrable levee. This map, according to Stein, is "The Bailout (Simplified)."

In the wake of Katrina, New Orleanians held signs aloft reading "THIS IS NOT AMERICA." But New Orleans *is* America. And America had been coming to resemble New Orleans with each passing year.

"O-bama!

  "O-bama!

  "O-bama!"

It was just after five in the evening on Sunday, November 2, and Priestess Miriam was leading a small second line down North Rampart. The second line was meant to bring good fortune to the man who the group of about a dozen marchers hoped would become the nation's forty-fourth president. As Priestess Miriam and the marchers crossed the intersection of St. Ann and North Rampart, and then danced the half block to the Voodoo Spiritual Temple, the chanting became louder: *"O-bama! O-bama! O-bama!"* Then, Priestess Miriam pushed open the clanging metal gates beside 826 North Rampart and led the second line into the courtyard behind Zack and Addie's former apartment, where the pro-Obama chanting quickly hushed to a whisper. Like a lot of second lines—which are improvisational by nature—the Priestess Miriam's pro-Obama second line was as fast as a late-afternoon thundershower in New Orleans, where the clouds seem to pull away as soon as the raindrops hit the ground.

This uniquely and unmistakably New Orleans moment—voodoo priestesses for Obama!—filled me with good feelings for the future. The horrors of the Bush years represented at 826 North Rampart—the breakdown of an Iraq vet and Katrina survivor that led to a brutal murder and suicide—was eclipsed by, to use a word overused for good reasons during the presidential campaign, hope. For me—and I think for many New Orleanians—this optimism stemmed not from Obama worship but from the simple and sensible expectation that we might have a president who would believe in the common good. Perhaps New Orleanians—and the rest of America—would no longer be, as Robert Solow put it in a great essay in the *New York Review of Books* during the fall of 2008, "trapped in the new 'You're on Your Own' World." Thankfully, just two days later, Barack Obama was elected president. In one of his first addresses to the nation as president-elect, he promised to put millions to work "rebuilding our crumbling roads and bridges." As the levee breaks of August 29, 2005, were among the most catastrophic examples of failed infrastructure in the nation's history, Obama's vows were particularly welcome in New Orleans.

But I could not savor uninterrupted the much-needed change in the country's leadership, or the feelings of jubilation and expectation in New Orleans, because I had to head to New York for a long business trip. I was worried about leaving my wife alone in New Orleans for an extended period of time, just as I had to do during my road trip to see Todd and Jeremy in the early spring of 2008. At first, my wife seemed to be safe and well without me—she had a coworker drive her home from work, and when she went out at night she made sure to be accompanied by friends. Early in the morning on December 20, however, I received a frightening text message from my wife. She had been out in the Marigny with our friends Billy Sothern and his wife, Nikki, and they'd all just been robbed at gunpoint. Billy is a street-savvy criminal defense attorney who represents defendants in death penalty cases. If there was anyone who I thought my wife would be safe with in New Orleans, it was Billy. When I got on the phone with my wife a few minutes after the text, she explained what had happened. At about 11:00 p.m., they all left the popular bar Mimi's in the Marigny and walked to Billy's car just a few feet away from the bar's entrance. My wife and Nikki got into the car and were speaking to Billy, who was standing on the sidewalk. Suddenly, two teenage boys appeared next to Billy. One pulled out a semiautomatic gun. The robbers ordered everyone to "empty your pockets." My wife and Nikki handed over their purses and Billy gave up his cash. The robbers then turned and fled. The police were called and arrived on the scene a few minutes later; as they filled out a report, a man rode up to the scene on his bike and explained that he had just been robbed in front of his house. The description of his assailants matched the boys who had just robbed them.

The next morning, Billy called his wife's cell phone company to turn off service on her phone, which had been taken in the robbery. Before Billy had the service shut off, he figured he would ask if any calls had been made on the phone since the robbery. Sure enough, someone—perhaps the robbers—had made a call to a number with a 504 area code. Stealing a cell phone and then making calls on it is just the sort of thing that New Orleans criminals—who are unaccustomed to any consequences for their actions—would do, so Billy went to the Fifth District police station to report the calls. A disinterested clerk took the information but no one ever called him back. Frustrated by the experience with the NOPD, Billy wrote an op-ed for the *Times-Picayune* on December 29:

> As of this writing, no one has called me to follow up on the calls made from the phone or, as far as I know, made any efforts to investigate the two potentially lethal armed robberies that occurred that night. Like many people in this town, I had to overcome real reluctance to report this crime and to try to assist in the investigation. . . . Anyone who reads the news in this town has no doubt read comments from our police brass shirking responsibility and blaming us citizens when asked about the high levels of crime in our city or about unsolved crimes like the murder two years ago of my friend, Helen Hill. The police say they cannot solve cases because we fail to cooperate and speak up. My experience gives me real reason to doubt that claim and suggests that any apathy in our communities about helping the police may be motivated more by the futility of the exercise than any lack of desire to see our streets made safer. I know that is why I have stopped calling.

Billy's op-ed resonated with New Orleanians who were frustrated by both the hundreds of armed robberies that occur in the city every year and the NOPD's inability to do anything to stop or apprehend those who perpetrate them. It certainly hit home with me. In my nearly two years of interviewing New Orleanians who had lost a friend or relative to murder, a common thread had emerged: the criminal justice system was failing at even its most basic functions. Calls from family members of the slain to homicide detectives went unreturned. Witnesses to violent crimes came forward only to find that cops were not interested in talking to them. Innocents were being questioned and even charged in homicides to which they had no plausible connection, all seemingly in an effort to simply close a case instead of achieving justice. Worst of all, *in 2008 there were no trials and no convictions in the 179 murders committed.* The criminal justice system was not just dysfunctional in New Orleans. It was dead.

I finally returned to New Orleans just before Christmas. Fortunately, my wife was handling the aftermath of the armed robbery well. Soon after unpacking I received a call from Lana, who sounded perhaps the best I had ever heard her. When I took her out to dinner at a French Quarter restaurant just before New Year's, she told me that as the trauma from the awful fall of 2006 had receded, long-forgotten memories of Zack were finally coming back. Over dinner, Lana told me that she'd recently remembered the very moment she discovered that Zack was dating Addie. It was the summer of 2005 and Zack, who returned from Iraq only a few months earlier and was struggling to get back on his feet financially, was living with Lana and the kids on the West Bank. One afternoon, Lana had found a poem written on notebook paper in Zack's clothing. In the poem, the author wrote of falling in love with an Iraq vet who was experiencing profound mental anguish from the war. Undeterred by the vet's troubles, the author vowed to rescue the "soldier boy." When Lana confronted Zack about the poem, he said that a friend and fellow Hog's Bar bartender named Addie had written the poem—but he insisted that it was written about someone else. Lana quickly debunked Zack's claim—after all, how many "soldier boys" who had just served in Iraq could Addie have known in New Orleans anyway? Right then, Zack sheepishly admitted that he was dating Addie.

There was a dark humor to the Addie story—it was ludicrous for Zack to think that he could convince Lana that the "soldier boy" poem was written for anybody but him, and it was sad to think now of Addie's intentions to save Zack. The mood at the table became even more serious when Lana began talking about Zack and Katrina. Lana rarely talks about that time period because she's rightly furious that the living Zack had been the subject of so much celebratory media attention, as she and the kids made do without his support. She said that initially Zack was optimistic about a reborn city. New Orleans, Zack had told Lana, was going to be a far better place. But when the evacuees started coming home that fall, Zack's anger rose and his optimism faded. Lana said that Zack's optimism died when "the lights came back on." The notion that the return to normalcy destroyed the morale of the holdouts had never been made clearer to me.

Lana also remembered that she'd held on to a few of Zack's belongings in a storage facility on the West Bank, but had not gone to claim them because it had been too emotionally difficult to do so. As we talked that night, she attempted to perform a mental inventory of the storage facility. Inside were mostly old clothes but also the remnants of an expensive vintage electric guitar that Zack had purchased years ago: Zack had smashed the guitar to pieces just before he killed Addie. Lana told me that she was shocked that Zack would have destroyed his beloved guitar, even during his long downward spiral, but it made sense to me, for that fall had been shearing away every part of his humanity: *"Fuck it all and fucking no regrets."*

The day after my dinner with Lana, Katrina was unexpectedly in the headlines again thanks to an oral history of the Bush years in *Vanity Fair*. "Katrina to me was the tipping point," Matthew Dowd, Bush's pollster and chief strategist for the 2004 presidential campaign, told the magazine. "The president broke his bond with the public. Once that bond was broken, he no longer had the capacity to talk to the American public. State of the Union addresses? It didn't matter. Legislative initiatives? It didn't matter. P.R.? It didn't matter. Travel? It didn't matter. I knew when Katrina—I was like, man, you know, this is it, man. We're done." Dowd's comments were the subject of heated debate in the blogosphere—was it Katrina, the intervention into the Terry Schiavo case, or the botched attempt at privatizing Social Security that doomed the Bush administration?—but in New Orleans the argument felt unsatisfying. Like the debate over who was right about the Iraq war, it was detached from real people. Katrina may have been a tipping point for a failed presidency but, more important, the breaking of the levees claimed thousands of lives and dealt a near fatal blow to a city that would have to claw back for survival for years to come.

With the arrival of the New Year, I felt more committed to participating in the New Orleans recovery, even after my wife's armed robbery, and even as more chaos arrived on the city's streets. Early in the morning on January 1, Adolph Grimes III, the twenty-two-year-old father of a seventeen-month-old son, was shot fourteen times by plainclothes police officers in Tremé. Grimes had just left his grandmother's home and was sitting in his SUV parked outside. What happened next is unclear: the NOPD says that the officers approached the vehicle and Grimes fired upon them, causing them to shoot back. Grimes's family disputed the NOPD's characterization of the shooting: they said that the officers did not identify themselves when they approached Grimes and that he did not shoot at them. And an autopsy by the Orleans Parish coroner's office revealed that Grimes was shot nine times in the back of his body. Both the NOPD and the FBI are investigating the incident, and Grimes's family is suing the NOPD. The next day, on January 2, a twenty-two-year-old man named Danny Platt slit the throat of his two-year-old son, Ja'Shawn Powell, and then dumped his tiny body in a playground. Danny's killing of Ja'Shawn was allegedly prompted by the fact that he owed four thousand dollars in child support payments to the child's mother. "I'm sorry about killing my baby," Platt said as cops walked him to a jail in front of a throng of reporters on January 3, adding that he had a "whole bunch of reasons" for doing so.

The citizens of New Orleans would not be bowed. A raucous second line was held in Ja'Shawn's honor, where the T.B.C. Brass Band played an ecstatic version of "I'll Fly Away" as marchers solemnly held up candles. And on January 9, Silence Is Violence—the group responsible for the massive Helen Hill march two years earlier—held a Strike Against Crime in which New Orleanians were urged to "find some way to express the toll violence takes on your individual life, the lives of your family and neighbors, and your jobs and businesses." New Orleanians posted signs made by Silence Is Violence reading "Crime Happened Here" at crime scenes around the city. To further commemorate the Strike Against Crime, Nakita Shavers, the sister of slain Hot 8 drummer Dinerral Shavers, led a morning motorcade that rode by the sites of several recent murders. At noon, Nakita joined Silence Is Violence and about fifty of its supporters as they convened on the front steps of city hall to read the names of 179 New Orleanians murdered in 2008.

For about a week afterward, there seemed to be a relative calm in the city, but then at about 11:25 p.m. on January 17, I received a text message from Billy: "Woman in her thirties shot in Quarter. You all fine I assume?" My wife and I had moved to the Marigny just after the presidential election and we were both safe at home, with our dogs, watching TV, when I received Billy's text. I then searched the Internet and discovered that a woman had been shot—and killed—during an armed robbery in the French Quarter at the corner of Governor Nicholls and Dauphine streets, just blocks from our old apartment on Burgundy Street. That night and early the next day, the coroner's office did not release the woman's identity, pending notification of her family. But on January 19, friends speaking to a reporter from the *Times-Picayune* identified the victim as Wendy Byrne, thirty-eight, a bartender at both Starlight by the Park (the North Rampart gay bar where Zack had tended bar) and Aunt Tiki's (a lower Decatur watering hole that both Zack and Capricho had delivered groceries to). Wendy was also close friends with Robin Malta and his sister Monica. Indeed, Monica tearfully told a reporter from a local TV news station that Wendy's murder had brought back the trauma of Robin's slaying. Wendy had a huge mane of curly black hair and was known as a talkative, gregarious bartender who loved to down a few shots of Jägermeister while working behind the bar. Wendy was every bit the Quarterican, an Addie without the edge. "You were our queen," read a note that a friend tacked up outside Aunt Tiki's soon after Wendy's slaying. The stories recounting Wendy's life even brought eerie reminders of Addie (WWL-TV on Wendy: "Slain Woman Was Popular Among Quarter Residents"; the *Times-Picayune* on Addie: "In Quarter, Victim's Artistic Side Shined").

Apparently, I was not the only one experiencing déjà vu. At noon on Friday, January 23, furious residents of the French Quarter and the Marigny gathered in the back room of Buffa's to discuss the wave of murders and armed robberies in their neighborhoods. Buffa's, of course, is the Esplanade Avenue bar where Zack had worked, and after one New Orleanian angrily pointed to Billy's *Times-Picayune* editorial about the NOPD's lack of follow-up in the armed robbery involving my wife as evidence of local law enforcement dysfunction, one speaker referenced Zack and Addie. "This is Groundhog Day for me," longtime French Quarter resident Jimmy Delery declared. "We've done this before." The crowd of about a hundred—which included city council members Arnie Fielkow and James Carter as well as newly sworn-in district attorney Leon Cannizzaro—sat in rapt attention as Delery spoke. Delery commanded respect because he had hosted "French Quarter Town Hall" meetings in Katrina's immediate wake, which covered everything from the rebuilding of the levees to combating crime at a moment when New Orleanians were yearning for civic engagement and any information they could get their hands on about the brand-new recovery. "It all started with the poor girl," Jimmy continued, "the poor girl who was cannibalized." Jimmy was wrong, of course; Addie had not been cannibalized by Zack. But he was right that the murder-suicide had opened a dark era in New Orleans of unsolved murders and what seemed to be ceaseless second lines to remember the slain. Indeed, several New Orleanians I'd spoken with while researching the murder-suicide had told me that "we knew we were not going to be all right" when the crime occurred. In the past, I'd brushed aside such comments as overly dramatic and perhaps not representative of the entire city's feelings about Zack and Addie. But hearing Jimmy Delery talk about Zack and Addie that day, I was reminded of what Jarret Lofstead of Nolafugees.com had once told me:

> In our chronicling of the city, the murder-suicide is a sort of Altamont.
> It's a levee breaking all its own, public evidence of the collapse of the era
> of good feelings after the storm, and a harbinger of the Bad Times to
> Come.

Bad times had undoubtedly come to New Orleans after the deaths of Zack and Addie, but what I had come to admire so much about the citizens here was the way in which they bravely confronted them. At 2:30 p.m. on Saturday, January 24, hundreds of mourners gathered for a second line for Wendy Byrne just outside Starlight by the Park, just two days after the parents of her alleged killers—Drey Lewis and Reggie Douglas, both fifteen, and Ernest Cloud, fourteen—turned them in to police. (All three suspects were booked with one count of first-degree murder; Douglas and Lewis will be tried as adults. As of this writing, a determination has not been made if the fourteen-year-old Cloud will be tried in juvenile or adult court.) Organizers of the second line asked that attendees dress in red—Wendy's favorite color—so there was a sea of red umbrellas, red feather boas, red balloons, and red dresses. The uniformity of color was set against the wild gender and ethnic makeup of the crowd: there was a drag queen with a tattered blond wig tottering on high heels; a little boy dressed in a black top hat, black dress shirt, and blue tie who looked like he'd been pulled from a Dickens novel; and, toward the front of the crowd, Amzie Adams, with his stark white beard and tall top hat, playing a washboard strapped to his chest. Standing there with Amzie so soon after yet another murder, and thinking of his remark that he'd tired of playing back-to-back jazz funerals, made me physically ill.

From Starlight by the Park, the marchers moved across St. Ann and then down Bourbon, making a right on Governor Nicholls toward the Mississippi. At the corner of Governor Nicholls and Dauphine streets—the very corner where Wendy was killed—the huge crowd stopped for a moment of silence. Such quiet, solemn moments are rare in New Orleans—mourners prefer a dirge or some raucous brass-band music to shake the devil off. But under a cloudy, gray sky, all that could be heard for blocks was the whirr of camera clicks capturing the scene. For several minutes, mourners silently placed candles and flowers on the street corner where Wendy was murdered, which was now marked by a "Crime Happened Here" sign. Then someone in the crowd yelled, "Jäger!" Another voice rose up: "Where's the Jäger?" In any other city, calling for a shot of Jägermeister while remembering a slain friend would have seemed inappropriate, but here it was not only true to Wendy but a statement of defiance: New Orleans would never stop being New Orleans.

The crowd of hundreds roared its approval and proudly held their drinks aloft. Then there were murmurings of just how to find a bottle of Jäger. When it was determined that no one in the crowd was carrying a bottle of the liquor, a man in a top hat, tattered black suit jacket, and white T-shirt broke through the crowd, pulled out a bottle of vodka from his messenger bag, and poured its contents onto the pavement. "God bless my soul," he said. "I hope I am good enough to wind up with her." Then he disappeared back into the crowd.

With that, Amzie and the band struck up a funereal dirge. And then a few minutes later, per second-line tradition, the band began to swing and we headed along Governor Nicholls toward the river. At Decatur we turned right and amassed in front of Aunt Tiki's, which was covered with flowers and signs remembering Wendy and protesting the murder rate in New Orleans ("To 'Ray Ray' and W. Reiley [*sic*]: Wendy's Blood Is on You!"). Amzie and the band launched into a sad yet defiant version of "St. James Infirmary," and marchers streamed slowly into Aunt Tiki's. Wanting to leave Wendy's friends to their mourning, I went down to

Molly's at the Market about a block away. When I made it through the door, I immediately noticed that Jack Jones was sitting at the bar by the jukebox. I waved my hand to get his attention and he came over and warmly embraced me. Then, for the first time since we'd met nearly two years before, Jack admitted that seeing me was always difficult because it brought back a rush of memories of Zack and Addie. Perhaps sensing that I'd just marched in the second line because of the sad and serious look on my face, Jack then embraced me again and said, "It's rough out there, man." Just then, I had a powerful sense of a feeling that had always been with me since we made our home in New Orleans: intense pride in this city that mourned its dead with such passion, and horror that the mourning arrived so often.

SOURCE NOTES

PROLOGUE

INTERVIEWS

Greg Rogers, November 11, 2007.
Fredy Omar, January 2009.
Tom Morovich, October 5, 2007.
Leo Watermeier, November 2006.
Andrei Codrescu, November 4, 2006.
Jed Bowen, March 2007 and February 2008.

SOURCES CONSULTED

Lucy Bustamante, "Police: Man Dismembered Girlfriend Before Jumping to His Death," WWL-TV news broadcast, October 19, 2006.
Andy Soltis, "Gal Pal Gumbo," *New York Post*, October 19, 2006.
Ryan Parry, "Man Cooks and Eats Girlfriend," *Daily Mirror*, October 20, 2006.
Cain Burdeau, "Dismemberment Murder Rivets New Orleans," Associated Press, October 27, 2006.
Walt Philbin and Laura Maggi, "Boyfriend Cut Up Corpse, Cooked It," *Times-Picayune*, October 19, 2006.
Ashley Morris, "Get It Right, Mooks," October 23, 2006, www

.ashleymorris.typepad.com/ashley_morris_the_blog/2006/10/get_it_
right_mo.html.

Joshua Clark, *Heart Like Water: Surviving Katrina and Life in Its Disaster
Zone* (New York: Free Press, 2007).

Bill Barrow, "Living in French Quarter Has Its Boons," *Mobile Register*,
September 14, 2005.

Poppy Z. Brite, "Ghost Stories and a Horror Story," October 19, 2006,
www.docbrite.livejournal.com/2006/10/19/.

Associated Press, "Survey: New Orleans Under 190,000 People," October 6, 2006.

Janet McConnaughey, "One-Third of Orleans Area Residents Polled May
Leave in 2 Years," *Insurance Journal*, November 29, 2006.

New Orleans Levee, "Allstate Called On to Change Name to Somestates,"
October 2006.

Naomi Klein, *The Shock Doctrine: The Rise of Disaster Capitalism* (New York:
Metropolitan Books, 2007).

Alex Berenson, "Holdouts on Dry Ground Say 'Why Leave Now?'" *New
York Times*, September 9, 2005.

1: SANTA MARIA

INTERVIEWS

Lori Bowen, February 2008.
Lana Bowen, March 17, 2008.
Katharina Friedrich, April 25, 2007.

SOURCES CONSULTED

Richard Wright, *The Outsider* (New York: HarperCollins, 1953).

"Homecoming Slated for Friday," photo from Santa Maria High School
newspaper, November 1, 1995.

The Armed Forces of the United States, Enlistment Document, May 12,
2000.

2: KOSOVO

INTERVIEWS

Lori Bowen, February 2008.
Jeremy Ridgley, February 26, 2008.
Eric Royer, September 21, 2007.

SOURCES CONSULTED

The State Department, "The Ethnic Cleansing of Kosovo; Fact Sheet based on information from U.S. Government sources," May 7, 1999, www.state.gov/www/regions/eur/rpt_990507_ksvo_ethnic.html.

Zackery Bowen, "Fragile Life," December 10, 1993, provided to the author by Lori Bowen.

Letter from Zackery Bowen to Lori Bowen, June 5, 2000, provided to the author by Lori Bowen.

Globalsecurity.org, "709th Military Police Battalion," www.globalsecurity .org/military/agency/army/709mp-b.htm.

Globalsecurity.org, "Operation Joint Guardian, Kosovo Force, KFOR," www.globalsecurity.org/military/ops/joint_guardian.htm.

Globalsecurity.org, "Camp Bondsteel," www.globalsecurity.org/military/ facility/camp-bondsteel.htm.

Letter from Zackery Bowen to Lori Bowen, March 24, 2001, provided to the author by Lori Bowen.

3: GIESSEN

INTERVIEWS

Todd Rauch, February 23, 2008.
Lana Bowen, March 17, 2008.
Mary Bosveld, March 2, 2008.
Larry Berreman, May 7, 2008.

SOURCES CONSULTED

Walter A. McDougall, "How Should Americans Prepare for the Most Likely Challenges Facing Them in the Next Generation?" *American Diplomacy*, December 1999.

Jean-Marie Colombani, "Nous sommes tous Américains," *Le Monde*, September 13, 2001. www.lemonde.fr/cgibin/ACHATS/acheter.cgi?offre= ARCHIVES&type_item=ART_ARCH_30J&objet_id=721875.

Michael R. Gordon and Bernard E. Trainor, *Cobra II: The Inside Story of the Invasion and Occupation of Iraq* (New York: Pantheon, 2006).

"President Bush's Address to the United Nations," September 12, 2002, www.archives.cnn.com/2002/US/09/12/bush.transcript/.

"Authorization for Use of Military Force Against Iraq Resolution of 2002," www.c-span.org/resources/pdf/hjres114.pdf.

Emily Slater, "Nipomo Mother Watches, Worries," *Santa Maria Times*,
    April 4, 2003.

4: BAGHDAD

INTERVIEWS

Todd Rauch, February 23, 2008.
Jeremy Ridgley, February 26, 2008.
Mary Bosveld, March 2, 2008.

SOURCES CONSULTED

Michael R. Gordon and Bernard E. Trainor, *Cobra II: The Inside Story of the
    Invasion and Occupation of Iraq* (New York: Pantheon, 2006).
Carl Robichaud, "Failings of the Rumsfeld Doctrine; Intense Air Power
    and Small Groups of Troops Didn't Win in Iraq or Afghanistan,"
    Christian Science Monitor, September 21, 2006.
Jim Garamone, "Battle Intensifies Around Nasiriyah," American Forces
    Press Service, March 23, 2003.
United States Army, "Attack on the 507th Maintenance Company,"
    July 17, 2003, www4.army.mil/ocpa/read.php?story_id_key=5056.

5: ABU GHRAIB

INTERVIEWS

Larry Berreman, May 7, 2008.
Todd Rauch, February 23, 2008.
Mary Bosveld, March 2, 2008.

SOURCES CONSULTED

Ewen MacAskill, "US Postwar Iraq Strategy a Mess, Blair Was Told," *Guard-
    ian*, March 14, 2006.
Michael R. Gordon and Bernard E. Trainor, *Cobra II: The Inside Story of the
    Invasion and Occupation of Iraq* (New York: Pantheon, 2006).
CNN, "Iraqi President Frees All Prisoners, Except 'Spies,'" October 20, 2002,
    www.archives.cnn.com/2002/WORLD/meast/10/20/iraq.amnesty/.
Letter from Zackery Bowen to Lori Bowen, July 18, 2003, provided to the
    author by Lori Bowen.

6: RAMADAN

INTERVIEWS

Jeremy Ridgley, February 26, 2008.
Todd Rauch, February 23, 2008.
Carl Shupack, October 10, 2007.
Larry Berreman, May 7, 2008

SOURCES CONSULTED

Daniel Williams and Anthony Shadid, "Saboteurs Hit Iraqi Facilities; Oil and Water Lines and Prison Targeted in New Ambushes," *Washington Post*, August 17, 2003.
Samantha Power, *Chasing the Flame: Sergio Vieira de Mello and the Fight to Save the World* (New York: Penguin Press, 2008).
Washington Post, "Two Years Later," www.washingtonpost.com/wp-dyn/ nation/specials/attacked/twoyearslater/.
WISC-TV, "News 3 Special Assignment: Baghdad," January 17, 2004, www .channel3000.com/news/2773178/detail.html.
Jesse Hamilton, "The War Comes Home," *Hartford Courant*, November 24, 2004.

7: HOMECOMING

INTERVIEWS

Lana Bowen, March 17, 2008.
Jeremy Ridgley, February 26, 2008.
Paul Sullivan, April 23, 2008.

SOURCES CONSULTED

Ariana Eunjung Cha, "Flaws Showing in New Iraqi Forces; Pace of Police Recruiting Leads to Shortcuts," *Washington Post*, December 30, 2003.
"Report of Medical History" form filled out by Zackery Bowen on August 25, 2004.
Stephen J. Palazzo, squad leader, "Developmental Counseling Form," April 23, 2004.
Dale J. Paff, command sergeant major, "Developmental Counseling Form," July 12, 2004.

Stephen J. Palazzo, squad leader, "Developmental Counseling Form," July 13, 2004.

Captain William A. Rodgers, "Memorandum for Zackery Bowen . . . 527th Military Police Company; Subject: Notification of Separation Under AR 635-200, Chapter 13, Unsatisfactory Performance," November 2, 2004.

Colonel Lou Marich, "Separation Under AR 635-200, Chapter 13, Unsatisfactory Performance," November 30, 2004.

E-mail statement on Zackery Bowen's discharge from Christian Deichert, June 3, 2008:

. . . In looking at Zackery's packet, I see that he had less than six years of service, so he wasn't entitled to a board hearing. He could still have requested one, but realistically, if he wasn't entitled to one it's very unlikely he would have been granted a hearing, and I would have told him that. More important, he didn't elect to submit any matters to the separation authority. From that I have to conclude that he did not want to contest the chapter.

I did not know until now that the separation authority picked a general over an honorable discharge in this case. In a chapter 13 separation, the separation authority has the discretion to choose either an honorable or a general discharge. Paragraph 3-7 lays out the things the separation authority should consider in choosing the characterization of service. The factors for a general discharge at paragraph 3-7b are, well, general. All it really says is that it is issued to a Soldier "whose record has been satisfactory but not sufficiently meritorious to merit an honorable discharge." Section 3-7b2 just means that you can only give a Soldier a general discharge if the reason for the separation (the specific chapter) authorizes it. Whether a particular Soldier's record is "not sufficiently meritorious" is entirely within the discretion of the separation authority.

That's a long answer, and I know it doesn't specifically answer your question. I don't have a good answer for you.

I spent a little less than two years working as a defense counsel, first in Wiesbaden, then deployed to Kuwait and traveling to Afghanistan and Iraq. Before that, I was a trial counsel (prosecuting attorney) for a year. In the two and a half years since my trial defense time, I have either worked with or supervised trial counsel.

In short, I have seen a lot of chapter packets during my time as a judge advocate.

I do not see a basis for the general discharge in this case other than the PT test failures themselves, and there would have to be more to justify it for me. Based on the packet, I don't understand the characterization of service, and I don't agree with it.

If Zackery had been entitled to a board and I represented him in the hearing, I would have laid out his record and argued that he deserved a chance to stay in and get his PT score back up. I would have argued that, if the board disagreed and decided he needed to be separated, he deserved an honorable discharge.

On the other hand, if I represented the Army in a separation board in this case, I would have had a hard time justifying a general discharge. Without more than the PT test failures, I would not have argued for one unless the chain of command recommended it, and if that were the case, I would have called them to testify to the board as to their reasoning.

I think that's as specific an answer as I can give you on the record. I hope this helps. Let me know if you have any follow-up.

Yours,

Christian Deichert

8: NEW ORLEANS

INTERVIEWS

Lana Bowen, March 17, 2008.
Ted Mack, January 22, 2008.
Dennis Monn, fall 2007.
Rob Van Meter, September 26, 2007.

SOURCES CONSULTED

Zackery Bowen, "one awfully long run-on paragraph," e-mail from Zackery Bowen to Lori Bowen, March 3, 2005.

Ned Sublette, *The World That Made New Orleans: From Spanish Silver to Congo Square* (Chicago: Lawrence Hill Books, 2008).

Delia Labarre, *The New Orleans of Lafcadio Hearn: Illustrated Sketches from the Daily City Item* (Baton Rouge: Louisiana State University Press, 2007).

NPR, "The French Quarter: Present at the Creation," *Morning Edition*, April 8, 2002, www.npr.org/programs/morning/features/patc/frenchquarter/index.html.

PBS, *American Experience: New Orleans*, transcript of chapter 11, www.pbs.org/wgbh/amex/neworleans/program/neworleans_11_trans.html.

John Pope, "Ruthie the Duck Girl Dies of Cancer at 74," *Times-Picayune*, September 12, 2008.

9: HOLDING OUT

INTERVIEWS

Capricho DeVellas, fall 2006–spring 2008.
Jack Jones, fall 2007.
Greg Rogers, November 11, 2007.
Lori Bowen, February 2008.
Lana Bowen, March 17, 2008.
Jed Bowen, March 2007 and February 2008.

SOURCES CONSULTED

Cathy Booth Thomas, Tim Padgett, and Steve Barnes, "Life Among the Ruins: As New Orleans Counts Its Dead, Some Defiant Survivors Plot the City's Comeback," *Time*, September 19, 2005.

CNN, Katrina Interactive Timeline, www.cnn.com/SPECIALS/2005/katrina/interactive/timeline.katrina.large/content.6.html.

Douglas Brinkley, *The Great Deluge: Hurricane Katrina, New Orleans, and the Mississippi Gulf Coast* (New York: William Morrow, 2006).

Ethan Brown, "Overcoming the Katrina Myth: Three Years after Hurricane Katrina, New Orleans Is Still Trying to Get the US Government to Focus on the Real Cause of the Disaster," *Guardian*, August 27, 2008.

Sandy Rosenthal, levees.org "Frequently Asked Questions," www.levees.org/faq.

Civil Engineering News, "Group Accuses ASCE of Wrongdoing in Katrina Investigation," April 1, 2008, www.cenews.com/article.asp?id=2795.

Paul Purpura, "Gretna Cops Win Round in Court; Pedestrians Barred from Bridge Suing," *Times-Picayune*, December 19, 2008.

Allen G. Breed, "French Quarter Holdouts Create Survivor 'Tribes,'" Associated Press, September 4, 2005.

Bill Barrow, "Living in French Quarter Has Its Boons," *Mobile Register*, September 14, 2005.

Alex Berenson, "Holdouts on Dry Ground Say 'Why Leave Now?'" *New York Times*, September 9, 2005.

Jesse Oxfeld, "Joe Francis Would Be So Proud," Gawker, September 9, 2005, www.gawker.com/124810/joe-francis-would-be-so-proud.

David Carr, "Singing into the New Orleans Night," *New York Times*, September 21, 2005.

Dan Baum, "Deluged: When Katrina Hit, Where Were the Police?" *New Yorker*, January 9, 2006.

Dan Baum, "Kajun's," *New Yorker*, September 19, 2005.

Rebecca Catalanello and Curtis Krueuger, "Forced Evacuation Mired in Constitutional Dilemma," *St. Petersburg Times*, September 9, 2005.

PBS Online NewsHour, "The High Costs of New Orleans Recovery," November 11, 2005, www.pbs.org/newshour/bb/economy/july-dec05/neworleans_11-22.html.

Charles Babington, "Some GOP Legislators Hit Jarring Notes in Addressing Katrina," *Washington Post*, September 10, 2005.

Frank Donze and Michelle Krupa, "Rebuilding the City Is Debate Theme," *Times-Picayune*, April 4, 2006.

The Preservation Hall Jazz Band featuring Clint Maedgen, "Complicated Life," www.youtube.com/watch?v=dzVCHv6FSbg.

10: THE SUICIDE KING

INTERVIEWS

Greg Rogers, November 11, 2007.

Capricho DeVellas, fall 2006–spring 2008.

Michael Fedor, fall 2007.

Dennis Monn, fall 2007.

Leo Watermeier, November 2006.

John Boutté, fall 2007.

Lana Bowen, March 17, 2008.

SOURCES CONSULTED

Antonin Artaud, *Collected Works*, 3 vols., trans. Victor Corti (London: Calder Publications, 1970), vol. 3.

Walt Philbin, Steve Ritea, and Trymaine Lee, "Katrina Survivalist's Descent into Madness," *Times-Picayune*, October 19, 2006.

Orleans Parish Criminal Court, Docket Master, Zackery Bowen, Case #468062, Poss. Marijuana 1st Offense, Bond $500.00.

11: THE WAKE

INTERVIEWS

Amzie Adams, August 28, 2007.

Tom Morovich, October 5, 2007.

Capricho DeVellas, fall 2006–spring 2008.

John Boutté, fall 2007.

Rob Van Meter, September 26, 2007.

Dennis Monn, fall 2007.

Tonya Bowen, February 26, 2008.

Priestess Miriam Chamani, November 2006.

SOURCES CONSULTED

Walt Philbin and Laura Maggi, "Boyfriend Cut Up Corpse, Cooked It,"
     Times-Picayune, October 19, 2006.

David Usborne, "Murder Most Mysterious: The House of Horror in New
     Orleans," *Independent*, October 20, 2006.

Tara Jill Ciccarone, "The Bad Places," from *Soul Is Bulletproof: Reports from
     Reconstruction New Orleans* (New Orleans: NOLAFugees Press, 2008).

Cain Burdeau, "Dismemberment Murder Rivets New Orleans," Associ-
     ated Press, October 27, 2006.

Cain Burdeau, "New Orleans Crime Rate on the Rise," Associated Press,
     November 2, 2006.

12: MURDER CITY

INTERVIEWS

Charles Shepard, April 16, 2007.

Capricho DeVellas, fall 2006–spring 2008.

Jack Jones, fall 2007.

Jeanette Kelly, fall 2007.

Greg Rogers, November 11, 2007.

Rick Teissier, fall 2007.

Amzie Adams, August 28, 2007.

Tom Morovich, October 5, 2007.

SOURCES CONSULTED

Delia LaBarre, *The New Orleans of Lafcadio Hearn: Illustrated Sketches from the
     Daily City Item* (Baton Rouge: Louisiana State University Press, 2007).

Peter Scharf, "New Orleans Murder Realities: We Need New Thinking,"
     e-mail to New Orleans mayor and city officials, April 20, 2008.

April 24, 2007, e-mail from 527th MP Co. to soldier.

Associated Press, "PTSD Cases Up About 50 Percent in 2007," May 28,
     2008.

Ari Shapiro, "In Post-Storm New Orleans, Murder Is a Fact of Life," NPR,
     All Things Considered, August 30, 2007.

Russell McCulley, "Baghdad on the Mississippi?" *Time*, January 12, 2007.

Nicole Gelinas, "Baghdad on the Bayou," *City Journal*, spring 2007.

Peter Scharf, "Reducing Murder in New Orleans," lecture presented to the Alliance for Good Government, September 7, 2007.

Associated Press, "Census Revises 2007 Population in New Orleans Area," January 15, 2009.

Gwen Filosa, "Two Die in New Orleans Shootings; Prominent Musician Killed While His Family Watched," *Times-Picayune*, December 26, 2006.

Brendan McCarthy, "Marigny Victims Worked to Leave Mark on City," *Times-Picayune*, January 6, 2007.

Brendan McCarthy and Laura Maggi, "Killings Bring the City to Its Bloodied Knees; Husband, Wife Just Two of 6 Shot in 24 Hours," *Times-Picayune*, January 5, 2007.

Katy Reckdahl, "Sour Note: Credit Problems Are Keeping Many Musicians Out of Musicians Village," *Times-Picayune*, January 2, 2007.

Walt Philbin, "Robbery, Murder Leaves Hole in the Community," *Times-Picayune*, June 28, 2007.

Staff Reports, "NOPD Investigating Two Homicides," *Times-Picayune*, June 11, 2007.

Laura Maggi, Brendan McCarthy, and Brian Thevenot, "New Orleans Breeds Bold Killers: Half of Murders Occur in Daytime," *Times-Picayune*, January 24, 2009.

Brendan McCarthy, "New Orleans Murder Rate Drops in 2008," *Times-Picayune*, January 1, 2009.

Foreign Policy, "The List: Murder Capitals of the World," September 2008, www.foreignpolicy.com/story/cms.php?story_id=4480.

Mark Van Landingham, "2007 Murder Rates in New Orleans, Louisiana," *American Journal of Public Health*, May 2008, vol. 98, no. 5, www.ajph .org/cgi/content/extract/98/5/776.

C. B. Forgotston, "How Have We Benefited?" forgotston.com, www .forgotston.com/2008/11/17/how-have-we-benefited/.

Associated Press, "5 People Killed in New Orleans Shootout," June 18, 2006.

Gwen Filosa, "Grand Jury Indictments Reinstate Charges in Two High-Profile Murder Cases," *Times-Picayune*, August 9, 2007.

The Happy Talk Band, *There There*, Gallatin Street Files, 2007.

Rod Amis, "Smoke & Mirrors: Ass Kicking Time in America," G21.net, www.g21.net/smomir29.htm.

Staff Reports, "Violence Claims More Victims," *Times-Picayune*, October 28, 2007.

Bill Walsh and Stephanie Grace, "Jefferson Parish Sheriff Harry Lee Dies," *Times-Picayune*, October 1, 2007.

Brendan McCarthy, "Gunmen Sought in Fatal Shooting at Detective's Eastern N.O. Home," *Times-Picayune*, November 10, 2007.

Gwen Filosa, "Crime Thrives Under 60-Day Rule; Blown Deadline Frees Hundreds of Suspects," *Times-Picayune*, February 12, 2007.

Associated Press, "Police Chief Won't Ask Guard to Extend Stay," January 29, 2009.

Metropolitan Crime Commission, Inc., "Orleans Parish Criminal Justice System Accountability Report, January 2007–June 2008," www.metropolitancrimecommission.org.

Cynthia Salerno, "In Search of the News Crew that Saved Her Life," Poynter Forums, www.poynter.org/forum/view_post.asp?id=10834.

Ethan Brown, "New Orleans' Epic Housing Crisis," *Guardian*, March 20, 2008.

Martin Scorsese, *The Last Waltz*, United Artists, 1978.

13: AUBURN, COLUMBUS

INTERVIEWS

Capricho DeVellas, fall 2006–spring 2008.

Peter Scharf, January 2008.

Paul Sullivan, January 14, 2008.

Lana Bowen, March 17, 2008.

Todd Rauch, February 23, 2008.

Jeremy Ridgley, February 26, 2008.

SOURCES CONSULTED

Phillip Carter, "Extraordinary Acts of Valor; For a Soldier, Going to War Is a Duty. Heroes Go Much Further," *Los Angeles Times*, November 11, 2006.

Thomas Ricks, "The War Over the War," *Washington Post*, February 28, 2008.

Deborah Sontag and Lizette Alvarez, "Across America, Deadly Echoes of Foreign Battles," *New York Times*, January 13, 2008.

John Hinderaker, "Crazed Veterans Spark Nationwide Crime Wave," Power

Line, January 13, 2008, www.powerlineblog.com/archives/2008/01/
019533.php.

NPR, "The War at Home," *On the Media*, January 25, 2008, www.onthe
media.org/transcripts/2008/01/25/01.

Clark Hoyt, "Stories that Speak for Themselves," *New York Times*, January 27, 2008.

Philip Weiss, "At Elite Graduation in N.Y., Not a Word About Iraq," July 4,
2008, www.philipweiss.org/mondoweiss/2008/07/at-elite-graduation-
in-ny-not-a-word-about-iraq.html.

Bob Herbert, "An Invisible War," *New York Times*, May 3, 2007.

14: OURSELVES ALONE

INTERVIEWS

Larry Berreman, May 7, 2008.
Paul Rieckhoff, spring 2008.
Leo Watermeier, spring 2008.
Chad Peterson, June 5, 2008.

SOURCES CONSULTED

Ashley Morris, "Sinn Fein: Ourselves Alone," February 19, 2006, www
.ashleymorris.typepad.com/ashley_morris_the_blog/2006/02/sinn_
fein_ourse.html.

Thom Kahler, "Where You're Most Likely to Get Robbed in the French
Quarter and Mariny Triangle," NOCrimeline, February 23, 2008, www
.nocrimeline.com/ 2008/02/special-report.html.

Brendan McCarthy, "Acquitted Murder Suspect David Bonds Back in
Prison," *Times-Picayune*, May 20, 2008.

Maureen Ryan, "David Simon Pays Tribute to a 'Wire' Fan," *Chicago Tribune*, June 13, 2008.

Terri Tanielian and Lisa H. Jaycox, "Invisible Wounds of War: Psychologi-
cal and Cognitive Injuries, Their Consequences, and Services to Assist
Recovery," Rand Corporation, www.rand.org/pubs/monographs/
MG720/.

Avram Goldstein, "Post-War Suicides May Exceed Combat Deaths, U.S.
Says," Bloomberg News, May 5, 2008.

"Post Traumatic Stress Disorder Treatment and Research: Moving Ahead
Toward Recovery," hearing before the Subcommittee on Health of the

House Committee on Veterans' Affairs, U.S. House of Representatives, 110th Cong., 2nd sess., April 1, 2008.

Charles W. Hoge, Dennis McGurk, Jeffrey L. Thomas, Anthony L. Cox, Charles C. Engel, and Carl A. Castro, "Mild Traumatic Brain Injury in U.S. Soldiers Returning from Iraq," *New England Journal of Medicine*, vol. 358, no. 5 (January 31, 2008).

Jane Norman, "Senate Hears Parents Push for Mental Care," *Des Moines Register*, May 2, 2007.

Jennifer L. Price, "Findings from the National Vietnam Veterans' Readjustment Study," United States Department of Veterans Affairs, www.ncptsd.va.gov/ncmain/ncdocs/fact_shts/fs_nvvrs.html?opm=1&rr=rr45&srt=d&echorr=true.

James M. McPherson, "War in the Mind," *Atlantic Monthly*, March 1998.

Mark Benjamin and Michael de Yoanna, "Death in the USA: The Army's Fatal Neglect," *Salon*, February 9, 2009, www.salon.com/news/special/coming_home/2009/02/09/coming_home_intro/.

Christopher Lee, "Official Urged Fewer Diagnoses of PTSD," *Washington Post*, May 16, 2008.

Paul Rieckhoff, "First Victory on GI Bill Today," *Huffington Post*, May 15, 2008, www.huffingtonpost.com/paul-rieckhoff/first-victory-on-gi-bill_b_101982.html.

Jim Webb, "Fact Sheet on GI Bill," May 22, 2008, www.webb.senate.gov/pdf/factsheetgi52208.pdf.

Associated Press, "GI in Famous Photo Defeated by 'Demons,'" July 21, 2008.

EPILOGUE: STILL HERE

INTERVIEWS

Capricho DeVellas, July 2008.
Jack Jones, September 2008.
J. Lofstead, August 17, 2008.

SOURCES CONSULTED

Louis Maistros, "Why Won't Ray Nagin Shut the Fuck Up?" HumidCity, September 14, 2008, humidcity.com/2008/09/14/why-wont-ray-nagin-shut-the-fuck-up/.

Mark Folse, "Buddy Can You Spare Some Bootstraps?" Tolouse Street,

October 21, 2008, toulousestreet.wordpress.com/2008/10/21/buddy-can-you-spare-some-bootstraps/.

Ramon Antonio Vargas, "Murder Victim Identified as Woman from Ohio," *Times-Picayune*, August 12, 2008.

Andrew Vanacore, "Feds Collect Files from Nonprofit," *Times-Picayune*, August 11, 2008.

Lee Zurik, "Did City Group do the Remediation Work It Claims to Have Done?" WWL-TV news broadcast, July 22, 2008.

Gordon Russell, "And the Winner Is . . . Unclear," *Times-Picayune*, August 14, 2008.

Michelle Krupa and Frank Donze, "Inside, Nagin's a Hero, Outside He's a Joke," *Times-Picayune*, August 22, 2008.

Kevin Allman, "'Excellence in Recovery,' the Aftermath, and Robert Cerasoli," Blog of New Orleans, August 23, 2008, www.blogofneworleans.com/blog/2008/08/23/excellence-in-recovery-the-aftermath-and-robert-cerasoli/.

MarketWatch, "In Grim Déjà Vu, New Orleans Awaits Gustav on Katrina Anniversary," August 29, 2008, www.marketwatch.com.

Ethan Brown, "The Trouble with Ray Nagin," *Details*, December 2008.

Times-Picayune, "Filmmaker Michael Moore expands on Gustav comments," August 30, 2008.

Glenn Beck, "Big Easy a Lost Cause?" CNN, *CNN Headline News*, August 29, 2007.

Banksy, "Outdoors," www.banksy.co.uk/outdoors/horizontal_1.htm.

James Andrews, "Got Me a New Love Thing," *A Bit of New Orleans*, NYNO Records, 1999.

Shaila Dawan, "A Long and Weary Bus Ride to Anywhere, Haunted by Memories," *New York Times*, August 31, 2008.

Kevin Allman, "Major Evac Problems Near Hattiesburg," Blog of New Orleans, August 31, 2008, www.blogofneworleans.com/blog/2008/08/31/major-evac-problems-near-hattiesburg/.

The City of New Orleans, "Post-Disaster Phased Re-Entry Plan," www.cityofno.com/pg-150-13-post-disaster-phased-re-entry-plan.aspx.

KTBS 3, "DSS to Address Post-Gustav Food Stamp Issues," TV news report, September 10, 2008.

Matt McBride, "Mayor Declares I Heart Wrecking Balls," HumidCity, September 10, 2008, www.humidcity.com/2008/09/10/mayor-declares-i-heart-wrecking-balls/.

The Sable Verity, "A Public Health Crisis in Houston: Ike-trina Update,"
    September 19, 2008, www.sableverity.com/2008/09/19/ike-trina-update-
    a-public-health-crisis-in-houston/.
Lisa Gray, "Abandoning the 'Independent,'" *Houston Chronicle*, September
    18, 2008.
Nouriel Roubini, "Public Losses for Private Gain," *Guardian*, September
    18, 2008.
Opinion Journal, "Wall Street Reckoning," *Wall Street Journal*, September
    15, 2008.
Paul Krugman, "Gordon Does Good," *New York Times*, October 12, 2008.
Ed Stein, "The Bailout Simplified," *Rocky Mountain News*, September 24,
    2008.
Robert M. Solow, "Trapped in the New 'You're on Your Own' World,"
    New York Review of Books, November 20, 2008.
President-elect Obama's weekly address, www.change.gov, November 22,
    2008.
Billy Sothern, "As Police Dither, Holdup Clues Grow Cold," *Times-Picayune*,
    December 29, 2008.
Laura Maggi, Brendan McCarthy, and Brian Thevenot, "New Orleans
    Breeds Bold Killers: Half of Murders Occur in Daytime," *Times-Picayune*,
    January 24, 2009.
Cullen Murphy and Todd Purdum, "Farewell to All That: An Oral History
    of the Bush White House," *Vanity Fair*, February 2009.
Brendan McCarthy, "Ministers Demand Justice in Killing of Adolph
    Grimes III," *Times-Picayune*, January 6, 2009.
WDSU, "Adolph Grimes Autopsy Report," www.wdsu.com/news/
    18640831/detail.html.
Brendan McCarthy and Molly Reid, "Father Kills 2-Year-Old Son, Dumps
    Him in Park, Police Say," *Times-Picayune*, January 3, 2009.
Silence Is Violence, "January 9 Strike Against Crime," silenceisviolence
    .org/article/131.
Brendan McCarthy, "French Quarter Mourns Bartender Murdered in
    Armed Robbery Attempt," *Times-Picayune*, January 19, 2009.
Laura Maggi, "Teenage Suspects in Wendy Byrne Murder May Be Tried as
    Adults, Judge Says," *Times-Picayune*, January 21, 2009.
Meg Farris, "Slain Woman Was Popular Among Quarter Residents,"
    WWL-TV news report, January 28, 2009.
Katie Moore, "Quarter Murder Suspect on House Arrest at the Time of
    Crime," WWL-TV news report, February, 27, 2009.

ACKNOWLEDGMENTS

Thanks to: my agent Ryan Fischer-Harbage at the Fischer-Harbage Agency; my editor, David Patterson; my wife, Kristen; my parents, Susan and Stanley Brown; my brother, Josh, and his wife, Claire; Lori Moffitt; Jed and Tonya Bowen; Lana Bowen; Capricho DeVellas; Paul Sullivan of Veterans for Common Sense; Paul Rieckhoff of the Iraq and Afghanistan Veterans of America; Michael G. Bracey; Katharina Friedrich; Billy Sothern and Nikki Page; Kevin Allman; John Boutté; Jeremy Ridgley; Peter Scharf; Mary Bosveld; Michael Tomasky; Aaron Gell; Justin Manask; Greg Watkins; Robert Melanie; Davey D.; Gino S.; Jarret Lofstead and everyone at Nolafugees.com; Seth Ferranti; Walter Johnson; Jeff Chang; Joshua Cousin; Rick Doblin; Ann del Llano; Clyde Smith; Todd Rauch; Dennis Monn; Amzie Adams; Jack Jones; David Sylvian and Richard Chadwick; Leo Watermeier; the Squirrel; Tom and all the folks at Octavia Books in New Orleans; Bob French at WWOZ; Sara Roahen; Thomas Neff; Ted Mack; Rob Van Meter; Eric Royer; Cynthia Salerno; Karen Gadbois; Joseph Corcoran; Grant Shaffer; Andy Salzer; Juan Carlos Castro; Mark Healy and Susan Kaplow-Healy; Robert Levine; Jon Berry, Aksel Schaufler, and Michael Mayer. Finally, huge thanks for the friendship and inspiration from the two incredible friends I lost far too soon, Joshua Shome and Dave "Disco D" Shayman.

ILLUSTRATION CREDITS

ABOUT THE AUTHOR

ETHAN BROWN has written for *New York* magazine, *The New York Observer*, *Wired*, *Vibe*, *The Independent*, *GQ*, *Rolling Stone*, *Details*, *The Guardian*, and *The Village Voice*, among other publications. He is the author of two previous books, *Queens Reigns Supreme* and *Snitch*. He lives with his wife in New Orleans.